A Diary of the Euro Crisis in Cyprus

Panicos Demetriades

A Diary of the Euro Crisis in Cyprus

Lessons for Bank Recovery and Resolution

Panicos Demetriades
University of Leicester
Leicester, UK

ISBN 978-3-319-62222-4   ISBN 978-3-319-62223-1   (eBook)
DOI 10.1007/978-3-319-62223-1

Library of Congress Control Number: 2017951553

Cover design by Samantha Johnson

Printed on acid-free paper

This Palgrave Macmillan imprint is published by Springer Nature
The registered company is Springer International Publishing AG
The registered company address is: Gewerbestrasse 11, 6330 Cham, Switzerland

To Sofia, Emma and Polis.

Foreword

Perhaps the standard image of the role of a Central Bank Governor is that of an aloof technocrat, dealing with the intricacies of monetary minutiae and econometric modelling, far beyond the ken of normal mortals. If that was also your own view, this book will come as a shock and a revelation. Central banking, especially the role of a Governor, can become unbearably exciting, especially in a crisis.

My friend, Panicos Demetriades, was dropped into his new role of Governor of the Central Bank of Cyprus starting in May 2012, slap-bang right into the middle of one of the most extreme financial crises of recent years; and such crises are no longer rare events. Cyprus may only be a tiny country, but this crisis was big enough, and sufficiently badly handled on occasions, to have international ramifications.

Although Panicos was only Governor for 2 years, May 2012 to April 2014, his period in office was action-packed, with one dramatic event following another so fast that at times it all must have seemed a blur. So he has a remarkable tale to tell, and he tells it most effectively, with short crisp sentences and short crisp chapters. Would you expect a book about Central Banking to be too exciting to put down, (despite no sex, and violence only of the verbal kind, though Panicos did receive death threats)?

Finance involves money, often lots of it. When a financial crisis hits, the way that such a crisis is resolved will determine who loses, or gains, and how much. So there are bound to be all kinds of vested interests, and many of such interests will have the funds and the power to try to swing the final outcome in the direction that they favour.

Demetriades' book is largely about the clash of interests, between local and European interests, between commercial banks and the Central Banking fraternity, between political parties, with even the Church, though in its Temporal rather than its Spiritual capacity, playing a role. And, to add piquancy to this mix, there were the Russian depositors in the Cypriot banks. The junior partner of any 'special relationship' is always likely to hope for more assistance from the senior partner than the latter will find it in their interests to give. Moreover, Panicos doubts whether the Russian depositors in the Cyprus banks were closely aligned with the Kremlin. But the hope of Russian funding support, as a deus ex machina, to replace the Troika, absorbed too much of the hopes, time and energy of Cypriot politicians.

The chapters on the boiling-point of the financial crisis give a vivid impression of the fog of uncertainty, (who was saying what to whom), the pressures of time, lack of sleep, legal uncertainties, etc. In such circumstances, those involved need to stick to their training about what can, and should, be done (and the reverse). Fortunately, Panicos had had a good training as a monetary economist.

This book should be on every reading list to train future generations of monetary economists and Central Bankers. It is also a 'must read' for anyone interested in the euro-crisis of 2012–2013 particularly, and in European recent political history more broadly. But beyond all that, it is a vivid and dramatic story. Read on.

Charles Goodhart
London School of Economics

Acknowledgements

I am indebted to Svetlana Andrianova, David Green, David Lascelles, Michael Olympios, Andreas Panayiotou and Michael Zannetides, all of whom provided comments to drafts of various chapters. I am particularly grateful to two other individuals who provided extensive comments on most chapters but wish to remain anonymous. Naturally, any remaining errors or omissions are my own responsibility.

This book would never have been written without the encouragement and support of many academics, graduate students, policymakers, international journalists and financial practitioners from a wide range of disciplines, including business, economics, economic history, European studies, finance, law, politics and sociology. Most of these individuals had listened to my talks at several universities, central banks or conferences in the UK and the rest of Europe or in other parts of the world and were intrigued by the twists and turns in the way in which the crisis unfolded and was managed by Cyprus, Europe and the IMF. I was also encouraged to write the book by former colleagues at the CBC, who wanted the world to learn the truth about what actually happened. Last but not least, I was encouraged to write this book by numerous relatives and friends, to whom I am particularly grateful for their support during some very difficult times.

I hope that my narrative lives up to everyone's expectations.

Contents

List of Figures

Prologue

When in March 2013 the euro looked like it was about to break up in Cyprus, I couldn't stop thinking that we were writing history. The future of Cyprus, Greece and possibly the rest of the euro area was at stake, although some politicians in Europe, who feared what might happen, were bravely trying to convince spooked markets that Cyprus was not systemic.

It wasn't just economic or financial history we were about to write. It was European political history. After all, the euro was, first and foremost, a project of peace. That was particularly important in Cyprus, an island at the eastern edge of Europe within close proximity of Israel, Lebanon, Syria and Turkey.[1] An island that had joined the European Union in order to safeguard its very own survival in a turbulent region. An island with nearly half its territory already occupied by Turkey, a country with weak institutions and a fragile democracy embroiled in religious and political turmoil and military conflicts. History teaches us that even small accidents can have profound consequences. I couldn't help feeling that there was a lot more at stake than the euro's future in March 2013 if we got it wrong.

When the euro was first introduced, I was not its greatest fan. Like many other economists, I could easily see many of its design flaws from the day of its inception. I was not, therefore, in the least surprised when the euro crisis erupted in 2009 and I wasn't at all surprised that it first surfaced in Greece. Like many other Greek Cypriots, especially one born and raised in Cyprus during the most turbulent period of its recent history in which

---

[1] Distances from Larnaca to Haifa, Beirut, Mersin and Latakia are 164, 127, 128 and 141 miles respectively.

Greece had played a major negative role, I had my fair share of exposure to the institutional weaknesses of modern Greece. I hasten to add that—as with many other of my compatriots—the failures of modern Greece in terms of economic management, take nothing away from my love for the country and my admiration of its ancient history, mythology and modern culture.

When I joined the ECB's Governing Council in early May 2012, I witnessed from within the superhuman efforts that were being made to make the euro work against a political environment that was becoming increasingly hostile towards the single currency and the idea of a united Europe. The ECB had its own limitations, not least because of its institutional set-up and the incomplete architecture of the euro, but I never questioned the determination of people there to keep the European dream alive. It certainly felt like an honour to belong to that group of individuals who were committed to do 'whatever it takes' to save the euro. The Outright Monetary Transactions (OMT) programme and the banking union were born at the same time as the Cypriot crisis was erupting. I was glad that the lessons we were learning from Cyprus were taken on board in the design of the banking union.

This book tells the story of the euro crisis in Cyprus, how it unfolded and how, in the end, we managed to avoid euro exit in March 2013, although we came pretty close. The story has many interesting twists and turns, which provide the main ingredients of the crisis, ranging from the influx of Russian money through politically connected Cypriot law firms to German pre-election politics and the portrayal of Cyprus as 'a playground for rich Russians' by the German media. In between those twists and turns, there is a tale of two Cypriot banks that became too big to fail, too big to save and, arguably, too big to regulate. Between them, Laiki and Bank of Cyprus grew to four times Cyprus' GDP and were able to use their financial muscle to capture the political process and the media, protecting themselves from more effective regulation and supervision that could have averted the crisis. The two banks' imprudent risk taking provided some of the other ingredients of the crisis, including reckless investments overseas and a massive exposure to Greece at the worst possible time of modern Greek economic history. The lax regulatory environment provided the 'plain vanilla' ingredient, for which the entire domestic banking sector was responsible: easy credit, which fuelled a housing boom and led to one of the highest levels of private sector indebtedness in Europe.

The crisis erupted only days after I took office as Governor of the Central Bank of Cyprus (CBC) on 3 May 2012, although it was simmering from the end of 2011 when Laiki and Bank of Cyprus declared record losses amounting to nearly one-quarter of the country's GDP from the Greek debt write-down. It was a crisis that lasted for over 12 months before it started to subside. During that period, the CBC had the unenviable task of preventing financial meltdown amidst very fragile local sentiment and hostile domestic political conditions. Following the Eurogroup agreement of the ill-conceived deposit levy on 15 March 2013, the CBC was forced to impose a bank holiday that was extended indefinitely when Cyprus's Parliament rejected the proposed levy and Cyprus came close to exiting the euro. The CBC was then tasked with the poisoned chalice of implementing the Eurogroup agreement of 25 March 2013, which involved applying newly acquired resolution powers to impose large losses on uninsured depositors. The CBC was also tasked with major bank surgery that included splitting the island's second largest lender Laiki into a good and bad bank and folding the good bank into Bank of Cyprus, which was recapitalised through the first ever application of the bail-in tool in Europe involving the conversion of uninsured deposits into equity. In addition, the CBC oversaw a major restructuring and recapitalisation of the large credit cooperative sector and introduced a range of new regulations and directives intended to prevent future crises. As if all that wasn't enough, the CBC was called upon to help introduce unprecedented capital controls in a manner that would allow their gradual lifting, which eventually happened within 2 years of their introduction.

Only 12 months after major surgery, at about the time I decided to step down, the banking system started showing signs of recovery and stabilisation. On 30 July 2014, the IMF described the stabilisation of the banking system as "a major achievement" and commended the "resolute measures that were taken upfront". Three years on, Bank of Cyprus shares started trading on the London Stock Exchange.

This book also tells a second story, one that has both a political but also a more personal dimension. It tells the story of an increasing political influence over the functioning of the central bank and the consequential erosion of its independence, which eventually led to my own resignation and return to the UK in April 2014. In that story, the CBC reluctantly acquired bank resolution powers that Cyprus' international lenders decided were best delegated to an independent central bank that had the technical capacity to use them in an effective and impartial manner. That story is about the toxic political fallout that was generated through the imposition of substantial losses on wealthy and influential investors. It is a story in which the main beneficiaries—the taxpayers and future generations who were spared the burden of bailing out the big banks—remain unwitting and underrepresented in the political system.

The storyline unfolds around key events in my diary, however, I make no apologies for not providing a rigid or even a sequential chronology. Although I describe some key meetings, I am more interested in recalling the big picture without going into all the minutiae of every event or every meeting (many of which are in any case subject to secrecy or confidentiality restrictions). I keep jargon to a minimum and, where necessary, try to present economic and banking concepts in a manner that makes them accessible to a general readership. For the more specialised readers, who may be looking for the technical details of the banking crisis and the policy lessons from Cyprus, I have included two chapters at the end (Chaps. 17 and 18) that should help satisfy their curiosity.

Most, if not all, of the material presented in this book, including my accounts of various events or meetings, is already in the public domain, although not necessarily in written format. Some of it, inevitably, is scattered around in interviews published in newspapers and much of it is in Greek. Some is published in formats such as radio or TV interviews that do not make it readily accessible, especially to an international audience. Bringing everything together in one book allows me to put together all the pieces of the puzzle, all in one place for easy reference. This is, in some sense, the book's contribution, to economic, financial and European history. I would also like to think that the book makes a contribution to the literature on banking crises, by providing some useful insights into the importance of political economy factors, which are often neglected by economists. Additionally, I hope that the lessons from Cyprus are useful for policymakers, especially those who are interested in banking regulation and resolution, as well as those interested in safeguarding the future of Europe's common currency.

Leicester, UK   Panicos Demetriades
February 2017

1

Baptism of Fire

Alarm Bells

3 May 2012. Barcelona. A delightful setting with views of the Mediterranean sea. Warm and sunny with only a slight breeze. My very first ECB Governing Council meeting, in the company of the Eurozone's central bankers. Everyone was very welcoming. It seemed like the perfect start, especially if one ignored all the security and the helicopters hovering above for much of the time.

It turned out to be the calm before the perfect storm. The alarm bells started ringing soon after the Governing Council meeting had finished. There was a call in my hotel room. It was Vasos Shiarly, the Cypriot minister of finance, whom I had yet to meet.

'Is that the Governor?' he asked. There was a sense of urgency in his voice.

'Yes' I replied, although I felt a bit uneasy using the title without even having gone through a handover ceremony. I had arrived in Barcelona the evening before straight from the UK, where I was an academic economist since 1990. There was no formal induction to prepare me becoming a Governor, other than signing the contract a few days earlier and signing the Code of Conduct for ECB Governing Council Members earlier that day.

'This is Vassos Shiarly, the minister of finance. May I call you Panicos?' he asked.

'Yes, of course', I replied.

Then came the question that startled me:

'Can we go to Athens together as soon as you have finished in Barcelona?'

© The Author(s) 2017
P. Demetriades, *A Diary of the Euro Crisis in Cyprus*,
DOI 10.1007/978-3-319-62223-1_1

'Why?' I asked.

'We need to get support for Laiki from the Greek government', he continued, without waiting for me to reply, 'Our banks have lost a lot of money because of them, you know from the Greek debt restructuring.[1] It is now Greece's turn to help us and Papademos understands that very well. We have to do our utmost to save our country', he added, 'and Greece owes a lot to Cyprus'. He referred briefly to the events of 1974 when the Greek junta organised a coup against President Makarios, which was followed by the Turkish invasion of the island.

It was well known that the Greek PSI resulted in massive losses for Cypriot banks. Overnight, they lost over €4 billion, an amount that was nearly a quarter of the country's GDP.[2] It was a big blow not just for the banks but for the wider economy, especially if the taxpayer had to bail them out.

Lucas Papademos was the Greek caretaker prime minister at the time. He took office soon after George Papandreou's resignation in November 2011. His remit was to form a coalition government that would continue to implement Greece's adjustment programme, so that Greece could continue receiving financial support from Europe and the IMF—and to take the country to an election. That election was to be held on Sunday, 6 May 2012.

I had no doubt that Papademos understood very well the implications of the Greek PSI for Cyprus. He was, after all, a distinguished economist who had not only served as Governor of the Bank of Greece during the country's transition from the drachma to the euro but was also the ECB's vice president during 2002–2010. From 2010 onwards, he served as George Papandreou's economic adviser. Thus, in all likelihood, he would have contributed substantially to the adjustment programme's design, even before he became prime minister. He would also have known, I am sure, the implications for Cyprus. But Greece was a country on its knees and his role was to make sure it didn't become even weaker.

I was taken aback by Shiarly's request. Not so much by the prospect of having to go to Greece with a begging bowl in hand on only my second day in office but because I realised the situation must have been pretty desperate for our minister of finance to want to ask for help from the outgoing prime minister of a country at the brink of bankruptcy. There was no way that

---

[1] The restructuring of Greek debt, known as the Greek PSI, reduced the value of Greek bonds held by the private sector by nearly 80%.

[2] See Chap. 17 for the precise numbers and figures.

Papademos would be able to commit the next government of Greece to dish out several billion euros to help Cypriot banks, even if he had wanted to. Whatever promises we managed to obtain from Papademos before Sunday's election, if any, would be worth very little after the election. There was, therefore, very little to be gained by seeking help from an outgoing government, let alone from a country that was in a dire economic state. I wasn't a politician but all that seemed like common sense to me. I made those points to Shiarly, not perhaps in exactly those words.

Vassos Shiarly wasn't a politician either. He was a commercial banker. A senior banker, in fact, who had only very recently retired from one of the top positions in the Bank of Cyprus. Paradoxically, a banker who became a finance minister in Demetris Christofias' self-proclaimed left wing government. That paradox, of course, made a lot of sense to me, as I had been following Cypriot politics quite closely since I was a teenager. Despite its name, the party that Christofias led (AKEL—Greek acronym for Progressive Party of Working People) was essentially a pragmatic left wing party not too dissimilar to the UK Labour Party of the 90s. He nevertheless felt that he needed a banker in the finance ministry to reassure markets, local businessmen and foreign governments that the economy was in a safe pair of hands. In any case, Christofias wasn't elected to reform the economy. His remit was to solve the Cyprus problem and, as a left winger, he was perceived by voters as being much closer to the Turkish Cypriot leader of the time, Mehmet Ali Talat, than any of the other contenders for the presidency.

Although Vassos was not directly responsible for the Bank of Cyprus' investments in Greek Government bonds, his views regarding the Greek PSI echoed those held by the higher echelons of the Cypriot commercial banking establishment. These were rather simple views, which appeared to be motivated by their instinct of self-preservation. The Greek PSI should never have happened, they argued. It was bad luck that it happened and it was grossly unfair to us Cypriots who had only been trying to help Greece by investing in Greek Government Bonds (GGBs). Vassos took this argument a step further. He thought that as Greece hadn't really considered the implications of the PSI for Cyprus, we could somehow be compensated for those losses.

However, these arguments failed to take into account that the acquisition of the GGBs violated two of the most basic principles of risk management: (i) that a very high yield normally reflects a very high risk and (ii) an investment portfolio should always be diversified (no prudent investor puts all their eggs in one basket). Yields on ten year GGBs started climbing from the onset of the Greek crisis at the end of December 2009. By January 2010, the spread between GGBs and German bonds widened to 4%. In April 2010, Greece's credit rating was downgraded to junk status, sending bond yields to double digits. Although there were some temporary dips, reflecting bailout agreements, yields on GGBs remained on an upward trend and reached 20% in early September 2011. Notwithstanding these developments, the two banks invested amounts that exceeded 100% of their respective equity capital in GGBs, dwarfing their holdings of other securities, including those issued by the Cyprus government.[3]

A banker turned finance minister should have more political acumen than that, I thought to myself, unless …well unless the situation is so desperate that desperate actions may be needed. So the alarm bells started ringing. I suggested we go to Greece as soon as there was a new government in office. He readily agreed. 'We should, however, meet as soon as you return to Cyprus', he said. 'The senior management of Laiki want to see us', he added.

We agreed to meet three days later, on Sunday, 6 May, soon after my plane had landed at Larnaca airport.

Central Banks, ELA and Some Financial History

The first sign of trouble was, in some sense, visible earlier that day, on the agenda of the ECB Governing Council meeting. It was the request by my predecessor for the non-objection by the Governing Council for the provision of Emergency Liquidity Assistance (ELA) to Laiki, the second largest Cypriot bank. This request had been submitted the week before the meeting, in line with standard Eurosystem procedures. At that time, however, neither Laiki nor Cyprus were an exception. There was, in fact a long list of ELA non-objection requests by several other central banks in the euro area, not just from the usual suspects—Greece, Ireland and Portugal—but also from others, including some 'core' countries. There was a crisis rummaging throughout Europe. During a financial crisis, it is perfectly normal for a central bank to be supplying liquidity to banks facing liquidity difficulties. It would have been surprising if that had not been the case: depositors flee from weaker to stronger banks and from weaker to stronger countries. It's a normal 'flight to quality' that is exacerbated during crises.

The last time a central bank refused to provide emergency liquidity was in the 1930s when the Federal Reserve misjudged the extent of the

---

[3]See Chap. 17 for more details.

damage its refusal to supply banks with liquidity would create. Some Fed Governors at the time subscribed to the 'real bills doctrine' and thought that during a contraction, central bank credit should also contract. They advocated that central banks should stand aside and allow troubled institutions to fail as this would allow a healthier financial system to emerge. Although other Governors believed that central banks should provide funds to solvent institutions that are affected by panics, the argument was won by the other side under the influence of Hoover's secretary of the treasury, Andrew Mellon, an advocate of the 'real bills doctrine'. Banks were, therefore, allowed to fail and the money supply was allowed to contract. Banks failed in large numbers. Deflation ensued which increased real debt burdens. Households and firms couldn't service their debts. Households reduced consumption and firms were liquidated. More banks failed and more firms and households went bankrupt. Industrial production collapsed and unemployment soared. The contraction spread worldwide. The Great Depression lasted a whole decade.

Since then, economists and central banks have learnt the lesson. The Fed could have prevented deflation by preventing the collapse of the banking system, by supplying emergency liquidity. During a bank panic that is precisely what is needed. Ben Bernanke was one of the most prominent researchers of that period. In 2002, as a member of the Federal Reserve, he acknowledged publicly in a conference to honour Milton Friedman, that the Fed's mistakes contributed to the 'worst economic disaster in American history' (Bernanke 2004). His stewardship of the Fed during the sub-prime crisis meant that in no way would those mistakes be repeated. Not surprisingly, the ECB behaved in a similar fashion, which was very reassuring.

Central banks have an obligation to act as lender of last resort to commercial banks in order to safeguard financial stability. That is what I had been teaching my money and banking students in the UK for over 20 years. I had always explained that the lender of last resort function was a safety valve that made an inherently unstable system much more stable. By its very nature, commercial banking is risky and prone to runs because of the maturity transformation that banks engage in: banks borrow at short maturities and lend at much longer ones. It is the very nature of banking. If all depositors try to withdraw their money simultaneously, no bank would have enough liquidity to sustain that. Even the healthiest banks would fail unless they can obtain emergency loans from the central bank. Banks are, in fact, vulnerable to runs. Even if a bank is solvent and even if all depositors know that, the mere belief that a bank could become illiquid—that is to say, not have enough cash to meet depositor demands—can trigger a run on deposits.

A bank run, in turn, can force even a solvent bank into insolvency, as it tries to obtain liquidity through fire sales of assets. One bankruptcy can trigger others, and an otherwise healthy banking system can collapse like a set of dominoes because of the interlinkages between banks.

Stability is, in some sense, a confidence trick and central banks play a critical role in safeguarding that confidence. When confidence shocks do occur—and they can occur without any rational reason—a liquid bank can quickly become illiquid, simply by meeting deposit withdrawals. Under normal circumstances, banks can borrow from each other in money markets. However, during crises, money markets 'freeze' because banks stop lending to each other. In a volatile and uncertain environment, where no one has perfect information, banks become overcautious about who to lend to since they know that even a sound bank can fail if one of its counterparties fails. Because of information imperfections—banks do not know enough about each other—only central banks are willing and able to supply sufficient amounts of liquidity to commercial banks during crises. This is, in fact, the *raison d'être* for the existence of central banks.[4] In the hypothetical scenario in which a central bank refuses to supply emergency liquidity to a bank that is large enough to have systemic consequences, one bank's failure can trigger the collapse of an entire banking system. Small banks do fail from time to time without systemic consequences, especially in countries with large banking systems, like the USA, that are able to fully protect depositors. However, in countries that are not able to protect all depositors, the failure of even a small bank, which does not threaten other banks directly, can cause runs on other banks by adversely effecting depositors' confidence in the system. Thus, even small banks can sometimes be considered 'systemic'.

This is widely accepted banking theory and quite a few economists have made a name for themselves by demonstrating the above in elegant mathematical models. The main question a central bank has to ask before supplying liquidity to an illiquid bank is whether that bank is solvent and able to repay the loan when normality returns. More often than not, however, that question does not have a clear-cut answer. Accountants are satisfied that a firm is solvent when it has positive net worth, i.e. when the value of its assets exceeds the value of its liabilities. In the case of banks, assets are by and large the loans and investments in bonds and other securities that a bank has

---

[4]See, for example, Charles Goodhart's (1988) excellent analysis of central banks in which he explains that the liquidity support by the Bank of England was the result of commercial banks demanding that the Bank of England acted in that way to safeguard the stability of the banking system.

made. The value of these assets can fluctuate considerably as the economy moves through the business cycle. During booms, the value of bonds and other securities tends to go up while during busts the value of bonds but also loans tends to decline, not least because some borrowers—individuals who lose their jobs or firms that fail—are unable to meet their loan repayments. The value of a bank's liabilities—money owed to depositors and other banks—is, however, pretty much fixed. This asymmetry creates fuzziness when it comes to questions of solvency.

It is largely for this reason that bank supervisors have in one sense stricter definitions for bank solvency than accountants and in another sense looser ones. Bank supervisors demand that banks have 'adequate' capital buffers, which enable them to absorb future losses, in line with internationally agreed standards. These standards are recommended periodically by the Basel Committee on Banking Supervision and have evolved considerably over the years.[5] Specifically, banks are required to hold a certain percentage of their risky assets in the form of capital so that if those assets lose value, there is a buffer that can absorb future losses under adverse but plausible scenarios. In this sense, a positive capital ratio that would satisfy accounting definitions of solvency may not be enough: nowadays, supervisory capital requirements could be as high as 12% or even 15% for larger and systemically important banks.

Bank supervisors, however, also recognise that a bank that fails to meet minimum capital requirements is not necessarily insolvent, as long as it has a credible plan to raise additional capital. Thus, a bank that is under-capitalised may be deemed to be 'dynamically solvent' if such a plan is in place. If that were not the case, we would see far more bank failures and more frequent financial instability.

Under-capitalised banks do, however, create headaches for supervisors as they are likely to be perceived as weak by depositors and other investors. As

---

[5]Basel I was introduced in 1988 and focused mainly on credit risk. It stipulated that internationally active banks should have a minimum capital ratio of 8% of risk-weighted assets and introduced five categories of credit, ranging from 0% for OECD government debt to 50% for residential mortgages and 100% for other private debt. Basel II was introduced in the mid-2000s and introduced additional risk categories, as well as three methods for measuring risk depending on the bank's risk management capacity. It also introduced two additional pillars in addition to the capital requirements pillar: the supervisory review process and disclosure requirements intended to enhance market discipline. Basel III introduced a macroprudential overlay that is intended to address 'systemic risk' (the risk of the financial system as a whole, which includes the interconnectedness between financial institutions), which is believed to have led to the Global Financial Crisis, which erupted in 2007–2008.

such, they have incentives to take on excessive risk or 'gamble for resurrection' and should therefore be closely monitored (Llewellyn 1999).

The Trigger

In 2011, the European Banking Authority (EBA) carried out EU-wide stress tests on 91 European banks, including Marfin Popular Bank (known as 'Laiki') and Bank of Cyprus. The results were published in July 2011. Both banks passed the test but only marginally; the passing capital ratio was set to 5% of risk-weighted assets under an adverse scenario of a 4% shock to real GDP. Banks that obtained a marginal pass, like the two Cypriot ones, were given until the end of June 2012 to raise fresh capital. They were also given targets of new capital to raise.[6] In order to protect financial stability, EU governments agreed that banks that failed to raise sufficient capital themselves would be supported by public funds. As a result, under-capitalised banks remained dynamically solvent from a supervisory viewpoint.

The Cypriot media that I had been following closely in the weeks and months before my appointment, were full of optimism that both banks would meet their capital targets. Bank of Cyprus was considered to be solid as a rock. No one seemed worried it would not meet its capital targets. Laiki was more of a concern, because it was widely believed that its former owner-chairman (a Greek tycoon by the name of Andreas Vgenopoulos—now deceased), had allegedly mismanaged the bank and used it to prop up the capital value of his own businesses. There was, however, plenty of optimism surrounding the new chairman of Laiki, Michael Sarris, who was in effect installed by my predecessor, Athanasios Orphanides, after Vgenopoulos was forced to resign as the bank's chairman at the end of 2011, following the losses from the Greek PSI and the bank's multibillion reliance on ELA.

Michael Sarris was considered a successful former minister of finance under the previous centre-right government of President Tassos Papadopoulos. It was hard not to like Sarris, a former central bank officer who maintained links with everyone who was anyone in Cyprus, while for three decades he worked at the World Bank in Washington DC. Sarris was something of a mentor to many of the Cypriots who worked or visited Washington DC.

---

[6]Details of the tests and results can be found on the EBA website: http://www.eba.europa.eu/risk-analysis-and-data/eu-wide-stress-testing/2011/results.

Sarris was also well liked by the local media. They followed and supported his every move, including his adventures in the Turkish occupied part of Northern Cyprus, until he made the unfortunate decision of accepting to become minister of finance in Nicos Anastasiades' government on 1 March 2013. During 2012, Sarris went globe-trotting from Brazil to China to find new investors. The press covered his every move. Reportedly, it was all very promising, although the months were passing by and there was nothing concrete. For the media and his political backers, Michael was a good guy, a successful former minister of finance as well as a friend of literally every Cypriot who mattered so it was hard not to be optimistic. Surely, all that optimism could not be misplaced?

Well, it was. On Sunday, 6 May at around 8pm, soon after my Cyprus Airways flight from Amsterdam landed at Larnaca airport, I entered my office at the Central Bank of Cyprus (CBC) together with finance minister Shiarly. It wasn't my first time in that office but it was my first time as the Governor. Laiki's chairman and former minister, Michael Sarris, arrived a few minutes later accompanied by Laiki CEO Christos Stylianides. They gave us the bad news: Laiki wasn't going to be able to raise €1.8 billion of new capital. It wasn't in fact going to be able to raise anything at all, they said, unless the government underwrote their share issue, in which case the issue would become more attractive to foreign investors. This was the feedback they had received by sounding out investors all around the world. If the government did not underwrite the share issue by the end of June, it would have to inject €1.8 billion into it, anyway, they said. With their plan, they explained, at least some private capital would be raised.

'How much do you think you can raise if you do obtain the government support that you need at this stage?' I asked them.

Initially, they were unwilling to answer that question. However, after a lot of pressure from both Vassos and myself, they suggested it could be up to €300 million. I said that I wanted a few days to ponder over it. I had not even had a chance to examine the numbers in depth yet or a briefing by the CBC staff who supervised Laiki. As it eventually turned out, although the government did underwrite Laiki's share issue, Laiki ended up raising just €3 million out of the €300 million that Sarris and Stylianides had indicated they would be able to raise. During the summer, and following several sessions where I had to do a bit more than just raise my eye brows, Sarris agreed to step down as chairman of the—by then—nationalised bank.

On Monday, 7 May 2012, one day after my first meeting with the Laiki bankers and the minister, my predecessor came to the central bank for the delayed handover ceremony. The ceremony was more of a farewell for him, as the changeover of Governor had already taken place in Barcelona. It was held in the bank's amphitheatre in the presence of board members and the CBC staff. At my request, journalists were not invited so as to avoid controversy—Orphanides had been rather vocal in expressing criticism of the president's decision not to reappoint him. However, the journalists and the camera crews were waiting for him outside the gates of the central bank. Someone had tipped them off that he was going to make a statement after the ceremony. Once the ceremony had finished, Orphanides went straight out to them. Besides attacking President Christofias, he went on to state that the Cypriot banking system was healthy up until 2 May 2012 but that he could not be sure what had happened since or what would happen next. He said nothing about Laiki's multibillion reliance on central bank funding, which included nearly €4.0 billion in ELA, nor about the difficulties it faced in raising private capital that led to its chairman's request for state aid on the very day of my arrival in Cyprus. As far as I was concerned, there was a time bomb laying under the foundations of the economy that needed defusing before the end of June.[7]

Bibiliography

Bernanke, Ben. 2004. *Essays on the great depression*. Princeton, New Jersey: Princeton University Press.

Llewellyn, David. 1999. *The economic rationale for financial regulation*. London, UK: Financial Services Authority.

Goodhart, Charles. 1988. *The evolution of central banks*. Cambridge, MA: MIT Press.

---

[7]Sarris' actions suggest that he did not want to break the bad news about Laiki before the changeover of Governor. Prior to that, he gave several interviews in which he made public his support for Orphanides' reappointment.

2

Entering a War Zone

...over the period 2004-2010, Cyprus *banks grew dangerously large through a combination of aggressive management and weak governance, compounded by a failure of the public authorities to appreciate the risks that the banks were running, and therefore to take effective measures to rein them in. At its height in 2009, the banking sector was equivalent to 9 times GDP, one of the highest levels in the EU.*

Independent Commission on the Future of the Cyprus Banking Sector, Final Report, 31 October 2013 (http://www.centralbank.gov.cy/media/pdf/LSE_ICFCBS_Final_Report_10_13.pdf).

EU Membership

The Cypriot banking sector started growing uncontrollably in 2004, the year that Cyprus became a full member of the European Union. By 2011, banking sector assets more than doubled to reach €141.0 billion, or 9.5 times GDP. In order to qualify for membership, Cyprus had to adopt the *acquis communautaire* (the body of legislation and regulations constituting EU law), including fully liberalising its hitherto tightly controlled financial system. The changes to the structure of the economy were, however, not

© The Author(s) 2017
P. Demetriades, *A Diary of the Euro Crisis in Cyprus*,
DOI 10.1007/978-3-319-62223-1_2

fully appreciated, largely because the motivation for joining the EU wasn't economic but political.

EU membership was, and still is, considered by the majority of Greek Cypriots as essential for the long-term survival of the Republic of Cyprus. Indeed, the biggest hurdle Cyprus faced in its desire to join the EU wasn't the island's tightly controlled economy but 'the Cyprus problem', i.e. the de facto division of the island since 1974. The Republic of Cyprus, which applied to join the EU in 1990, only controls the southern part of the island. The northern part representing 36% of the Republic's territory is, at the time of writing, controlled by the 'Turkish Republic of Northern Cyprus', a pseudo state recognised only by Turkey. Nicosia, the capital city, remains at the time of writing, the only divided capital city in Europe.

It is largely because of the tragic events of 1974 that EU membership came to be considered as essential for national survival by the majority of Greek Cypriots. With the Cyprus problem uppermost in most people's minds, the key economic challenges facing Cyprus, including the institutional changes that needed to be made, received little more than passing attention. The common misconception was that the economy was sufficiently robust to withstand any shocks from EU membership, which, at any rate, would be mostly positive. Few recognised the risks emanating from a fully liberalised financial system and hardly anyone thought that the banking system, if left unmanaged, could become the source of another national disaster.

Early on during my period in office, I came to realise that many politicians and journalists had little, if any, appreciation of European institutions. Few, for example, understood that central bank independence is one of the cornerstones of economic and monetary union. Even fewer appreciated why. For many Cypriot politicians and journalists, central bank independence was a European curiosity that simply had to be embedded in Cypriot legislation and then conveniently forgotten.

Neither the Greek Cypriots' determination to join the European Union nor Cypriot politicians' casual respect for European rule of law can be adequately understood without gaining a deeper appreciation of the island's turbulent pre- and post-independence history, to which much of the rest of this chapter is devoted.

Turbulent History: From Ancient Times to British Rule[1]

'He who would become and remain a great power in the East must hold Cyprus in his hand. That this is true, is proved by the history of the world during the last three and a half millenia from the time of Thutmes III of Egypt to the days of Queen Victoria'. These were the words of the German classical archaeologist Gustav Hirschfeld in 1880, soon after the British took over Cyprus from the Ottomans in 1878.[2] These wise words, which remain as relevant today as they were in 1880, not only neatly encapsulate the island's strategic importance but also hint at the source of its turbulent—and at the same time rich and fascinating—history. For while Cyprus is only the third largest island in the Mediterranean—it is smaller than Sicily and Sardinia—its close proximity to the Middle East is second to no other European land. Modern-day Turkey and Syria can be seen from Cyprus with the naked eye, while Beirut, Haifa, Port Said and Alexandria are all within easy reach by sea.[3]

Cyprus was settled by humans during the Palaeolithic period: water wells, believed to be among the oldest in the world, which date back over 9000 years, provide the first evidence of human presence on the island and indicate the sophistication of these early settlers. The neolithic settlements of Khirokitia and Kalavasos, near Limassol on the south coast, which date back to 5800 B.C., provide further evidence of a relatively developed civilisation. The discovery of copper at around 3000 B.C., from which the island seems to have derived its name, transformed Cyprus into a centre of trade by attracting traders and settlers from the region, as well as Egyptian invaders around 1500 B.C. The Minoan traders were the first Greeks to visit Cyprus and although they never settled on the island, their highly developed civilisation became a source of cultural influence on its inhabitants. Achaean and Mycenaean traders followed from around 1400 B.C. but they only started settling on the island towards the end of the Trojan war (around 1184 B.C.). The Achaeans and Mycenaeans were followed by the Dorians around 1100 B.C. During that period, ten independent city kingdoms were founded,

---

[1]This section draws on a number of historical and other sources, including Hill (2010), Trimikliniotis (2012), Hitchens (1997), Karageorghis (1968).

[2]See Hill (2010).

[3]For example, the distance from Larnaca to Beirut is 112 nautical miles while the distance from Limassol to Haifa is 139 nautical miles.

which gradually adopted the Greek language, religion and culture.[4] Cyprus, in turn, exerted its own influence on the Greek mainland and became an integral part of Greek religion, culture and mythology. One of many examples of such influence relates to Aphrodite, the Greek goddess of love and beauty whose mythical birthplace was on the western part of the island.

The Assyrians were the first foreign power to occupy Cyprus in ancient times, following the victory of King Sargon II in 709 B.C. Assyrian direct rule lasted for four decades and was followed by around 100 years of relative independence. The island was then conquered by the Egyptians around 570 B.C. and the Persians around 545 B.C. Alexander the Great put an end to Persian rule in the late fourth century BC. The Ptolemaic period that followed—which also turned Egypt into a Hellenistic kingdom and Alexandria into a city of Greek culture—resulted in the full Hellenisation of the island.

The Ptolemaic period ended in 58 B.C., when Cyprus became part of the Roman Empire. The people of Cyprus were converted to Christianity during the first century AD by the Apostle Paul, who travelled to Cyprus with the Levite Barnabas, who was a native Cypriot. The Church of Cyprus became independent in 431 AD. Cyprus became part of Byzantium after the division of the Roman Empire into East and West and remained as such until it became a target of the crusaders in the twelfth century AD. In 1192, Issac Comnenus, the last Byzantine Governor of Cyprus, conceded control of the island to Richard the Lionheart, who had landed in Limassol a year earlier in search of his bride Berengaria. Later that year, Richard sold Cyprus to the Knights Templar who passed it on to the French Lusignans, which resulted in Latin being declared the official language. In 1196, they established the Latin—Roman Catholic—Church and started persecuting the independent Eastern Orthodox Church of Cyprus. The Lusignans remained in control of the island until 1489, when the Venetians bought the island from Catherine Cornaro, the last Lusignan Queen of the island, who was subsequently forced to abdicate. The Venetians fortified the island to protect it from frequent Ottoman raids. Venetian rule lasted until 1571 when the island finally fell to the Ottoman Turks, following the historically famous siege and naval blockade of Famagusta on the island's south-eastern coast, which lasted eleven months.[5]

---

[4]The ten kingdoms were: Salamis, Kition, Amathus, Kourion, Paphos, Soli, Tamassos, Ledra, Idalium and Chytri.

[5]These events provide the historical setting to Shakespeare's *Othello*, that tells the story of the commander of the Venetian garrison defending Cyprus against the Ottoman Turks.

Ottoman rule lasted over 300 years, during which the supremacy of the Greek Orthodox Church was restored and Catholicism displaced. It was, by and large, a period of economic and cultural oppression. During Ottoman rule, the Archbishop—the head of the Greek Orthodox Church of Cyprus—was recognised as the sole representative of the Greek Cypriot population. The Church was also given power to govern and raise taxes from the local population, all of which raised the status of the Archbishop from a religious leader to 'ethnarch'—ethnic leader. In addition to the Archbishop, the Greek Cypriots elected a Dragoman, an official 'interpreter' chosen from candidates nominated by the Archbishop. The Dragoman played a significant administrative and diplomatic role as the leading intermediary between the Christian population and the Ottoman rulers.

The importance of this period for modern times cannot be overstated. This was the period during which a new ethnic group, the Ottoman Turks, mainly soldiers and their families, were incentivised to settle in large numbers on the island. This development, combined with the rise of nationalism in the twentieth century, was to lead to significant ethnic tensions in modern times between the Greeks and Turks of Cyprus, which culminated in the invasion of the island by Turkey in 1974.[6]

Cyprus came under British rule in 1878, following a secret convention with the (by then) weakening Ottoman Empire. The convention obliged Britain to use the island as a base to protect the Ottoman Empire from Russian aggression. Cyprus' strategic importance for Britain was related to the opening of the Suez Canal nine years earlier, which made the island a particularly useful naval outpost as it could be used to protect the sea route to India, Britain's most important overseas colony at the time. With the onset of World War I in 1914, Britain found itself on opposite sides of the Ottoman Empire and, as a result, rescinded the convention and annexed the island. In 1925, Cyprus became a Crown colony and remained under British colonial rule until 1960. Although the island remained largely underdeveloped, under British rule Cypriots enjoyed greater freedoms compared to Ottoman times, including freedom of speech and access to formal education, which was largely provided by the Greek Orthodox Church. This facilitated the emergence of Greek nationalism and its vision of Greater Greece, which eventually led to the idea of 'enosis'—union of Cyprus with Greece.

---

[6]See, however, Panayiotou (2006) for a more nuanced sociological perspective on the historical conflict between Greek and Turkish Cypriots.

At the same time, the poor living and working conditions of much of the population during the 1920s led to the rise and propagation of left-wing ideas, influenced by the Bolshevik Revolution of 1917. The Communist Party of Cyprus, established in 1926, declared its support for independence, thereby providing a plausible alternative to enosis. A non-nationalist alternative gained further ground and momentum with the establishment in the 1940s of AKEL—the Progressive Party of the Working People—the mass party created by the communists and trade unions when the Communist Party was disbanded by the British colonial administration. AKEL rejected nationalism from the outset and sought to unite Greek and Turkish Cypriot workers in their struggle for better working conditions.[7] In 1947–1948, AKEL embarked on negotiations with the British on self-government. However, the right, which was both more staunchly pro-enosis but also more pro-British (until the mid-1950s) objected to the idea of an independent, or even, initially, a self-governing Cyprus. Meanwhile, the idea of partition of Cyprus along ethnic lines started gaining ground among the Turkish Cypriots.

Troubled History: From EOKA to Christofias

Cyprus gained its independence from Britain in 1960, following a four-year campaign against British rule by a Greek Cypriot guerrilla organisation named EOKA (National Organisation of Cypriot Fighters).[8] EOKA, whose goal was 'enosis' was led by Georgios Grivas, a Cyprus-born retired officer in the Greek army with a distinguished military record in the 1919–1922 Asia minor war against Turkey. During the EOKA campaign, Grivas adopted the pseudonym 'Digenis', after a Greek hero who had defended the borders of the Byzantine empire against Ottoman attacks.

Grivas was a highly controversial character because of his extremist, far-right political views. During the German occupation of Greece, he founded and led a secret organisation named 'X', which collaborated with the Nazis against the communist-led Greek resistance.[9] Grivas was also a fierce Greek nationalist with extreme anti-Turkish views; he could never accept that Cyprus could aspire to be anything other than a part of Greece. He showed

---

[7]For a comprehensive history of AKEL and the left-wing movement in Cyprus, see Katsourides (2014). Note, however, that over the years AKEL's position on independence fluctuated.

[8]For a fascinating British soldier's perspective on EOKA, see Bell (2015).

[9]See, for example, Hondros (1983), Richter (1985) or Close (1995).

little tolerance for those who were prepared to consider the future of Cyprus as an independent state. In his memoirs, he referred to his campaign not only against the British but also against the 'communists and the Turks'. Hundreds of Turkish and Greek Cypriots, whom he branded 'traitors' or 'collaborators', were assassinated by EOKA under his orders, in addition to similar numbers of British soldiers and civilians.

In the late 1950s, as a reaction to the Greek Cypriots' demands for 'enosis', Turkish Cypriots began advocating 'taksim', the partition of Cyprus into Greek and Turkish parts and their respective union with Greece and Turkey.

During British rule, the Greek Orthodox Church remained the leading institution representing the interests of Greek Cypriots as had been the case during Ottoman times. The Archbishop continued to play the role of 'ethnarch'.

In 1950, the Church acquired a new, young and charismatic leader, Archbishop Makarios. Makarios had studied theology and law at Athens University, before heading to Boston University in the USA to embark on his doctoral studies, funded by a World Council of Churches scholarship. Makarios, who was from the Paphos district, rose quickly through the ranks of the Church and became Archbishop and leader of the Church at the age of 37.

Makarios was a leading advocate of the principle of self-determination for Cyprus well before the start of the EOKA campaign. Given the demographics, self-determination, if granted by the British, would in all likelihood have resulted in the island's union with Greece from the early 1950s. Although the extent of Makarios' collaboration with Grivas during the EOKA campaign remains uncertain, what is known with certainty is that the British Governor of the island, Sir John Harding, believed that Makarios was the spiritual leader of EOKA. Perceived as a threat to British rule, Makarios was secretly removed from the island by British forces in March 1956, less than a year after the start of the EOKA campaign. He remained in exile (in the Seychelles) for three years.

Makarios returned to Cyprus in 1959, after an agreement reached in Zurich between Britain, Greece and Turkey to establish an independent Republic of Cyprus, with Britain maintaining military bases on the island. Makarios, who was a pragmatist, realised early on that 'enosis' was not a realistic prospect for Cyprus. Although initially against the Zurich agreement, he was eventually persuaded by the Greek and British governments to endorse it and contributed to its further refinement in London. In December 1959, soon after his return to the island, Makarios was elected as the first president of the newly established Republic of Cyprus, defeating his opponent, George Clerides, who had been supported by AKEL.[10]

The 1960 constitution envisaged power sharing between the Greek and Turkish communities on the island. In an attempt to protect the Turkish Cypriot (T/C) minority from the Greek Cypriot (G/C) majority, it provided for over-representation of Turkish Cypriots at all levels of government and the civil service. It also provided the T/C minority with veto power over important decisions. The arrangement did not last long. Continuous friction between the two communities over power sharing led Makarios to propose changes to the ethnic restrictions agreed in London and Zurich, with the aim of creating a more efficient public administration. The T/C community, however, responded by withdrawing completely from the government and civil service in December 1963, from the lowest ranking civil servant to the Vice-President of the Republic, Dr Fazıl Küçük. As a result, the position of vice-president, which was intended by the 1960 constitution to provide an important check and balance on the powers of the president, has remained vacant since 1963.

By contrast, other positions that were intended by the 1960 constitution for Turkish Cypriots, such as those of Deputy Attorney General and Deputy Chief of Police, were, over time, filled with Greek Cypriots, by appealing to the so-called law of necessity, so that the state could remain functional.

UN peacekeeping forces were deployed on the island in 1964 and have remained ever since. They were not, however, able to prevent further episodes of intercommunal strife. The Turkish Cypriots withdrew into enclaves and formed their own administration in 1968.

On 15 July 1974, there was a military coup against Makarios, ordered by the Greek junta in Athens. Turkey invaded the island five days later, claiming it had the right to do so in order to protect the T/C minority under the Zurich-London agreement. By mid-August, Turkish military forces occupied 36% of the island, defeating an under-equipped and demoralised Greek Cypriot National Guard. Around 200,000 Greek Cypriots (representing about one-third of the G/C community) fled for safety to the southern cities of Limassol and Larnaca. At the same time, an agreement was reached

---

[10]George Clerides attracted about one-third of the vote. His son, Glafcos Clerides, had better luck: he was elected president in 1992 and served until 2002.

between the two sides to move 60,000 Turkish Cypriots to the areas controlled by the Turkish army, with the help of British and UN forces.

The coup against Makarios, which triggered the Turkish invasion, was the pinnacle of a campaign of violence, terror and intimidation directed against Makarios and his supporters by right-wing nationalists, who justified their actions by claiming that they were continuing to fight for 'enosis'. There were in total four assassination attempts against Makarios, but also numerous bomb explosions, frequently outside police stations.

In 1968, Makarios was re-elected to the presidency with an overwhelming 96% majority against Takis Evdokas, a nationalist candidate who had the support of the Greek military junta. Makarios' popularity did not, however, prevent the junta from stepping up the campaign against him. In 1971, the junta secretly dispatched colonel Grivas back to Cyprus with a new remit: to destabilise the government with the ultimate aim of overthrowing Makarios. Prior to his return, Grivas had publicly accused Makarios of being a traitor. For Grivas, it was enough that Makarios had abandoned the aim of 'enosis'. Makarios had also shown leanings towards the left in the 1968 elections, something which Grivas could not tolerate. On his return to Cyprus, Grivas founded the paramilitary organisation EOKA B, which launched a terror campaign against Makarios and his supporters.

By that time, Makarios had become a prominent figure in the non-aligned movement worldwide, alongside Egypt's Gamal Abdul Nasser and Yugoslavia's Josip Tito. This development, which coincided with the height of the cold war, certainly alienated the USA, which had expected a more pro-western stance from him. Makarios was branded 'the Fidel Castro of the Mediterranean' (see, e.g. Hitchens 1997) in view of his moderate beliefs and tolerance of communism, fuelling the Greek junta's determination to overthrow him. After all, the colonels' 'revolution' of April 1967 was mainly intended to save the Greek nation from what they saw as widespread communist infiltration.

In addition to Grivas and EOKA B, the junta also used its control of the Greek Cypriot National Guard, which was managed by officers from Greece, to undermine Makarios and the rule of law. It funded three new newspapers which started a propaganda war against Makarios. Grivas' supporters infiltrated the local police force, upon which Makarios depended for his own security, and stole weapons and ammunition to arm the paramilitaries of EOKA B. Makarios' dual role as head of state and head of the Greek Orthodox Church, or perhaps because of his Christian beliefs, resulted in extraordinary levels of tolerance and forgiveness, even of the people who repeatedly attempted to kill him. However, violence escalated during the period 1971–1974 and he was forced to create a special police force, staffed by loyal supporters.

In an attempt to regain control, Makarios removed from the Cypriot police force a number of police officers who had openly revolted against him. The most prominent was Chrysanthos Anastasiades, who was the head of the Limassol police force and had been dismissed by Makarios for assisting EOKA B.[11] On 15 July 1974, soon after the presidential palace and the archbishopric in Nicosia were attacked by National Guard tanks and artillery, the paramilitaries, with help from National Guard conscripts, attacked Limassol's main police station, which was being defended by Makarios' newly created special police force. On 16 July 1974, Chrysanthos Anastasiades was installed as the director of the Limassol police force by Nicos Sampson, the new president chosen by the Greek junta.

Within three days of the Turkish invasion of the island on 20 July 1974, the Greek junta collapsed. Support for Brigadier Dimitrios Ioannides, the secretive dictator who had taken control of the junta in late 1973, dwindled.[12] Ioannides quickly lost the support of senior military officers once it became obvious that, either through his actions or his incompetence, Cyprus was, in effect, being handed over to Turkey. General Phaedon Gizikis, who had been installed as a figurehead president in November 1973, asked Constantinos Karamanlis, a veteran politician who had been residing in Paris since 1963, to form a government. Without backing from Greece, the President of Cyprus, Nicos Sampson, who had been installed by Ioannides, resigned after just eight days in office. Glafkos Clerides, speaker of the House of Representatives (and subsequent President of the Republic during 1992–2002), took over the presidency of the Republic and gradually helped to restore constitutional order. Makarios, who had fled the island from the British air base in Akrotiri on 16 July 1974, returned to the island in December 1974. By that time, he had secured sufficient international

---

[11]Chrysanthos Anastasiades was the father of the current President of Cyprus, Nicos Anastasiades. A photograph of the young Nicos Anastasiades, a lawyer, with the defendants outside the court has been used to link him to the defence of EOKA B in court.

[12]Ioannides had replaced George Papadopoulos who was removed following the student uprising at the prestigious Metsovion Polytechnic, which ended in bloodshed. It is believed that Ioannides, a hardliner who was the head of the military police, staged the events in order to justify Papadopoulos' removal, as the latter was planning a softening of the military's grip. Ioannides formed a puppet government comprising of individuals who would take orders from him. It is widely believed that the individuals he chose for various ministerial roles were not consulted, but were rounded up by the military police and ordered to take up office.

support to ensure that his government was recognised as the lawful govern-ment of the whole island.

Sixteen years later, Cyprus applied to join the EU and eventually did so in 2004. A lot had happened in the period between the coup and invasion of 1974 and the island's application for EU accession in 1990. Cyprus, like any country wishing to join the EU, needed to have stable institutions guaran-teeing democracy, the rule of law, human rights and respect for and protec-tion of minorities, before it could apply.

Negotiations for EU membership began in 1998. Although the island remained divided, notwithstanding numerous attempts at reunification, the reasoning that was given by the European Commission in its support for Cyprus' EU membership was that it would bring '…increased security and prosperity and that it would help bring the two communities on the island closer together'.[13]

As part of the process of gaining EU membership, Cyprus, like all can-didate member countries, had to adopt the *acquis*. Among the numerous legislative changes that were introduced, the country had to amend the 1960 constitution and banking laws in order to strengthen the independ-ence of the central bank. The 1960 constitution allowed the President of the Republic to dismiss the central bank Governor at will. The same was true of the deputy Governor, a position earmarked for a Turkish Cypriot, aimed at providing cheques and balances on the powers of the Governor. The deputy Governor could be removed from office by the Vice-President of the Republic. What also had to change was the government's veto power on the central bank's board of directors. Before this change, the government had complete control over all central bank strategic decisions, through the minister of finance, whose representative on the central bank board had veto power. The 1960 constitution was amended so that the Governor and deputy Governor could only be removed from office through a judicial pro-cess, if they were either no longer capable of carrying out their duties or if they had committed a 'grave offence'. Following EU membership, addi-tional protection of central bank independence was provided by the Treaty of Establishment of the European Union, which in practice means that any national decision to remove a sitting Governor from office needs to be rati-fied by the European Court of Justice.

---

[13]See European Commission, Press Release Database: http://europa.eu/rapid/press-release_DOC-93-5_en.htm.

EU membership, along with the financial liberalisation it entailed, brought with it unprecedented levels of euphoria, which fuelled the unchecked growth of the banking system in the years that followed. With a secure future within the EU, Cyprus' banking system began to attract capital inflows from Russia and other former 'eastern bloc' countries, looking for a safe, tax-efficient, home. By that time, Russia had begun its own return to prosperity, following more than a decade of transition. Geographically, historically, culturally and, more recently, politically, Cyprus offered all that nouveau-rich Russians wanted from a safe haven. Cypriot law firms, closely connected to the banks and local politics, were the key conduit in this process, acting as 'introducers' of wealthy Russian clients (often politicians themselves) and frequently receiving commissions from the banks for these services (Demetriades 2015).

Europe had hoped that EU membership would act as a catalyst for reunifying the island. In 2004, a preliminary agreement, known as the Annan Plan, was brokered by the United Nations. However, the G/C community rejected the Plan in a referendum after President Tassos Papadopoulos made an emotional appeal on television stating that he could no longer support the agreement, citing last minute changes intended to secure the support of Turkey.

The only Greek Cypriot political leader who supported the Annan Plan was, in fact, Nicos Anastasiades. Anastasiades' stance won him western plaudits and laid the foundations for his election to the Presidency in 2013, as it helped to transform his public image into that of a moderate centre-right politician with a pragmatic outlook on the Cyprus problem. By contrast, Tassos Papadopoulos became comparatively isolated internationally and began losing support domestically. In the 2008 presidential elections, Papadopoulos, who stood for re-election, came third, although by a small margin. Ahead of him were Dimitris Christofias, leader of AKEL, and Yiannakis Kasoulides who was the conservative candidate backed by Democratic Rally (DISY). Anastasiades, the leader of DISY, did not stand, fearing a backlash because of his support of the Annan Plan. The elections were won by Christofias, who made renewed efforts at reunification soon after his election. At that time, the Turkish Cypriot leader was Mehmet Ali Talat, also a left-winger. Given the traditionally good links that AKEL had maintained with their fellow left-wingers on the Turkish Cypriot side, expectations for a settlement were rather high and go some way in explaining Christofias' electoral success. These expectations were not realised, in part because Talat lost the 2010 election to Dervis Eroglu, a nationalist who was less inclined to seek compromise. Nevertheless, the convergences that were achieved during that period provided the basis for the present round of negotiations when a new pro-solution Turkish Cypriot leader was elected in 2015.

Christofias' term coincided with the start of the global financial crisis in the USA and the beginning of the Eurozone crisis. Christofias, who was educated in the former Soviet Union and frequently boasted about his communist ideals, nevertheless appointed a banker as his finance minister. This was a clear signal to everyone that it was 'business as usual' when it came to the running of the economy. These, however, were not usual times. Christofias and his first finance minister, Charilaos Stavrakis, were criticised for being too slow to recognise that the global financial crisis would sooner or later affect Cyprus. The country's public finances rapidly deteriorated with the bursting of the property bubble in 2009, which was triggered by Britons selling retirement and holiday homes. Christofias was also criticised for increasing pension and other social security spending, which was, perhaps, the only 'socialist' policy that he had managed to implement.

The biggest criticism of Christofias, however, arose as a result of the devastating explosion at the Evangelos Florakis naval base near Mari that occurred on 11 July 2011. The explosion resulted in the death of 13 military and fire service personnel. It also damaged the nearby electricity generation plant, the largest on the island, resulting in widespread blackouts. The explosion was caused by the inappropriate storage of 98 containers of ammunitions destined for Syria from Iran that were seized by the US navy in the Red Sea from a Cypriot flagged, Russian-owned, vessel and offloaded in Cyprus. Critics alleged that Christofias had turned down offers from the USA, the UK and Germany to dispose or safely destroy the ammunitions, fearing an adverse political reaction from Syria. Following the explosion, the media mounted an attack on Christofias and thousands of people, encouraged by opposition political parties, demonstrated outside the presidential palace demanding his resignation. The explosion triggered the withdrawal of centrist DIKO from Christofias' coalition government, which resulted in a de facto minority government of the left, as AKEL had no majority in Parliament. Christofias became more and more isolated but did not yield to the demands of the demonstrators and the opposition political parties. With the continued support of AKEL, he remained in office until the end of his term, although he was vilified by the local media, with the exception of the left-wing daily *Haravgi*.

Back to the Present

I met Dimitris Christofias for the first time in March 2012, following an invitation that I had received from his office a few days earlier. By that stage, Christofias had decided not to reappoint my predecessor and was looking for a replacement. My name had been put forward by several people who had followed my career since leaving the Central Bank of Cyprus in 1990 to become an academic in the UK. At that meeting, Christofias shared with me the circumstances of my predecessor's appointment, which, although fascinating, encapsulated the way in which Cypriot politics and policymaking were conducted.

Christodoulos Christodoulou was the Governor before Orphanides. He had only served one term and the then President, Tassos Papadopoulos, decided not to reappoint him because of differences over Laiki. At that time, Papadopoulos, who was the leader of centre-right Democratic Party (DIKO), and Christofias, who was the leader of AKEL, were allies—they had formed a coalition government together.[14] Tassos asked Christofias his views about the two candidates he was considering for the governorship. One of them was Athanasios Orphanides, an economist working at the Federal Reserve Board in Washington, D.C., with impeccable research credentials in the field of monetary policy.

Christofias happened to know Orphanides' parents well because both of them belonged to AKEL. The other candidate was a respected and successful academic econometrician based in the USA whom, however, Christofias did not know. Orphanides was born in Brno in the then Czechoslovakia during the depths of the cold war to a Greek mother and a Greek Cypriot father. His parents had met in the Socialist Republic of Czechoslovakia. His father was a student there while his mother, who had been a young resistance fighter during the German occupation of Greece, fled Greece at the end of the Greek civil war, like many other communists.

For Christofias, it was an obvious and easy choice; he recommended Orphanides without any difficulty over the other candidate.[15] What Christofias was not aware of, given the solidly red credentials of Orphanides'

---

[14]The relatively modest percentages of DIKO meant that they needed support from either the left or the right to win an election.

[15]Orphanides was also recommended by the then finance minister Michael Sarris. who was well acquainted with Orphanides' career as they both had spent large parts of their careers in Washington D.C. Sarris was a World Bank economist before returning to Cyprus to take on the role of finance minister.

parents, was that Athanasios had acquired views on economic management that could not be further removed from those of his parents. Later on, when Orphanides started to publicly espouse his strong pro-market views, Christofias came to the conclusion that this child of the left had been converted to the 'neoliberal ideology' prevalent in the USA. However, by that time, it was too late for Christofias to do anything, other than wait for Orphanides' term to end. Christofias, for all his stubbornness and somewhat romantic socialist beliefs, had considerable respect for EU institutions, including that of central bank independence.

When it came to banking supervision, it appeared as if Orphanides had adopted a Greenspan-style laissez-faire stance towards the big banks. It was thus no surprise that the bankers wanted his reappointment. They offered higher deposit rates than anywhere else in Europe, which helped them to attract billions of foreign currency funds. These were used to lend to domestic property developers, paying little attention to systemic risk, thereby helping to fuel an unprecedented property bubble with the help of strong demand from wealthy Russians.

Early during his term, Orphanides made a relatively feeble attempt to prevent the property bubble from inflating further by suggesting the introduction of a ceiling on the loan to value ratio for primary and secondary residences. The proposal was, however, abandoned as soon as it encountered resistance from politicians and property developers. No further attempt was made to contain property lending, which could have been achieved through tighter regulation or stricter corporate governance. For example, if the number of independent directors on bank boards had been increased to achieve majority-independent boards, it would, in all likelihood, have resulted in more prudent lending standards and lower appetite for risk. Instead of being reigned in, property developers' influence over bank boards increased. In one obvious case of conflict of interest that remained unchecked, Theodoros Aristodemou, a large property developer connected to the Bank of Cyprus' largest shareholder—which happened to be Cyprus' Greek Orthodox Church—became Chairman of the Bank in 2008. As the rules on connected lending to bank directors and the definition of non-performing loans (NPLs) remained lax until mid-2012, asset quality in banks continued to deteriorate. Cyprus, according to the latest statistics at the time of writing, continues to have one the highest ratios of corporate lending to GDP in Europe as well as the highest ratio of NPLs. At 49%, NPLs in Cyprus dwarf Italy's NPL ratio which stands at 17%. Even Greece, which experienced seven consecutive years of recession, has an NPL ratio that is two percentage points lower than Cyprus'.[16]

Lax lending standards were not the only source of poor asset quality. Both Laiki and Bank of Cyprus started expanding in the 'new lands of opportunity'—Russia, Ukraine and Romania. The Bank of Cyprus paid over €1 billion to acquire and support a Russian retail subsidiary—Uniastrum bank—lacking any synergies with its core business. It continued to expand in Greece up until 2011 as it saw the Greek crisis as an opportunity to grow at the expense of their Greek competitors. Bank of Cyprus and Laiki became, through their advertising expenditure, the main funders and financiers of the local media. Not surprisingly, the media made little attempt to mention the excessive risks undertaken by the two banks. Even when the rating agencies started downgrading Cyprus because of its large banking sector and the exposure to Greece, the media remained relatively silent on the issue.

Some of the politicians who backed the bankers through thick and thin worked in law firms that benefited directly by 'introducing' Cypriot banking services to their rich Russian clients. Others were closely connected to property developers and other big business. With the successive downgrades, the excesses of the banking sector became increasingly difficult to sustain, even with all the help from the local media.[17] The supporters of the bankers needed a scapegoat. Christofias became an easy target, especially after the naval base explosion. The credit rating downgrades mentioned the link between banks and public finances—a small country could not support a large banking system without sound public finances. This was a very clear warning but it was ignored by the political establishment, including Parliament which had a duty to call the CBC to account for the growing risks in the financial system.

With the help of large sections of the local media, the causes of the downgrades were systematically distorted so as to put the blame entirely on Christofias and the deterioration of the public finances. Some of his critics—including Orphanides—went as far as to say that the Christofias gov-

---

[16]See EBA Report on the Dynamics and Drivers of Non-Performing Exposures in the EU Banking Sector, published 22 July 2016. https://www.eba.europa.eu/documents/10180/1360107/EBA+Report+on+NPLs.pdf.

[17]An article by the columnist and chairman of the investors' Association, Michael Olympios, which appeared in Politis—a major newspaper—entitled 'Too big to save' (which was inspired by a similar article of Joseph Stiglitz) alarmed the CEO of Bank of Cyprus. According to Michael Olympios who had a conversation with the editor in chief, Andreas Eliades threatened to cut €50,000 worth of advertising, forcing the paper to drop his column. The events were described in a sworn testimony in court during one of the criminal cases against Bank of Cyprus and some former executives.

ernment should have vetoed the Greek PSI in order to protect the Cypriot banking system.[18]

Against this background, whoever Christofias had chosen to replace Orphanides, was bound to face hostility, unless they were an 'insider'. Bankers wanted the party to go on and so did the developers as well as the businessmen who benefited from easy credit. The media was equally reliant on the banks for easy credit and advertising revenues, especially after economic conditions begun to deteriorate in 2010. Lawyer-politicians and those politicians who depended on developers and big businessmen had every interest to maintain the status quo. However, with Laiki failing to raise private capital and needing state support, the party was nearing the end, although the news had been kept secret until after the changeover of Governor at the central bank. Bank of Cyprus was also destined to request a bailout, although it did not reveal this until after its AGM in June 2012.[19] The party had to go on for as long as possible.

I certainly wasn't an insider. Perhaps that is why Christofias appointed me. Or maybe it was because my own grandfather, Christodoulos Petrou, had been a key figure himself in the left-wing movement. He was among the founders of the metal workers union in the 1930s. Later on he became a successful entrepreneur, but remained firm in his beliefs and continued to hire employees from the union he helped to found—which by then had become affiliated to AKEL—both Greeks and Turks. His workshop, which was named 'Μηχανουργείο ο Πορσεβίκος' ('Bolshevik metal works') was located on the boundary between the G/C and T/C communities in Limassol. It was never damaged or vandalised, even though the area was at the centre of several episodes of intercommunal violence. His Turkish-Cypriot workers had a deep respect for him and helped to protect him, his family and his business.

---

[18]Christofias, however, confided in me that he was never briefed about the effects the PSI would have on the Cypriot banks. By contrast, on 19 April 2011, when Greek debt restructuring was being publicly floated, Orphanides gave an interview to Reuters in which he claimed that Cypriot banks could withstand Greek debt restructuring. Specifically, he said: 'With respect to the exposure of Cypriot banks to Greek debt, we have examined the situation and we have come to the conclusion that even though there is exposure in our banking system, that exposure is manageable because our banks are very well capitalized. So even in the highly unlikely situation, if you wanted to run the counter factual, for example, of imposing losses on the holdings of Greek debt, our banks would manage to weather that'. See: http://www.centralbank.gov.cy/media/pdf/INTE_GOVINTERVIEW_190411.pdf.

[19]A Cyprus Securities and Exchange Commission investigation subsequently fined the bank for failing to promptly announce to shareholders the capital shortfall. The bank and the bankers involved are now facing criminal charges over this and related violations.

Media hostilities started even before my appointment was announced. My 'Bolshevik' roots were exposed by the gossip columns. My popular writings were scrutinised by the 'serious' press, who competed among themselves as to how much they could distort and criticise my 'Keynesian' views, as if being a Keynesian was equivalent to being a reckless revolutionary. My sceptical views on Europe and the role of Germany in the EU were described as explosive and dangerous, not only for Cyprus but also for the whole of Europe.

The hostilities continued unabated after my appointment was announced and during all of my 23 months in office. According to the critics—which included the bankers whose banks needed large bailouts and my predecessor—I was part of 'a communist conspiracy to destroy the banks'.[20],[21]

On Sunday, 6 May 2012, during my late night meeting with the Laiki bankers, I was struck by the flashing lights of the gigantic Turkish flag on the Nicosia side of the Pentadaktylos mountain, that seemed designed to intimidate the G/C population, as it was visible from literally everywhere in Nicosia and beyond.

I had clearly entered a war zone. In more ways than one.

Bibliography

Bell, Martin. 2015. *The End of Empire: Cyprus: A Soldier's Story*. Barsnley, South Yorkshire: Pen & Sword Books.

Close, David. 1995. *The Origins of the Greek Civil War*. London: Longman.

Demetriades, Panicos. 2015. "Political Economy of a Euro Area Banking Crisis", London School of Economics, Financial Markets Group, Special Paper Series,

---

[20]'According to reliable sources, PIMCO, in collaboration with AKEL and Demetriades, had been plotting the demise of Cyprus banks for several months before PIMCO came to Cyprus', Vassilis Rologis, a former chairman of Bank of Cyprus, exclaimed in my presence at a parliamentary session that was looking into the causes of the crisis in 2013. Aristodemou, the property developer who took over from Rologis in 2008 at the helm of Bank of Cyprus, hailed his 'agreed' sale of Venus Rock, a massive development near Paphos financed by Bank of Cyprus, to a Chinese investor at approximately €300 million in the summer of 2013 as tantamount to disproving the results of the independent diagnostic exercise, as, he claimed, the property prices he obtained were above forced sale values used by PIMCO. By June 2014, and notwithstanding generous government support in the form of visas for Chinese property buyers and town planning relaxations, Aristodemou's company was forced to admit that the sale had fallen through.

[21]Parliament's inquiry, in fact, endorsed the bankers' views that the capital needs of the banks were exaggerated, failing to note that, even after the banks were fully recapitalised using PIMCO's adverse scenario, the capital buffers of banks remained thin and well below banks that had been bailed out in other countries.

No. 245, *The Cambridge Journal of Economics*, forthcoming. doi:10.1093/cje/bex001.

Hill, George. 2010. *A History of Cyprus Volume 1: To the Conquest by Richard Lion Heart*. Cambridge: University Press. Cambridge Library Collection.

Hitchens, Christopher. 1997. *Hostage to History: Cyprus from the Ottomans to Kissinger*. London and New York: Verso.

Hondros, John Louis. 1983. *Occupation & Resistance: The Greek Agony*. New York: Pella.

Katsourides, Yiannos. 2014. *History of the Communist Party in Cyprus: Colonialism, Class and the Cypriot Left*. London: I.B. Tauris.

Karageorghis, Vassos. 1968. *Cyprus*. Geneva: Nagel Publishers.

Panayiotou, Andreas. 2006. Models of Compromise and 'Power Sharing' in the Experience of Cypriot Modernity. *The Cyprus Review* 18 (2): 75–103.

Richter, Heinz. 1985. *British Intervention in Greece*. London: Merlin Press.

Trimikliniotis, Nikos, and Umut Bozkurt (eds.). 2012. *Beyond a Divided Cyprus: A State and Society in Transformation*. New York: Palgrave Macmillan.

3

A German Question

'Panicos, why do you need the Russians in Cyprus?' asked the most senior German official at the ECB, as soon as he sat down for our lunchtime
meeting on Thursday, 14 June 2012 in one of the highest floors of the
Euro tower, where the ECB used to be located. I was taken aback by his
bluntness. Asmussen was the only German national on the ECB's executive
board—the committee of six individuals that has the responsibility for the
day to day running of the institution. Besides the President (Mario Draghi)
and the Vice President (Vitor Constanzio), the executive board comprises
four additional members, each with a different portfolio of responsibilities.
Asmussen's remit included overseeing programme countries: Greece, Ireland,
Portugal and Spain. In other words, he had day-to-day oversight of all the
economic adjustment programmes in the euro's troubled periphery. The
troika officials of the ECB reported to him.

Surely what the Russians were doing in Cyprus could not be the top priority of a meeting that was meant to deal with the practical steps Cyprus
needed to take in order to apply for financial assistance from Europe, I
thought to myself. I was, however, to be proven wrong by subsequent developments. The link between Russia and Cyprus came to be uppermost in
German policymakers' minds in the months to come. And the agreement
between the Cypriot government and the Eurogroup that was struck in the
early hours of 25 March 2013, reflected that: Russian depositors ended up

© The Author(s) 2017
P. Demetriades, *A Diary of the Euro Crisis in Cyprus*,
DOI 10.1007/978-3-319-62223-1_3

making a multibillion contribution to saving Cyprus, although initially no one knew how much of the bailed-in money belonged to Russians.[1]

During the autumn of 2012, the links between Russia and Cyprus became one of the main preoccupations of the popular press in Germany (more on this in Chap. 7). Germany was entering a pre-election period and the Cyprus bailout became a new battleground as it offered an interesting, albeit exaggerated, Russian angle: 'Why should the German tax-payer bail out rich Russians in Cyprus?' they asked. It was a question that would resonate well with German public opinion, in the light of the long-standing animosity between the two nations. Many Germans will never forget that a part of Germany—known as the 'German Democratic Republic'—remained firmly under the control of Soviet Russia until the collapse of the Berlin wall in 1989.

Linking the Cyprus bailout to Russia became a powerful weapon with which opposition parties in Germany, including the Social Democrats and the Greens, could attack the government of Angela Merkel for allegedly being careless with German taxpayers' money. Bailing out Greece and the other countries of the periphery was already pretty bad for any German government tasked, however reluctantly, with saving the euro. Bailing out Russian oligarchs in Cyprus sounded even worse. It was close to political suicide.

Not surprisingly, following the emergence of such stories in the German press, the links between Cyprus and Russia and, more formally, the willingness and ability of Cyprus to fight money laundering, ranked very high in the agenda of the political discussions that eventually led to the Eurogroup agreement on Cyprus in late March 2013. It also became clearer as we got closer to those critical programme negotiations that unless there was some form of Russian contribution to the Cypriot programme, the German Parliament was unlikely to agree to the bailout. The form of the contribution, however, remained vague until March 2013.

Asmussen may well have been anticipating those hard-hitting questions from the German press as he may have been privy to political discussions in Germany about Cyprus. Angela Merkel, the German Chancellor, was

---

[1]We eventually found out that about half the deposits that were bailed-in (converted to equity) belonged to Russian nationals. One-third belonged to residents, including small and medium size enterprises that were the backbone of the economy, that lost much of their working capital. There were also tragic cases of orphans who lost the insurance compensations they had received following the death of both their parents in the Helios air crash of 2009.

already criticised at home for being too soft on Greece, even though many Greek citizens thought exactly the opposite.

Asmussen was the last person to arrive in the room on the 35th floor of the Euro tower with excellent views of Frankfurt from above, smallish but more than adequate for a discrete lunch among six people, comprising the Governor of one of the smallest central banks in the Eurozone with two of his colleagues—a senior director and an economist specialising in public finance—and three senior ECB officials. Jörg was one of three ECB executive board members present. The other two were the ECB's chief economist, Peter Praet and Benoit Coeurè, both of whom arrived punctually for our meeting a few minutes earlier.

Asmussen had a hard stance on the periphery. He was expected to in some sense. I assume he felt pressure from German public opinion and the popular media in Germany, which portrayed the ECB as being too soft on the periphery. As the only German national on the ECB executive board, the spotlight in Germany was on him. His blunt, remarks about the periphery need to, therefore, be understood in this light. At the ECB, he replaced his compatriot Jurgen Stark who had stepped down because he felt that the ECB was becoming soft on inflation. Jörg himself didn't stay very long at the ECB. In late 2013, he went back to a government position in the coalition government that was formed by Angela Merkel.

What struck me at the time was that, as if by an unwritten rule, a German national had, almost by default, the primary responsibility for all the problem countries of the European periphery at the ECB. Otherwise known as the 'programme countries', the set of four, soon to increase to five, included big problem Greece, Portugal, that was also highly problematic, although less so than Greece, Ireland, that was generally considered well-behaved, and latecomer Spain, that was somewhat less of an issue. Indeed, Spain never had a full adjustment programme. Its programme focused only on cleaning up its troubled banking sector, which had been hit by the bursting of the Spanish property bubble.

Cyprus was next in line for an adjustment programme. It was likely that Asmussen would end up playing a key role during difficult programme negotiations in the weeks and months ahead. Indeed, that turned out to be the case, although it was considerably later than we initially anticipated. In the words of Nicos Anastasiades, Asmussen was the ECB official who 'had put a gun to his head' by threatening to cut off ELA to Cypriot banks if he had not accepted the 'deposit haircut'.[2]

This was, of course, a politician's spin on Eurosystem rules, made in order to justify the U-turn from his pre-election pledge that he would never accept a deposit haircut. The rules themselves, to which Asmussen was alluding to, are simple: they prohibit the ECB from funding an insolvent bank that has no credible plan for being recapitalised. The adjustment programme was intended to fully address capital shortfalls and restore the sustainability of public finances. Without one, the banks were insolvent.

A lot ran through my mind before attempting to answer Assmussen's blunt and completely unexpected question. It seemed that the world of UK academia that I occupied before setting off on my euro adventure had no connection with the harsh European realities of 2012; Germans certainly felt that they were called upon to pay for the excesses of the south. Or it may have been that politicians in Germany felt that Cyprus provided an opportunity to inflict some pain on Russia for the Berlin wall, which was still vivid in their memory. One can only speculate.

I gave him the long answer. I explained that the two countries, traditionally, had close links between them, dating back to the introduction of the Greek alphabet into Russia by Cyrillus and Methodius and pointed to the shared Orthodox religion. There were also political links going back to the Soviet times. President Christofias, for example, studied in Russia and spoke fluent Russian. Many other Cypriots, who studied in the USSR, also spoke Russian. This, in turn, meant that those Russians who didn't speak English and visited Cyprus, either for business or pleasure, would be able to communicate well with the locals. Politically, Soviet Russia consistently supported Cyprus in the United Nations. In post-Soviet times, the same support was provided by the Russian Federation. Then there was the climate and geography that made Cyprus even more attractive for Russians than for other European nations—a three and a half–hour direct flight from Moscow in a southerly direction would take them to the warmest and sunniest country in the European Union. On top of that, there was a good environment for doing business, which included the lowest corporate tax rate in Europe. Numerous double tax treaties with many countries, including Russia, a high

---

[2]Pikis, G. M., Kramvis, A. and Nicolaou, E. (2013), Έκθεση Τριμελούς Ερευνητικής Επιτροπής για τη Διεξαγωγή Έρευνας Σχετικά με την Κατάσταση στην οποία Περιήλθε το Τραπεζικό Σύστημα και η Οικονομία της Κυπριακής Δημοκρατίας (*Report of the Tripartite Committee on the Investigation in Relation to the State of the Banking System and the Economy*).

standard of professional services by lawyers and accountants, and a sound legal system based on English common law, all of which were valued by Russian businessmen. Last but not least, Cyprus offered a relatively safe environment to many Russian families with young children as well as good international schools. As a result of all this, Cyprus was indeed attractive to Russians. Not for all the reasons Asmussen and the German popular press had in mind.

Asmussen wasn't persuaded. He seemed like he had already made up his mind. The links between Russia and Cyprus were, for him, less saintly than I had described. Why did Russian oligarchs find Cyprus so attractive? Why are Cypriot banks full of Russian money? The lowest corporate tax rate in the Eurozone obviously had something to do with it, but it wasn't everything. The 'business model' of Cyprus was not sustainable, he added, although he did not elaborate much on that. All this had to change if Cyprus was to become a programme country, he exclaimed. I assumed—wrongly as it later turned out—that this was more to do with the corporate tax rate of Cyprus than with the need for Russians to somehow contribute to the Cyprus bailout. A small increase in the corporate tax rate may be unavoidable, I thought to myself. That would not be good but would it have the lethal effect on the 'business model' that Asmussen seemed to have in mind?

The meeting was meant to be a secret one. Not so much because it was a formal Eurosystem meeting, it certainly wasn't. We just wanted to make sure that it didn't have unintended consequences in Cyprus. If word came out, it may well have resulted in political wrangling that could have delayed or even derailed the application. Christofias' government was in its last year of office. It was certainly trying to avoid having a programme at all cost. A troika programme is politically costly for any government, more so for a government of the left. Austerity measures are unpopular. Labour reforms, including abolishing wage indexation, which everyone knew was on the cards, was anathema to the governing party and to the trade unions. The pro-European right and centre-right opposition were making matters worse. Instead of criticising the government for not having applied for a much-needed and delayed adjustment programme, it chose to criticise it for pushing the country to the arms of the troika. The opposition's position was that all that the economy needed was to fix the public finances which could be done without a troika programme. They wanted to blame public finances and, by extension, the government for all the ills of the economy, and could not do so by admitting that it was in fact the bloated banking sector that was *the* major issue. They couldn't blame the government for the condition of Laiki and k of Cyprus, as it had no responsibility over banking supervision.[3] They ould, however, try to blame it, as they did, for the state of public finances, although the statistics did not lend support to those claims, since Cyprus' public debt to GDP ratio was no worse than Germany's.[4]

I was, in fact, the first Cypriot official to remark publicly, within days after I took office, that an adjustment programme for Cyprus could not be ruled out and that it should not be demonised. This wasn't because I was an admirer of such programmes. Far from it. As an academic, I was very critical of the Greek programme. I thought austerity wouldn't work, precisely because I strongly believed that fiscal multipliers were high, even before the evidence was so clear. I felt, however, that Cyprus had little choice if it wanted to remain a member of the Euro area. Even a delay in the application could have meant that we would have had to interrupt liquidity supply to the banking system, which essentially would have meant shutting down the banks and, consequently, the economy down. What many people do not appreciate—and that includes many economists who don't study banking—is that banks, besides intermediating between savers and borrowers, provide a public good. They provide the payments system without which an economy will cease to function, as no transactions can take place.

I went to the meeting with Asmussen, Praet and Coeurè prepared to answer questions about the banks as well as about the public finances. However, none of that was needed. As I came to realise with the passage of time, the ECB already knew most of what there was to know about Cyprus. The ECB staff working on Cyprus maintained such good relations with the CBC staff that frequently they had access to local banking system data even before the CBC Governor did.

Asmussen stood up and left first from the meeting, in the same brisk manner with which he arrived. He was going straight into some other important meeting. I was left with the impression that for him the most challenging issue relating to Cyprus was the link between Russia and the banking sector and this had to somehow be to be addressed by the programme. It seemed that the rest for him was relatively straightforward.

---

[3]Moreover, by blaming the banks the opposition would have alienated an important ally—the Governor of the Central Bank who maintained till his final hour in office that the only problem with the Cypriot economy was public debt and excessive public spending.

[4]In December 2011, public debt in Cyprus was 71% of GDP, which was 10% points below the mean of the EU and lower than Germany's 78.7%. By contrast, private indebtedness was 286% of GDP and the third highest in Europe (See Demetriades 2015). Revised figures from Eurostat now show Cyprus' debt to GDP ratio at the end of 2011 as being 65.2%. By contrast, private indebtedness was 286% of GDP and the third highest in Europe.

A good dose of austerity could easily fix the public finances, which, after all were in much better shape than was the case in Greece. As far as the banking sector was concerned, again the process was straightforward. We had to carry out an independent diagnostic exercise, consistent with international norms, to establish the precise capital needs of the banking system, following the examples of Greece, Ireland, Portugal and, more recently, Spain.

Asmussen's departure gave us the opportunity to have a broader discussion with the other two senior ECB officials on some of the more mundane aspects of the application, including the practicalities involved. The formalities were, in fact, rather simple. All that was needed was a letter from the Cypriot Minister of Finance to the IMF and the European Stability Mechanism in which the government stated that it was applying for financial support for the country's banking system and public finances.

On a lighter note, we also exchanged views on the term 'troika', which the public associated with negative connotations. Somehow, the International Monetary Fund, the European Commission and the European Central Bank seemed to resonate better on their own than when grouped together to form the 'troika' of institutions. Even the left wing politicians, who were highly critical of the IMF, nevertheless have a lot of respect for the views and status of the institution. The same was true for the Commission and the ECB, although neither of these institutions attracted as much historical criticism as the IMF did over the years. This was a case where $1+1+1$ summed up to less than one.

This strange arithmetic had probably a lot more to do with Greece, which Cypriots followed closely, than anywhere else. In Greece, one troika programme after another was widely believed as having failed: they pushed the country into a deeper and deeper recession and very high rates of unemployment, with no sign of light at the end of the tunnel. That was largely because the troika had significantly underestimated the effects of fiscal austerity on output, which resulted in lower than predicted government revenues (e.g. Kitromilides 2016).

It turned out that the IMF debt sustainability analysis was too heavily influenced by the dominant paradigm in macroeconomics. This paradigm is associated with a most peculiar result known as 'Ricardian equivalence' (e.g. Barro 1989). It predicts that cuts in government spending have no real effects because rational households, who optimise over an infinite horizon because they care about their offspring, recognise that cuts in government spending or higher taxes now will—sooner or later—result in lower taxes. In this strange world, which new classical economists believe in, capital markets are perfect: households are able to borrow and lend as much as they need to in order to smooth out income fluctuations. As a result, their consumption paths are relatively smooth and fiscal austerity has little or no effects on spending.[5]

This world could not be further from reality. In fact, quasi-experimental evidence from Italy has shown that cuts in local government spending have led to sharp falls in consumption expenditure (e.g. Acconcia 2014). The IMF itself subsequently recognised its mistakes over Greece but it was too late by then. Fortunately, in the case of Cyprus the IMF's debt sustainability analysis that followed learnt from those lessons.[6] As a result, one round of austerity proved more than enough to achieve the fiscal objectives of the programme. It also helped, of course, that the taxpayer didn't pay the bill for bailing out the two largest banks.

We emerged from that lunch with a much clearer idea of what we needed to do to move forward with Cyprus' application for financial assistance. We also discussed and agreed on the necessity and importance of liquidity provision during the programme negotiations. The ECB understood very well the lessons from the Great Depression. We were, however, none the wiser about German intentions for little Cyprus.

Bibliography

Acconcia, Antonio, Giancarlo Corsetti, and Saverio Simonelli. 2014. Mafia and public spending; evidence on the fiscal multiplier from a quasi-experiment. *American Economic Review* 104 (7): 2185–2209.

Barro, Robert J. 1989. The Ricardian approach to budget deficits. *Journal of Economic Perspectives* 3 (4): 37–54.

Blanchard, Olivier J., and Daniel Leigh. 2013. Growth forecast errors and fiscal multipliers, NBER Working Paper 18779.

---

[5]These ideas were reflected in the IMF's debt sustainability analysis for Greece through the use of very low 'fiscal multipliers'—these are the parameters that measure the impact of government spending on GDP. The IMF systematically under-predicted both the depth and the duration of the recession in Greece using fiscal multipliers that were too low. All this forced the IMF to change its views on fiscal multipliers (see, for example, Blanchard and Leigh 2013).

[6]In one of the early meetings with the troika, I insisted that they read some of the more recent academic literature that demonstrated that the value of multipliers during a contraction was much higher than one. At a meeting with Christine Lagarde, the IMF director, at the Presidential Palace in September 2012, and in the presence of President Christofias, she thanked me for those comments and assured me that they were being taken on board by the IMF staff.

Demetriades, Panicos. 2015. Political economy of a euro area banking crisis. London School of Economics, Financial markets group, Special paper series, No. 245, *The Cambridge Journal of Economics*, forthcoming. doi: 10.1093/cje/bex001.

Kitromilides, Y. 2016. *Greece and the eurozone crisis: An evaluation.* Cyprus Economic Society Discussion Paper No. 2 (December 2016).

4

Buying Time

At the European Council meeting on 26 October 2011, EU national governments agreed that they would be providing a backstop for banks that needed recapitalisation following the Europe-wide stress tests carried out by the European Banking Authority (EBA) in 2011. The idea was that banks would try to raise capital privately and governments would stand ready to cover any capital shortfalls. This was intended to ensure that the publication of the EBA results in December 2011 did not affect depositors' confidence adversely. Without such backstops, bank runs by depositors were likely.

In the case of Cyprus, the backstop's credibility came under question because the government had lost access to international capital markets in May 2011. At the end of 2011, however, the Cypriot government managed to secure a loan of €2.5 billion from the Russian Federation, which was hailed as a big success locally, although the terms of that loan were not particularly favourable.[1] That loan certainly raised hopes within Cyprus and even among some in Frankfurt, albeit to a lesser extent, that the backstop for Cyprus' banks could ultimately be provided by the Russian government.

In Cyprus, there were high hopes that the backstop would not be needed. Bank of Cyprus was certainly believed to be solid as a rock, notwithstanding the losses from the Greek PSI. This view was propagated by the local media:

---

[1] The interest rate on the Russian loan was 4.5% p.a. compared to less than 1% that Greece was paying on its loans from the international creditors (there was, however, no conditionality attached). See: http://www.euractiv.com/section/europe-s-east/news/russia-bails-out-cash-strapped-cyprus/. The government did not, at the time, disclose that the agreement with the Russian Federation was that the loan had to be repaid in full five years later.

© The Author(s) 2017
P. Demetriades, *A Diary of the Euro Crisis in Cyprus*,
DOI 10.1007/978-3-319-62223-1_4

it was unthinkable that the country's largest bank, and the oldest, would not be able raise sufficient capital. Laiki was more of a problem. The bank was no longer considered as strong as it used to be and that was reflected in its rapidly falling share price.[2] However, its new chairman, Michael Sarris, who took over from Greek tycoon Andreas Vgenopoulos at the beginning of 2012, exuded sufficient confidence to create the expectation that it would still be able to raise enough capital. Cyprus' third systemic bank, Hellenic, was also considered to be robust as it had not suffered any significant losses from the Greek PSI.

In Frankfurt, however, the mood was rather different. Before I took over, the ECB had been asking questions of my predecessor, Athanasios Orphanides. It was demanding to know how the Cypriot government would be able to provide a credible backstop. Following advice from Orphanides, Kikis Kazamias, who had been the minister of finance prior to Vasos Shiarly,[3] came up with two solutions. The first one was a new Russian loan, which, although somewhat uncertain wasn't completely discounted; indeed even at the ECB, some senior people believed that this might be forthcoming because of the 'special relationship' between Cyprus and Russia. The second option involved the government issuing recapitalisation bonds and exchanging them with Laiki shares in a direct equity-bond swap. This was, of course, neither novel nor ingenious, although it was presented as such by the mainstream local media. It was, in fact, remarkably similar to the blueprint created by the Irish government during 2010 in its attempt to recapitalise Anglo Irish Bank (AIB) and Irish Nationwide Building Society (INBS), without entering an IMF/EU adjustment programme. Both institutions were facing growing liquidity and solvency problems, as a result of risky lending to the property sector, notwithstanding earlier bailouts and guarantees offered by the Irish government. By 2010, following several government bailouts of Irish banks, the country's public debt was beginning to reach unsustainable levels. As a result, the Irish government was no longer able to borrow the massive sums required to recapitalise these institutions from international financial markets. It, therefore, resorted to issuing 'promissory notes', which were in essence IOUs that promised the bearer future coupon and principal payments. These notes were pledged as collateral for

---

[2]Laiki had raised capital amounting to €480 million euro in February 2011 through a rights issue at €1.0 per share, the largest issue ever until that time. By October of that year, the stock was already trading at below 40 cents and there were no signs of it stabilising there.

[3]Kazamias resigned in February 2012 stating health reasons.

ELA purposes to the Central Bank of Ireland. However, their value, and consequently their contribution to the banks' solvency, came under the scrutiny of the ECB. By November 2010, the ECB was so uncomfortable with the situation that its President, Jean-Claude Trichet, wrote a secret letter to the Irish minister of finance, Brian Lenihan, explaining that the ECB would be forced to cut off ELA to Irish banks if the Irish government continued refusing to apply for an adjustment programme.[4]

The provision of ELA by national central banks requires the non-objection by two-thirds majority of the Governing Council of the ECB. My predecessor was of course there, as Cyprus became a member of the euro zone on 1 January 2008. Trichet's warning to Lenihan had the clear consent of the Governing Council since it stated: 'It is the position of the Governing Council that it is only if we receive in writing a commitment from the Irish government vis-à-vis the Eurosystem on the four following points that we can authorise further provisions of ELA to Irish financial institutions'. The conditions included the Irish sending a request for financial support to the Eurogroup (the euro area finance minister's informal meeting), with the commitment to undertake fiscal consolidation, structural reform and financial sector restructuring and recapitalisation, in agreement with the European Commission, the IMF and the ECB.

Orphanides should, therefore, have known better, in the light of the Irish experience and his insights into the workings of the Eurosystem. The issuance of a bond by a government that had no access to international capital markets and that no one other than Laiki's shareholders was prepared to accept, would surely not have been sufficient to avoid an adjustment programme. It would have been little more than a 'paper' bailout, yet Orphanides' actions seemed to suggest that he thought Cyprus could succeed where Ireland had failed. The only plausible explanation for such behaviour is that he was simply buying time. Orphanides' term of office was due to expire on 2 May 2012 and although he made it no secret that he was seeking to be reappointed, it was also no secret that Christofias was extremely reluctant to reappoint him, because of the icy relations between them. If Laiki's problems became public in March 2012 through a bailout request, Orphanides' chances for reappointment would probably have evaporated altogether. There was no escape from the fact that Laiki's deterioration happened under his watch. The bank's capital position was so dire

---

[4]Although in Ireland the existence of the letter was known, it wasn't until November 2014 that the ECB made it public, together with related correspondence. See Appendix 1.

that at the end of March 2012 Laiki's external auditors warned its management that their audit would be qualified. The bank was about to report massive losses for 2011 that would have wiped out most of its capital. The day after the management received the auditors' letter, its senior management appealed to the finance minister for financial assistance in the form of underwriting an issue of €1.8 billion. At the same time, the bank was bleeding deposits by the day. Laiki's board feared that a bank run was imminent as many branches were trying to dissuade depositors from withdrawing their money. There was every reason that the bank should have requested a bailout within days from the auditor's letter in late March since the letter made it clear that there was no other viable prospect. However, finance minister Shiarly also chose to wait. My appointment to the Governor's position was made on 28 April 2012—only four days before Orphanides' term expired. Shiarly waited until I took office on 3 May 2012 before proceeding with the bank's request for government support.

As a result of Trichet's letter to Lenihan, the ECB was—and still is—widely criticised by the Irish media for its 'blackmailing' tactics. However, the ECB had little choice, given its legal set up. The ECB, unlike most other central banks, is prohibited by the EU Treaty from printing money to finance government deficits, either directly or indirectly. The monetary financing prohibition stems from Article 123 of the Treaty and complements the ECB's price stability mandate. In contrast to most other central banks that have multiple objectives, the ECB, which was modelled on the Bundesbank blueprint, has one primary objective: price stability. Price stability is, in turn, translated into an inflation target that is below but close to 2% per year.

If the Irish government had not applied for an adjustment programme that would restore the soundness of its public finances, Ireland could well have been the first country to leave the euro area, assuming Trichet's 'blackmail' wasn't an empty threat—which we will never know. In June 2012, Cyprus was beginning to receive the same treatment as Ireland. Not surprisingly, the ECB decided that the 'ingenious' swap wasn't a good idea. However, given the fragile political conditions, the ECB did not publish its legal opinion on the matter until six months later when the recapitalisation had been completed.

It was made increasingly clear to me during my first few visits to Frankfurt that the plan that was put together by Kazamias and Orphanides was problematic from its inception. The government had to borrow, either from another government or from the European Union and the IMF.

Realistically, the only government that may have been prepared to lend money to Cyprus at that time was Russia, which had already shown willingness to help the island, to the surprise of many in Europe. Christofias was certainly confident that another Russian loan could be secured. He had talked to the Russian ambassador who was positive. He also talked to Putin, who was, however, non-committal. It seemed that the Russian government had reservations but hadn't rejected the request out of hand. Putin reportedly said they needed time to examine it.

By the middle of June 2012, time was running out. It had already run out for Orphanides who wasn't reappointed, but who nevertheless continued to argue that the Cypriot banking system was in good shape until the day he left the CBC. It had run out for Sarris, the chairman of Laiki, who had managed to scrape €3.0 million from investors instead of the €300 million he had promised to raise at our first meeting on 6 May or the €1.8 billion he needed. It was also running out for Christofias who had nothing concrete from the Russian government.

The final blow came in the third week of June, when Fitch informed us that they were about to downgrade the credit worthiness of the Republic to junk status. Up to that time, it was the only rating agency that had maintained Cyprus' rating at investment grade. The reason that Fitch gave for the downgrade was that '…the Cypriot banks will require a material increase in their capital. Financial exposure to Greece has been the main driver of Cyprus' deteriorating credit profile…[t]he three large domestic banks, Bank of Cyprus, Cyprus Popular Bank and Hellenic Bank represent a large contingent liability for the sovereign'(Fitch ratings update, Cyprus, 4 July 2012).

The Fitch downgrade meant that Christofias had to be persuaded to apply for an IMF/EU bailout without any further delay. I knew his views, and he would certainly not be happy. I spoke to him on the phone on Friday, 22 June.

'Mr President, it is my duty to inform you of the consequences of the downgrade', I said, starting the conversation rather ominously. I continued with more or less what Trichet said in his letter to Lenihan, although at that point of time I wasn't even aware that such a letter existed.[5] I explained to

---

[5] I first learnt about that letter a year, or so, later when the proposal to release it was discussed at the ECB.

him that if his government did not apply for a bailout, the CBC would not be able to supply ELA to Laiki. The Fitch downgrade meant that the plan to recapitalise Laiki with the unfunded bond could only work if the government entered an adjustment programme, which would address solvency concerns, as it would aim to eventually restore the government's access to international markets. I explained that if we were forced to cut off ELA, Laiki would have to be liquidated, with catastrophic consequences for the economy. We would have a banking collapse, a widespread bank run and paralysis of the payments system. Moreover, the state would be required to pay for the insured deposits of Laiki, which it wasn't in a position to do so because the Deposit Insurance Fund had only €130 million, approximately, so it would, in effect, be defaulting on its obligations.

'Your choice Mr President', I concluded, 'is a simple one: you need to choose between chaos, in the form of a double default of the sovereign and a systemic bank, and order, in the form of a programme that will stabilise the banking system, public finances and the economy'.

I feared his response. I thought he would react with rage. Instead, his response was very calm. He said: 'Well, if you say so, then it must be so, I trust you. We will apply. But we will only apply to Europe, not to the IMF'. That was obvious as far as he was prepared to go to save his dignity. Like many of his comrades, he disliked the IMF. It was an organisation that had always been portrayed in stark terms by *Haravgi*, the party's newspaper. It thus came as a surprise to him later on, during the negotiations with the troika that the IMF wasn't the evil organisation he had always thought they were. In fact, on some occasions, it was more supportive of Cyprus than the other two institutions comprising the troika.[6]

That phone call was a very important step forward for Cyprus, yet few people knew it happened and even fewer understood its importance at that time or even later.

---

[6]For example, in the early stages of the discussions, the discussions, the IMF had put forward the idea that the banks could have been recapitalised directly from the European Stability Mechanism. Europe, however, was not prepared to accept that.

Although I was relieved, I wasn't sure how to handle the IMF issue. In the end, the ministry of finance had to handle it. With some difficulty, the ministry explained to the president that Europe wanted the IMF on board, there was no other way. He conceded that one too.

On 25 June 2012, the same day that Fitch announced its downgrade, the Republic of Cyprus officially applied for financial support from Europe and the IMF.

Between us, the minister and I had succeeded in persuading a reluctant president to accept the need for a financial adjustment programme. Vassos had been saying to me from the first day we met: 'You are the only one who can persuade Christofias to apply. I tried many times but I failed'.

It all seemed, however, easier than I expected. Later on, the reason for this became clear: Christofias was also buying time.[7]

Appendix: Irish Letters

Source: European Central Bank

https://www.ecb.europa.eu/press/html/irish-letters.en.html

'On 6 November 2014, the Governing Council of the European Central Bank decided to publish a letter written by former ECB president Jean-Claude Trichet on behalf of the Governing Council to then Irish Finance minister Brian Lenihan in November 2010.

With this decision, the ECB honoured the European Ombudsman's call for the Governing Council to re-consider the release of the letter. The Governing Council also decided to disclose a further three letters that were part of correspondence between the ECB and the Irish authorities in the run-up to the official application of Ireland for support under an EU/IMF adjustment programme.

---

[7]Christofias continued to believe until well into the autumn of 2012 that it was a matter of time before another Russian loan would materialise.

Also included below are public documents with statements and positions of the ECB on Ireland'.

EUROPEAN CENTRAL BANK

EUROSYSTEM

Jean-Claude TRICHET
President

Mr Brian Lenihan
Tánaiste and
Minister of Finance
Government Buildings
Upper Merrion Street
Dublin 2
Ireland

Frankfurt, 19 November 2010
L/JCT/10/1444

Dear Minister,

As you are aware from my previous letter dated 15 October, the provision of *Emergency Liquidity Assistance (ELA)* by the Central Bank of Ireland, as by any other national central bank of the Eurosystem, is closely monitored by the Governing Council of the European Central Bank (ECB) as it may interfere with the objectives and tasks of the Eurosystem and may contravene the prohibition of monetary financing. Therefore, whenever ELA is provided in significant amounts, the Governing Council needs to assess whether it is appropriate to impose specific conditions in order to protect the integrity of our monetary policy. In addition, in order to ensure compliance with the prohibition of monetary financing, it is essential to ensure that ELA recipient institutions continue to be solvent.

As I indicated at the recent Eurogroup meeting, the exposure of the Eurosystem and of the Central Bank of Ireland vis-à-vis Irish financial institutions has risen significantly over the past few months to levels that we consider with great concern. Recent developments can only add to these concerns. As Patrick Honohan knows, the Governing Council has been asked yesterday to authorise new liquidity assistance which it did.

But all these considerations have implications for the assessment of the solvency of the institutions which are currently receiving ELA. It is the position of the Governing Council that it is only if we receive in writing a commitment from the Irish Government vis-à-vis the Eurosystem on the four following points that we can authorise further provisions of ELA to Irish financial institutions:

1)   The Irish government shall send a request for financial support to the Eurogroup;

2)   The request shall include the commitment to undertake decisive actions in the areas of fiscal consolidation, structural reforms and financial sector restructuring, in agreement with the European Commission, the International Monetary Fund and the ECB;

3)   The plan for the restructuring of the Irish financial sector shall include the provision of the necessary capital to those Irish banks needing it and will be funded by the financial resources provided at the European and international level to the Irish government as well as by financial means currently available to the Irish government, including existing cash reserves of the Irish government;

4)   The repayment of the funds provided in the form of ELA shall be fully guaranteed by the Irish Government, which would ensure the payment of immediate compensation to the Central Bank of Ireland in the event of missed payments on the side of the recipient institutions.

I am sure that you are aware that a swift response is needed before markets open next week, as evidenced by recent market tensions which may further escalate, possibly in a disruptive way, if no concrete action is taken by the Irish government on the points I mention above.

Besides the issue of the provision of ELA, the Governing Council of the ECB is extremely concerned about the very large overall credit exposure of the Eurosystem towards the Irish banking system. The Governing Council constantly monitors the credit granted to the banking system not only in Ireland but in all euro area countries, and in particular the size of Eurosystem exposures to individual banks, the financial soundness of these banks and the collateral they provide to the Eurosystem. The assessment of the Governing Council on the appropriateness of the Eurosystem's exposure to Irish banks will essentially depend on rapid and decisive progress in the formulation of a concrete action plan in the areas which have been mentioned in this letter and in its subsequent implementation.

With kind regards

Cc.: Mr Brian Cowen, Prime Minister

5

"Two" Big to Fail

My first six weeks in office coincided with unprecedented political turmoil in Greece, which unleashed a huge wave of financial contagion in Cyprus.

A Greek Tsunami

The Greek election of 6 May 2012 delivered a hung Parliament. After failed attempts to form a government by each of the three largest parties, a second general election was set for 17 June. The risk of a 'Grexit'—Greek exit from the Eurozone—started to loom large over both Greece and Cyprus. SYRIZA, the coalition of the radical left, which came a close second in the election of 6 May, was determined to renegotiate the terms of the bailout. If it won the election, many commentators were predicting that the country would be starved of essential bailout funds and be forced to leave the Eurozone. Greek depositors were withdrawing hundreds of millions of bank notes every day from Greek banks and stashing them in safe deposit boxes or at home. There was flight to quality: euro bank notes were much safer than euro bank deposits, as the latter could be redenominated into a different currency overnight.

Laiki, which was clearly perceived as a weak bank, was haemorrhaging deposits from its Greek branches. During May and June 2012, it experienced deposit outflows of around €2 billion—around 10% of its total deposit base. It was certainly critical to stabilise the bank through a much-needed capital injection. I thus had no choice but to agree to plans to

© The Author(s) 2017
P. Demetriades, *A Diary of the Euro Crisis in Cyprus*,
DOI 10.1007/978-3-319-62223-1_5

recapitalise the bank by the state, although it was obvious to me that those plans would have to be accompanied by an IMF/EU adjustment programme application. I, therefore, had the daunting task of trying to prepare public opinion that an application for a bailout was unavoidable.

Financial journalists were beginning to appreciate the need to protect—'ring-fence'—Cypriot banks from a possible Greek tsunami, although few understood the implications of Grexit for Cyprus. The Cypriot government's responsibility for insured deposits in Greece was in euros, while the loans to Greek businesses and households—would be redenominated to new drachmas and probably lose much of their value in no time. The Greek assets of Cypriot banks amounted to €25 billion, roughly 140% of Cyprus' GDP. Back of the envelope calculations suggested that Cyprus could lose between 50% and 60% of its GDP overnight by the black hole that would be created by Grexit. In all likelihood, Grexit would be followed by Cyprexit.

Protecting Cyprus from Grexit was, therefore, of utmost urgency. In my very first month in office, I paid a visit to my Greek counterpart at the Bank of Greece, George Provopoulos. Provopoulos had no objection to ring-fencing as long as we were able to recapitalise the Greek branches before converting them into subsidiaries; as such they could be folded in—or sold on—without impacting on the parent banks in Cyprus. The branches would have to be subjected to stress tests, which were likely to reveal significant capital shortfalls. There was no spare money in the Greek programme to recapitalise them, Provopoulos said to us. In any case, the branches of Cypriot banks in Greece were not the responsibility of the Greek taxpayer.[1] Building defences against Grexit was proving to be easier said than done.

In the Footsteps of Alexander

Amidst all the negative developments affecting Laiki, it was rather refreshing to receive the Bank of Cyprus CEO, Andreas Eliades, on 29 May 2012 and to hear from him that his bank was sound. Eliades assured me that the bank had nearly achieved its capital target. He also said that any shortfall was so small that it could easily be covered by a disposal of non-core assets. He explained they were in advanced negotiations to sell their insurance

---

[1]The irony was that in April 2011, Marfin Egnatia—a Greek lender—was converted from a subsidiary of Laiki into a branch, thereby transferring the responsibility of recapitalising that bank to the Cypriot taxpayer.

subsidiary, which would be more than sufficient to cover any capital shortfall.

I was, however, less than reassured by what followed. Eliades went on to argue that he saw the Greek crisis as more of an opportunity than a threat for the Bank of Cyprus. He was proud that they had continued to expand during the Greek crisis, while other banks were contracting. In 2011, at the height of the Greek crisis, Bank of Cyprus opened 11 new branches in Greece, he boasted. This was beginning to sound odd, if not altogether reckless, but I had more pressing problems on that day than curtailing Eliades' grandiose plans.

Eliades was a highly ambitious and confident man. He rose through the ranks to become the bank's CEO in Greece and eventually became the CEO for the bank's worldwide operations. During the Eliades era, Bank of Cyprus grew its business within Greece and expanded aggressively into new markets such as Romania, Russia and the Ukraine. That represented a break from decades of tradition, which dictated that the bank should be present only in countries in which there was a significant Greek Cypriot community. The UK and Greece were such countries as was, to a lesser extent, Australia. The bank thought—rightly—that it could attract business from Cypriot ex-pats and that it would also be able to hire staff from the community that spoke the language and shared common values with its clientele in those countries.

One of Eliades' most risky investments was the majority acquisition of Uniastrum Bank in Russia, only weeks after the collapse of Lehman in 2008. The purchase price was $576 million, which turned out to be grossly inflated. In 2015, the bank sold its shares in Uniastrum for $13 million and was pleased that it eliminated that risk. From this investment alone, Bank of Cyprus recorded losses approaching €1.0 billion.

Laiki had similar, if not more questionable, ambitions under CEO and Chairman Andreas Vgenopoulos, who acquired a controlling stake in 2006 with CBC's consent. Laiki acquired banks in Romania, Russia, Serbia and the Ukraine, which turned out to be poor investments. In Greece, it took over Marfin Egnatia bank, a small but troubled lender that belonged to Vgenopoulos himself. The bank was involved in various scandals, including loans to monasteries that were used to prop up the shares of Marfin Investment Group (MIG), Vgenopoulos' group of companies. This act alone—which my predecessor's critics think he could and should have stopped—turned a Greek bank that was very much the responsibility of the Greek government into a large contingent liability for Cyprus. Insured deposits in Marfin Egnatia, for which the responsibility was transferred from Greece to Cyprus, were about €5.0 billion. The responsibility for providing

ELA to Marfin Egnatia, a bank that was bleeding deposits, was shifted from Greece to Cyprus. Indeed, Laiki's reliance on ELA began six months later, and was largely the result of deposit outflows from the branches of former Marfin Egnatia.

The excesses of Laiki and Bank of Cyprus did not cease to surprise me in my first few weeks in office. I nearly fell off my chair when I first heard that between them, Bank of Cyprus and Laiki were employing 3000 people in the Ukraine. I had an even bigger shock when I first saw European bank rankings that used bank balance sheet size relative to GDP. Our banks topped the table. Number one in the European Union was Bank of Cyprus with 211% of GDP. Number 2 was Laiki with 190% of GDP. Two banks from one of the smallest countries in Europe. An island state with a population of less than one million people, that was bigger only than Malta. How was all this allowed to happen?

Capture

With their combined balance sheets exceeding four times the size of the economy, nearly everyone in Cyprus depended on these two large banks, often in more ways than one. It is, of course, normal for households and businesses to depend on banks for credit. However, in Cyprus the dependencies went much, much, further than what could be considered normal. To start with, bank credit itself was provided abundantly. So much so, that by 2011, private sector indebtedness had reached 286% of GDP—it was the third highest in Europe; Bank of Cyprus and Laiki accounted for roughly half the indebtedness of households and firms. Moreover, between them, Bank of Cyprus and Laiki employed over 5000 people in Cyprus alone; they were considered excellent employers, as they offered good pay and good employment conditions. Many staff at the CBC had spouses or children who worked for one of the big two. Importantly, the media depended on them for advertising revenues, more so during the crisis when other advertising was drying up. They also depended on them for credit, which seems to have been on favourable terms. I began to understand how such a small island state could sustain six daily newspapers and four fully fledged TV stations, each with their own news bulletin.

Arts, culture and charities also depended on them, as the banks contributed generously to various worthy causes, and established their own cultural foundations (e.g. the Bank of Cyprus Cultural Foundation), medical institutes (e.g. the Bank of Cyprus Oncology Centre) and research institutes. Universities depended on them for supporting conferences, sponsoring chairs (e.g. the prestigious Bank of Cyprus Chair in Finance at the University of Cyprus), student prizes and research funding. No wonder few, if any, dared question let alone criticise the bank's excessive risk taking.[2] When a bank's balance sheet reaches 20–30% of GDP, it is considered systemic. When it is 200% of GDP, it is not just systemic. It is controlling. An entire society was completely captured.

On a good day, the grandiose ambitions of Bank of Cyprus and Laiki reminded me of King Alexander the Great of Macedon who, by the age of 30, created one of the biggest empires in the ancient world, extending well into Asia and North Africa. But even the most romantic admirers of Great Alexander recognise that his ambitions were over the top. By the time he reached India, his army was exhausted and homesick. His troops decided they wanted to go home. In similar vein, I've heard that Bank of Cyprus had difficulty sending 'troops' to manage their overseas subsidiaries. Many were complaining of the risks. Some of these new markets were dangerous to life, let alone property. In their most costly investment, Uniastrum, they sent five staff from Cyprus, but only one of them had the nerve to remain. I wondered how they thought they could manage 220 branches with one person.

The similarities with Alexander, however, end there. Whereas Alexander managed to spread Greek culture well beyond the borders of modern Greece, I suspect that the only legacy that will be left behind by the reckless expansions of the big two will be the losses suffered by their shareholders and creditors.

Gambling for Resurrection

There was a repeat performance when I met the Bank of Cyprus chairman, Theodoros Aristodemou, for the first time. This was two weeks after my meeting with Eliades, on Wednesday 13 June. Aristodemou was equally optimistic as Eliades. 'Our bank will not need state help', he boasted. As if that wasn't enough to convince me, I had a visit from their entire board of directors on 17 June. The message was the same, loud and clear: 'We will

---

[2] A commentary by Andreas Paraschos, chief editor of *Kathimerini Cyprus*, reproduced in an Appendix to this chapter, is indicative of the extent of media capture by the banks. *Kathimerini Cyprus* is a weekly newspaper partly owned by the prestigious Greek daily newspaper *Kathimerini*.

not need state help, we are in the process of selling our insurance subsidiary and that would cover any shortfall, which is not expected to be more than €200 million, anyway'. On that occasion, Eliades was playing second fiddle to Aristodemou. I asked Aristodemou to explain to me why they had made such large losses from the Greek PSI, indeed why they had a risk concentration of over 100% of their own capital in Greek Government Bonds. He gave me the most remarkable answer:

> We had Mr Papademos visit us', he said, 'after he stepped down from the ECB. He assured us that there will not be any restructuring of Greek debt'.

Papademos was Governor of the Bank of Greece from 1994 to 2002 and Vice President of the ECB from 2002 to 2010. In 2010, he was an adviser to the Greek Prime Minister George Papandreou. He then became caretaker Prime Minister of Greece, following Papandreou's resignation in November 2011.

It was a naive, if not altogether arrogant, answer for a bank chairman to be using to justify a gamble that didn't pay off: they had 'invested' around 100% of the bank's capital into a single financial instrument, which, by any definition, constituted an excessive concentration of risk. Moreover, it wasn't just any instrument. It was, according to financial markets, the riskiest sovereign bond in Europe not least because it reflected what markets saw as the necessity of Greek debt restructuring. Yet Bank of Cyprus' leaders behaved as if they knew better.

Aristodemou either didn't understand the basic principles of banking and finance or assumed that his political connections meant that he could play the game better than the markets. Or it could just have been a feeble post facto excuse for a massive gamble that didn't pay off. After all, before the PSI was agreed by the private sector, the official line in Europe was that the restructuring of the debt was unnecessary. I very much doubt that a central banker like Papademos would give anything other than the official version away, which was, in any case, well known.

Aristodemou stepped down in the summer of 2012 citing health reasons. A year later, when the press got hold of a report prepared by the Bank of Cyprus on its 20 largest corporate exposures, it became public information that loans to companies connected to Aristodemou had reached several hundred million euros, the vast majority of which were non-performing. No wonder the bank's CEO could get away with taking excessive risks in Greece and elsewhere, when the board chairman depended on the bank's executives for approval of his loans.[3]

Corporate governance was certainly lax throughout the banking system. It was partly the result of a lax regulatory framework, in which even the definition of NPLs fell short of international norms, which stipulate that a loan be classed as an NPL once it is 90 days overdue. In Cyprus, such loans were considered performing if they were backed by sufficient collateral. The regulatory framework was, however, tough on bank directors with NPLs, who could be disqualified on grounds of lack of fitness and probity. Many bank directors, including Aristodemou, would not have qualified had the NPL definition been brought into line with international norms earlier.

The Business Model

How did Bank of Cyprus and Laiki, as well as the rest of the banking system, become so big?

Part of the reason was, of course, the euphoria that followed the island's accession to the EU in 2004, which contributed both to capital inflows and banking risks being underestimated. That was Cyprus' Minsky moment, very much in line with the financial instability hypothesis put forward by Minsky (1992) whereby during a boom risks are underestimated and eventually lead to crisis. However, that does not fully explain the influx of foreign money into the country's banks and the property market. For that one needs to look more closely at the banks' business model, which involved attracting funding from wealthy foreign clients.

The origins of that model had a lot to do with the island's transformation during the 1980s into an 'offshore' business centre. At that time, Cyprus, and in particular Limassol, marketed itself as a more stable regional alternative to Beirut, which had been the region's business hub until Lebanon descended into civil war. In the 1990s, Cyprus' offshore status, common law legal system, double tax treaties and geography proved an attraction to new Russian and Ukrainian entrepreneurs aiming to avoid high domestic taxes or corrupt courts to settle business disputes. Although Cyprus lost its 'offshore' status when it joined the EU in 2004, Russian and Ukrainian

---

[3]It is worth adding that both Aristodemou and Eliades, alongside other senior bankers, are now facing criminal charges over the purchases of Greek Government Bonds and, in particular, about the methods used to conceal the risk in the bank's accounts.

company registrations remained buoyant as Cyprus opted for the lowest corporate tax rate in Europe (10%). Moreover, by the early 2000s, Cyprus already possessed a large and successful industry of law and accounting professionals who were quick to exploit the opportunities offered by post-communist Russia and other countries of the former USSR.[4] Cypriot law and accounting firms helped these entrepreneurs set up thousands of companies in Cyprus and acted on their behalf in numerous legal disputes.[5] They also facilitated the opening of bank accounts in the country's banks, which had geared themselves up for attracting the business of wealthy foreign clients by setting up international business divisions.[6]

The business model revolved around politically connected law firms and the wider interest group of professional services, including accountancy firms, other law firms and banks. These 'introducers', were the catalysts for Russian business and capital inflows. Bank of Cyprus alone had around 1.900 introducers.

Mixing law, politics and business were not unusual in Cyprus (see, for example, Stavrakis 2012).[7] Members of the Parliament who were not practicing lawyers were an exception rather than the norm. The practice of law was not limited to politicians elected to Parliament. It was also quite common at the highest levels of government. Indeed, four out of seven presidents since Cyprus gained its independence from Britain in 1960 have been lawyers.

Politicians did not refrain from exercising influence over the affairs of banks. This happened through control of the Central Bank of Cyprus board, which was the bank's supervisor, or through control of commercial bank boards or the committees of credit cooperatives. Before Cyprus joined the EU, the CBC had limited, if any independence, from the government, as the government could exercise a veto on central bank decisions through its representative on the CBC's board of directors. Moreover, the president had the constitutional right to dismiss the CBC Governor at will. Given

---

[4]Stavrakis (2012) names the law firm of Nicos Anastasiades, the current president of Cyprus, as one of the first to enter the Russian market.

[5]Deakin (2016) analyses the weakness of the Russian legal system, which explains why Cyprus law often acts as a substitute because of its common law characteristics and fair courts.

[6]For more details on the Cyprus business model, see Lascelles (2013) or Stephanou (2011b).

[7]Charilaos Stavrakis was a senior banker in Bank of Cyprus who became the first finance minister in the government of Demetris Christofias. His book provides anecdotal evidence of cronyism and corruption on the island. He was quoted by Cyprus Property News (20 February 2012) as saying that 'some people who entered politics poor have subsequently become very rich'. See: http://www.news.cyprus-property-buyers.com/2012/02/20/corruption-in-cyprus-at-all-levels-says-former-minister/id=0010765.

the CBC's role as supervisor of the banking system, this translated into near complete control over the affairs of banks, including, for example, the authority to approve changes in bank ownership, fitness and probity checks for bank directors and issuing directives that governed lending and corporate governance within banks.

When Cyprus became a member of the EU in 2004, the constitution was amended to protect the independence of the CBC. The government lost the right of automatically dismissing the Governor at will. It also lost its veto power on the CBC's board. Old habits, however, die hard. Politicians continued to try to exercise influence over central bank decisions using their influence over board members, whose independence is not protected by law, and by exerting indirect pressure on central bank Governors through the use of their influence over the media, Parliament and the legal system, arguing that the Governor's independence is limited to matters of euro area monetary policy.

Cypriot lawyer-politicians had a clear advantage over other lawyers in attracting Russian business. In post-communist Russia, success in business without political connections or political backing is challenging, if not altogether impossible. In Cyprus, many lawyer-politicians had direct links with banks. Some of these links allegedly involved banks paying lawyers lucrative commissions for introducing wealthy Russian depositors (known as 'introducer fees').

The links between banks and lawyer-politicians helped to ensure that banks avoided close scrutiny when they began to take on excessive risks. As the central bank was accountable to Parliament for its banking supervision function, Parliament had every right and every obligation to exercise parliamentary scrutiny. Although the rating agencies made it abundantly clear that the banks represented a growing contingent liability for the country's public finances, during 2007–2012, Parliament refrained from asking the CBC penetrating questions relating to how these risks were being managed. Instead, the opposition parties that represented a majority in Parliament during the Christofias period deflected attention from the banks by focusing parliamentary discussions on the deterioration in public finances and increases in social spending. The media, which depended on the banks for advertising, adopted the same stance. So much so, that critical articles about banks' risk taking were censored.[8] By the time Parliament woke up

---

[8]Testimony was given in a recent court case by Michael Olympios, Chairman of the Cypriot Investor's Association, whose column in the newspaper *Politis* was cancelled because it was critical of Bank of Cyprus. The bank threatened the newspaper with reduced advertising expenditure. The case involves criminal charges against the Bank of Cyprus concerning market manipulation.

to the enormous contingent liability that had been created by the banking system, it was far too late to do anything.[9]

Appendix: A Commentary in Kathimerini Cyprus

«Όταν μια επιχείρηση ΜΜΕ, ξεκινά την κάθε νέα χρονιά, έχοντας διασφαλισμένο διαφημιστικό κονδύλι πέραν του ενός εκατομμυρίου από μία μόνο τράπεζα και τα ανάλογα από τις άλλες, τότε ο καθείς αντιλαμβάνεται ποιός υπαγορεύει τους όρους του παιχνιδιού. Όταν παράλληλα, ΜΜΕ λάμβαναν δάνεια εκατομμυρίων και μεγάλα παρατραβήγματα με «ευκολίες πληρωμής», τότε ποιός δημοσιογράφος μπορούσε να τα βάλει με τις τράπεζες, χωρίς να χάσει τη δουλειά του; Υπάρχουν κι άλλα, όπως οδηγίες τραπεζιτών για πιέσεις, π.χ. προς την εποπτική αρχή ή για προστασία της εποπτικής αρχής. Τα είδαμε και στο πολύ πρόσφατο παρελθόν να συμβαίνουν σε σύμπραξη τραπεζιτών, πολιτικών και ΜΜΕ.»

Η «δουλειά» από ποιούς γινόταν, αν όχι από δημοσιογράφους, αυλικούς του συστήματος ή και αιχμάλωτούς του;...

Έχουμε ευθύνη και οι δημοσιογράφοι για την κατάσταση στην πατρίδα μας; Έχουμε.»

Α. Παράσχος, Διευθυντής, Καθημερινή Κύπρου

9 Δεκεμβρίου 2012

Translation

'When a media enterprise starts each year having already secured an advertising budget over one million euros from just one bank and analogous amounts from others, then everyone understands who dictates the rules of the game. When in addition to this, media enterprises received loans amounting to millions and large overdrafts with "convenient repayment terms", then how could any journalist take issue with the banks without losing their job?

There is much more, like instructions by bankers for exerting pressure, e.g. on the supervisory authority [the CBC]. We have also seen in the very recent past collusion between bankers, politicians and the media.

Who did this job, if not the journalists, loyal servants of the system or its prisoners?

---

[9]For greater analysis of how the risks were ignored, see Lascelles (2013).

Do we have responsibility, us journalists, for the condition of our country? We do'.

Andreas Paraschos, Editor, Kathimerini Cyprus
9 December 2012

Bibliography

Deakin, Simon. 2016. *The Role of Law in Economic Development: The Case of Russia.* Mimeo: University of Cambridge.

Lascelles, David. 2013. *Independent Commission on the Future of the Cyprus Banking Sector,* Final Report, 31 October 2013. http://www.centralbank.gov.cy/media/pdf/LSE_ICFCBS_Final_Report_10_13.pdf.

Minsky, Hyman P. 1992. The Financial Instability Hypothesis. Working Paper No. 74 (May), Levy Economics Institute of Bard College.

Stavrakis, Charilaos. 2012. *Economy in Politics and Politics in the Economy* (in Greek).

Stephanou, Costas. 2011b. The Banking System in Cyprus: Time to Rethink the Business Model? *Cyprus Economic Policy Review* 5 (2): 123–130.

6

Too Big to Save?

The Diagnosis

Philip was clearly an old hand at the IMF. When he broke the news about his top-down estimates of the capital needs of the domestic banking sector, he had a grin on his face. It looked like he had done this sort of thing before. Many times.

'Your country is bankrupt', he exclaimed.

'The amount needed to recapitalise the banks and credit cooperatives is €13.5 billion', he continued. That was nearly 80% of the country's GDP, which, if true, would have been a new world record. In terms of the fiscal cost, the costliest systemic banking crisis up to that point had been Indonesia in 1997 at 57% of GDP (Laeven and Valencia 2013).

Philip appeared very proud of his work. His expression was not too dissimilar to that of a doctor who had just discovered what was wrong with a patient that no one else had been able to detect. It was as if his kind of diagnosis was the *raison d' être* for the Fund's existence. Now that they had the correct diagnosis, the Fund's troops could be parachuted on to the island to administer the right IMF medicine.

Philip's remarks were made in front of all the troika chiefs of mission, several representatives from the ministry of finance and a number of CBC officials. All the seats around the large meeting table in the Governor's office, which could easily sit 12 people, were taken. In fact, additional chairs were brought in, so there were probably around 20 people in the room.

© The Author(s) 2017
P. Demetriades, *A Diary of the Euro Crisis in Cyprus*,
DOI 10.1007/978-3-319-62223-1_6

There was a momentary silence while the Cypriots looked at Philip and at each other in disbelief. I then started questioning his methodology, with help from the CBC's more experienced supervisors, who started probing him on the more technical details.

Philip stood firm but he started becoming defensive. He reluctantly revealed that his working assumption relating to the value of collateral held by the banks was a very simple one: the collateral was assumed to have zero value. His thinking was that the legal framework was such that it would take a very long time for banks to repossess property. This was, in fact, true, but one of the aims of the programme would be to modernise the legal framework on foreclosures, so that banks could recover some of the collateral.

Philip's second line of defence was that the property market would collapse, anyway, given that the economy would be entering a long and deep recession. So, any attempt to sell foreclosed properties would be doomed to fail, he explained.

I countered his arguments: 'Yes, prices will decline but will not drop to zero, and, as all economists know, at zero price there will be an infinite number of buyers prepared to buy'.

He started scrapping the bottom of the barrel for his third line of defence: 'I have done this sort of work many times before', he said. 'I was spot on with my estimates in the case of the Savings and Loan (S&L) crisis and I had assumed zero collateral values back then, which was a good approximation for the outturn', he added.

Having been familiar with the S&L crisis, as part of my academic work, I explained that the S&L crisis was not a good comparison with the situation in Cyprus. I pointed out that Cyprus was a much smaller as well as a much more open economy than the USA. The property market could easily recover with a relatively small influx of foreign investment. This also meant that when prices eventually bottomed out, there would be a quick recovery.

Philip did not respond directly to my arguments but instead turned to other members of the troika for support. It was time to reveal the CBC's own, rough and ready, preliminary estimates of the capital needs of the banking system. These were still pretty large but only around half of Philip's. Philip did not concede but others, who had much less at stake, recognised that his estimates were only a starting point. Even his IMF colleagues became reluctant to endorse them.

It was, however, agreed that much more work was needed to be done and that Philip's estimates provided us with an upper limit. The Commission and the ECB said that they would carry out their own top-down estimates using more realistic assumptions. In any case, everyone agreed that we would need bottom-up estimates, which would involve looking at the loan portfolio of each bank in some detail in order to get an accurate picture of the capital needs. The troika mission chiefs suggested that for that kind of exercise to be reliable, an independent consultant needed to be appointed as soon as possible. There was no disagreement on that. It was the only way to convince markets and the rating agencies, which would have helped to find private investors. It was also agreed that the appointment of the independent consultant would be carried out by a steering committee composed of all the institutions of the troika and representatives of the Cypriot authorities (the ministry of finance, the CBC and the supervisor of the credit cooperatives). In addition, there were to be representatives from the European Banking Authority (EBA) and the European Stability Mechanism (ESM). It was also agreed that the same committee would provide the necessary parameters that the consultant needed to carry out the stress tests (i.e. the parameters relating to the baseline and adverse scenarios needed for the stress tests).

Nothing in Cyprus stays secret for very long. The next day the headlines in Phileleftheros—the largest circulation daily—read: 'Cypriot banks' capital needs estimated at €10 billion'. I don't know how *Phileleftheros* arrived at that figure. Perhaps it was the midpoint between the IMF's and the CBC's preliminary estimates. Or perhaps someone had fed the newspaper that figure in order to cause a stir.

It was, of course, a relief that they didn't publish Philip's number. Still, €10 billion was equivalent to 57% of Cyprus' GDP. Coincidentally, it was the same order of magnitude as Indonesia in 1997. This wasn't, of course, surprising as an order of magnitude (although, as the CBC's own estimates suggested it may have been at the top end of plausibility); the banking system in Cyprus became very large relative to GDP, so bailing it out was likely to be costly.

Such a high figure immediately raised the question of whether the country could afford to bail out the domestic banks. At the time, the public debt-to-GDP ratio was just over 70% so adding another 57% would take it to 127%. We all thought that 120% of GDP was the magical figure that the IMF would use in its debt sustainability analysis, in light of the Greek experience. But the important question is how debt dynamics behaved after that. Without a full debt sustainability analysis, no one could say whether that kind of bill was affordable. Debt could go over 120% for a year or two but it could start declining to more reasonable levels if the government started creating fiscal surpluses. The cost of borrowing also comes in. An adjustment programme offered very low costs of borrowing, relative to market rates.

A low-interest rate combined with a positive growth rate can make a large amount of public debt affordable.

Another Conspiracy Theory

Phillip and his IMF team arrived in Cyprus well before the troika teams. They were part of a confidential technical assistance mission that came to the island several weeks earlier to carry out a top-down diagnostic analysis of the banking system and the credit cooperative sector.

I agreed to such technical assistance at the first IMF constituency meeting I attended, which took place in Bucharest during 15–17 June 2012. I saw no reason to refuse the IMF's offer.

'It would be an opportunity for you to find out the real state of the Cypriot banking system at the start of your term, and no one would blame you for what you had inherited', the senior female IMF official explained. She was, of course, correct, but only in theory. In practice, neither she nor I fully appreciated the extent to which the media and politicians were captured by the interest groups that centred around the banks. Stories relating to the banks were twisted and distorted. Myths and conspiracy theories were easily created. Soon after the €10 billion figure was published by *Phileleftheros*, a new conspiracy theory was borne: the figure was, supposedly, my own estimate. The conspiracy theory being peddled by the media was that I had given the figure to the troika in order to satisfy the communist president, who wanted to destroy the banks. The facts were, of course, very different. Besides the fact that it was the IMF that came up with the figures that were used to justify the €10 billion figure leaked to the press, Christofias never mentioned anything to me that was even remotely related to the banks' capital needs. He wanted the CBC to get on with its job and did not want to interfere with its work, especially after the tense relationship between him and my predecessor.

The government spokesman, Stephanos Stephanou, did, however, on more than one occasion express real fears to me over the banks' capital needs: he was worried that a large bill to recapitalize the banks could be used by the troika to extract more concessions from the Republic. The notion that the AKEL government wanted to destroy the banks was nothing more than absurd propaganda. But cheap propaganda can work.

The propaganda machine found a pretext to ignore the real facts. It claimed that the troika had only recently arrived in Cyprus, therefore they couldn't have produced estimates of the banks' capital needs so quickly.

The propaganda machine was helped by the fact that the IMF's technical assistance mission was confidential. On this occasion there was no leak. Or if there was one, those who had access to this information must have decided that they didn't want the facts to get in the way of a good conspiracy theory. The banks, after all, were indirectly paying the bills. Indeed, the Bank of Cyprus doubled its advertising budget during the crisis.

By the time the troika visited again in November 2012, the three troika institutions came to agree that the bill would not be more than €10 billion. The preliminary Memorandum of Understanding that had been agreed did, in fact, have the number €10 billion in square brackets, indicating that it was the upper limit of the amount needed to recap the banks.

A few months later, PIMCO, the consultant appointed to carry out the independent diagnostic estimate came up with a figure that was not far off €10 billion. This provided more 'evidence' for the conspiracy theorists. They arrived at the conclusion that PIMCO must have been part of the communist plot to destroy the Cypriot banking system. The fact that PIMCO was the world's biggest asset manager and that there couldn't be a more capitalist company than that was conveniently ignored.

On 4 July 2014, only a few months after the publication of a parliamentary inquiry into the causes of the crisis that had claimed that PIMCO exaggerated the capital needs of the banking system, Bank of Cyprus was forced to raise additional capital of €1 billion. This was in order to pass the ECB stress tests that were being carried out just before the establishment of the Single Supervisory Mechanism in the euro area. The stress tests used data from the end of 2013 whereas the bank had been fully recapitalized based on PIMCO's adverse scenario in July 2013. The facts, once again, suggested that, if anything, PIMCO underestimated the capital needs of the banking system.

The propaganda machine hasn't, to date, managed to reconcile these facts with the conspiracy theory of exaggerated capital needs. I suspect it never will. It will just not let them get in the way.

Bibliography

Laeven, Luc, and Fabian Valencia. 2013. Systemic banking crises database. *IMF Economic Review* 61: 225–270.

7

A Russian Playground

Within days from 25 June 2012, the date that Cyprus applied for financial assistance from Europe and the IMF, troika technocrats started descending on the Island. The teams were large, as they contained economists with different specialisations, including banking and public finance specialists, competition economists and lawyers. I met regularly with the mission chiefs and took part in discussions about banking sector issues. By the end of July, the troika submitted its proposals to the government, covering banking sector, public finance, labour and structural reforms and left the island. In August, Europe goes on holiday. Crises are put on hold.

Not surprisingly, Christofias didn't like the troika proposals. There was too much austerity, he felt, and it was falling disproportionately on the weaker segments of the population. He and his labour minister, Sotiroulla Charalambous, a feisty lady trade-unionist, were strongly against the labour reforms proposed by the troika, which they saw as dismantling decades-long labour struggles.[1] Privatisation of state-owned enterprises, which were to cover telecommunications, ports and electricity supply, was also an issue, although, surprisingly, these reforms were not seen as a priority by the troika. Christofias also had issues with banking sector reforms, particularly those relating to credit cooperatives. The troika was proposing that the coops be brought under the supervision of the CBC. Hitherto, they were supervised by a department of the ministry of commerce that had a dual role: to promote the development of cooperatives as well as to regulate them. There

---

[1]The abolition of wage indexation was a prime example of this.

© The Author(s) 2017
P. Demetriades, *A Diary of the Euro Crisis in Cyprus*,
DOI 10.1007/978-3-319-62223-1_7

was certainly an inherent conflict in the dual mandate and it didn't take the troika technocrats very long to spot that.

The banking sector reforms proposed by the troika were, by and large, reasonable. They were addressing not only the symptoms but, more importantly, the deeper underlying causes of the crisis. Besides shoring up capital buffers, the proposed reforms included a significant strengthening of the regulatory framework, tighter corporate governance for the banks, which involved having boards with majority independent directors, and improved lending standards to ensure that banks were lending on the basis of ability to repay rather than the availability of collateral.

There were also proposals relating to strengthening the anti-money laundering (AML) framework, which included carrying out a specialised audit. This created considerable friction. The ministry of finance didn't want money laundering mentioned at all in the Memorandum of Understanding (MoU). It could create the wrong perceptions about Cyprus, the minister of finance argued. After all, he argued, Cyprus received good evaluations by Moneyval[2] and was ranked no worse than most other European countries, including Germany. The troika wasn't convinced. Their response was that if we had nothing to hide, we had nothing to worry about. In fact, the audit could help to silence the critics in Europe. They were, of course, correct.

Christofias instructed his ministers to come up with counterproposals. He was much more concerned about austerity, labour reforms, the credit cooperatives and privatisation than the AML audit. While Europe was on holiday, officials from various ministries were working on their counterproposals. On 30 August 2012, I was invited to a meeting at the presidential palace, chaired by the President, which was to discuss the counterproposals. The CBC's role was limited to advising, primarily on banking sector reforms, although our views on other reforms were also welcome.

I witnessed a government in disharmony and under pressure. Christofias was clearly unhappy with his minister of finance, Vassos Shiarly.[3] His ministry's proposals were much too close to the proposals of the troika: they were certainly not consistent with the president's ideology, in that there was little attempt to protect the most vulnerable in society. 'Who is in government?' Christofias wondered. The ministry's line of defence was that to generate large amounts of fiscal savings, it would be impossible to completely ring-

---

[2]The Council of Europe's Committee of Experts on the Evaluation of Anti-Money Laundering Measures and the Financing of Terrorism.

[3]In his memoirs, published in 2016 in Greek, Christofias mentions that he had considered replacing Shiarly but he was discouraged from doing so by senior figures in AKEL.

fence the weakest segments of society, unless taxes were raised, which they were rather reluctant to do.

I asked if VAT offered some room for manoeuvre: at 17.0% it was still low by EU standards. Although Christofias thought it was a good idea the ministry officials thought, based on recent experience, that a higher rate would not generate much additional revenue. I wasn't entirely persuaded. In an economy where a lot of spending is from tourists, a 1% higher rate of VAT could certainly generate more revenue. When the VAT rate goes up, people may well postpone consumption by a few months—or bring it forward before it goes up—but sooner or later they start to consume again. The ministry relented and said they would consider it. I had no doubt this would be something that the troika would welcome. That wasn't enough, however. More savings needed to be generated through expenditure cuts. Christofias sent the proposed cuts back to the drawing board, with instructions to produce the required savings but with greater progressivity in the fiscal measures—he genuinely wanted to protect the most vulnerable.

Meanwhile, Christofias set himself the task of avoiding the troika altogether, by obtaining another loan from Russia. Christofias, who was educated in Moscow during the Soviet era, spoke fluent Russian and had a soft spot for the country. At every meeting we had at the presidential palace he briefed us about his increasingly desperate attempts to talk to the Russian President, Vladimir Putin. He was going to make everything possible to get a loan from Russia. Eventually, he did talk to Putin during the summer of 2012 but received a lukewarm response. I suspect Putin had other concerns than safeguarding workers' rights in Cyprus, a country where per capita income was much higher than in Russia. However, as far as I was aware, Putin never explicitly said no to Christofias' request. In the months that followed, Christofias continued to hope that Russia would turn out to be the *Deus-ex-machina* that would save Cyprus from the troika.

In March 2013, when the new right-wing government of Anastasiades came to power, I was expecting all this to change. Anastasiades was a self-proclaimed pro-European and his party, DISY, aligned itself in the European Parliament with the European Popular Party; Mrs. Merkel pledged her support to him in a brief visit to Cyprus during the pre-election campaign. The finance minister, Michael Sarris, was well known for his free-market views: he was an advocate of privatisation, labour reforms, low taxes and fiscal austerity. I was, however, proven wrong. Anastasiades' government continued to view Russia as a potential 'savour' of Cyprus from the troika, very much like Christofias' government. However, the reasons for the new government's 'special relationship' with Russia had—as we shall see later on—little to do with ideology or international politics.

September 2012 turned out to be a very busy month. Cyprus had the presidency of the European Union during the second half of the year and there was an informal Ecofin meeting that Cyprus was hosting during 13–15 September. Ecofin meetings are meetings of all EU finance ministers that are also attended by central bank Governors. It's the only occasion in Europe when central bank Governors get to hear what the finance ministers discuss.

On the evening of 13 September 2012, Christofias received Christine Lagarde, the IMF's new managing director at the Presidential Palace. The next day, he received Mario Draghi, the ECB president and Jean-Claude Juncker, who, at the time, was the Eurogroup's chairman. He invited me to all these meetings. Although the discussions could not have been more civilised the differences of opinion on the kind of reforms needed were obvious. Christofias was, nevertheless, delighted when all three of his guests separately confirmed that Cyprus, with a debt to GDP ratio of less than 70%, wouldn't be needing a bailout if it were not for the banks' capital needs. However, who was to blame for the crisis was of little interest to his guests, all of whom emphasised the need for a speedy agreement with the troika. They were certainly getting impatient.

I am not sure that Europe and the IMF appreciated the extent to which hosting that Ecofin meeting delayed Cyprus' response to the troika proposals. Resources at both the ministry of finance, which was the only ministry involved in all the proposed reforms, and the CBC were stretched. Parliamentary populism made matters worse. In their infinite wisdom, parliamentarians tried to save public money by freezing all hires and promotions in the public sector. Even temporary staff could not be hired. This was certainly not the troika's idea. The troika wanted the overall public sector pay bill to be reduced through a combination of a smaller size public sector and wage restraint. However, they certainly didn't want the public sector to be paralysed through lack of new hires or demotivated through lack of opportunities for career progression. Parliament went out of its way to make sure that the CBC was included in the freeze. It took nearly a year to correct this. At the most critical time, the CBC was under-resourced. What made matters worse was a record number of early retirements at the same time as the freeze was imposed. Throughout the public sector, a large number of staff close to retirement age opted for early retirement because of fears over pension reforms. Within a few months, CBC staff numbers declined by 10% to less than 300.

Christofias decided that he would invite the troika back to the island soon after Cyprus' Independence Day on 1 October. However, the troika couldn't return before early November because of the annual World Bank/IMF meetings that were to be held in Tokyo during 11–13 October. The more senior members of the troika were attending.

Time was running out. The ECB was getting impatient. At the Governing Council meeting of 4 October 2012 in Ljubljana, I was asked to explain to the Cypriot president that the ECB would soon be setting a deadline for ELA provision to Cypriot banks. I sent a confidential letter to Christofias a few days later warning him about the likely consequences. I copied the minister of finance, Vassos Shiarly. Afterwards, Vassos said to me: 'You have done your duty. Now the responsibility is off your shoulders'.

The Commission was also getting impatient. It was of the view that matters for Cyprus could turn sour if an agreement wasn't reached before Germany entered its own pre-election period. The Commission was prophetic. On 5 November 2012, an article appeared in *Der Spiegel* with the following title:[4]

Bailing out oligarchs: EU aid for Cyprus a political minefield for Merkel

The opening paragraph stated: 'Last Friday, the sun was shining in this paradise for Russians. The sky was a deep blue and the palms along the beach promenade swayed in a light breeze as the temperature climbed to 29 degrees Celsius (84 degrees Fahrenheit) before noon. No doubt Limassol offered a welcome relief from the cold and wet autumn weather of Moscow. Russians appreciate this spot on the southern coast of Cyprus'.

It wasn't an advertisement of the Cyprus Tourism Organisation. The article went on to say that Cyprus was virtually bankrupt, because its economy was dragged down by the recession in Greece and billions of losses from Greek government bonds bought by Cypriot banks that were now worthless. It explained that the Cypriot government had applied for EU aid and that Putin's Russia already provided a loan of €2.5 billion but wasn't prepared to provide more. The killer paragraphs followed:

Now the euro countries, and especially Germany, will have to step in with a €10 billion aid injection to prop up the island's banks. That will confront

---

[4]http://www.spiegel.de/international/europe/german-intelligence-report-warns-cyprus-not-combating-money-laundering-a-865451.html.

Angela Markel, Finance Minister Wolfgang Schauble and their European colleagues with a major dilemma because a secret report written by the German foreign intelligence service, the Bundesnachrichtendienst (BND), outlines who would be the main beneficiaries of the billions of euros of European taxpayers' money: Russian oligarchs, businessmen and Mafiosi who have invested their illegal money in Cyprus.

The Russians don't just love Cyprus for its great climate. The shell companies here are conveniently anonymous, the banks discreet and the taxes are low. Dirty money bestowed a lasting boom on Cyprus and the inhabitants of "Limassolgrad" are still doing well.

I am not sure if that secret service report ever existed—my own high-level contacts in Germany suggested there never was one. That didn't matter, however. The stage was set for the German opposition to challenge Merkel for her intention to use German taxpayers' money to 'guarantee deposits of illegal Russian money in Cypriot banks'.

The article ended by quoting one Merkel confidant: 'Cyprus isn't an economic problem, it's long since become a political one'.

Soon after the article was published, we were informed by troika technocrats that there was no way the German parliament would approve the bailout funds for Cyprus without some form of contribution from Russia. However, the specific form of that contribution remained vague until March 2013. It could easily have been another loan from the Russian government.

It was also made clear to us that Cyprus needed to be seen to be cleaning up its act on money laundering—even if it had done a lot already. Perceptions against a hostile climate were important.

The anti-money laundering framework was, in fact, the first item that European leaders wanted to discuss with the newly elected government of Nicos Anastasiades in March 2013. His election was welcomed by European leaders, as he was viewed in Europe as more pro-European than Christofias. Anastasiades, however, was an inhabitant of 'Limassolgrad'. And not just an ordinary inhabitant. His immediate family co-owned one of the biggest law firms in Cyprus, which bears his name and whose main business was to provide a variety of legal services to rich Russians who wanted to register companies in Cyprus. According to the press, Anastasiades had flown to his first European Council meeting in a private jet belonging to a Russian oligarch 'friend', allegedly to save public money. I learnt from my sources in Brussels that EU leaders were—to put it mildly—unimpressed.

8

A Bank Run and a Tearful Agreement

November 2012 was a tough month. The troika descended on Cyprus but the negotiations started falling apart. President Christofias and his labour minister were reluctant to accept the labour reforms. There was also disagreement over other reforms, ranging from the management of gas reserves to privatisation of the ports, telecommunications and electricity. There was some glimmer of hope regarding the reforms of the regulatory regime for credit cooperatives. We managed to convince the President and the troika that we could find a compromise if we adopted the Dutch model, in which Rabobank oversees the regional coops and Rabobank itself is supervised by the central bank. The minister of commerce, however, whom Christofias respected a lot, wasn't persuaded: the department for cooperative development that had responsibility for supervising the coops, was part of his ministry and the senior people there who had his ear, were campaigning vigorously against these reforms. We were clearly stepping on their turf.

On several occasions, the minister of finance and I explained to the President, who was still trying hard to get a loan from Russia, that the banking system would collapse if we failed to reach agreement with the troika soon. I explained to him the implications of the ECB deadline. He was becoming increasingly irritated with both his finance minister and me.

'What do you mean collapse? You two are trying to blackmail me', he said on one occasion and stormed out of the meeting. Shiarly and I looked at each other. We were getting nowhere but we remained calm. Vassos looked like he was thinking of the exit option.

© The Author(s) 2017
P. Demetriades, *A Diary of the Euro Crisis in Cyprus*,
DOI 10.1007/978-3-319-62223-1_8

Christofias returned a few minutes later in a calmer mood. He wanted to know more. 'What do you mean by a collapsing banking system? I don't understand what you are talking about'.

At least he was honest about it. What bankers and economists who specialise in banking take for granted isn't necessarily obvious to non-specialists. Specialists know that a systemic bank that is twice the size of the economy without liquidity is like a nuclear bomb laid under the foundations of the economy that is about to explode. But it's not that easy to explain why. It certainly has a lot to do with the payments system and the interconnectedness of an economic system. For a politician, however, all that can sound like meaningless jargon. What does it mean for ordinary people?

I promised to produce a document that explained everything, drawing on real world examples. I went back to my office and dug out pictures from the Great Depression with thousands of people queuing outside banks that appeared closed. I asked Argyro Procopiou, one of the CBC's most experienced supervisors, to produce a document summarising what happened then, which included those pictures. My thinking was that for politicians what mattered more was how a bank collapse would impact on the lives of ordinary working people.

As if the President's procrastination wasn't enough of a problem, someone from the CBC, who was aware of the ECB's decision to impose a deadline on the supply of liquidity to Cypriot banks, leaked the news to Nicos Anastasiades, the leader of the main opposition party, DISY, whom nearly everyone expected to win the next presidential election. Anastasiades took immediate action. He wrote a letter to Christofias saying that if the ECB cut off liquidity to the Cypriot banking system, it would be catastrophic. That was true, of course. But he went on to threaten Christofias with criminal prosecution, if that happened. He wrote a very similar letter to me. I replied politely, explaining the risks to financial stability if the confidential ECB information he had access to was made public. At that time ELA was still a blessing for Anastasiades. It wasn't until March 2013 that it became a curse.

On Friday, 16 November 2012, when negotiations between Christofias' government and the troika looked like they were going nowhere, an article appeared in *Alithia*—the mouthpiece newspaper of DISY. The article explained in no uncertain terms what the ECB would do in case an agreement wasn't reached.

Troika chiefs thought that a bank run was imminent. We started monitoring outflows from ATMs on an hourly basis. Some positive news was desperately needed to avert a bank run. We worked throughout the weekend to try and reach a preliminary agreement between the troika and the CBC on banking sector reforms—this still needed the government's consent. We were determined to get there before the banks opened on Monday. There were still many issues that required the consent of the ministry of finance, who absented themselves from the meetings. As soon as we had an agreement, we immediately issued a press statement. I also wrote to Christofias informing him. It was also the perfect opportunity to remind him in writing of the consequences of him failing to reach agreement with the troika on the rest of the programme.

The CBC's initiative to come to a preliminary agreement with the troika on banking sector reforms was hailed by the media as a big step forward. Suddenly, I became a hero rather than a villain. Not so for Christofias' government, however, which, paradoxically, was attacked for allowing the CBC to come to an agreement on banking sector reforms, without its consent.

The bank run was, nevertheless, averted. Or, rather, postponed. A couple of days later, Christofias decided he had had enough with the troika and decided to send them home. Anastasiades, in turn, decided to call a press conference the following day, in which he would explain to the Cypriot people what Christofias' decision meant for the banking system. There was speculation that he would warn of the impending catastrophe and ask for Christofias' resignation and an early election.

I was en-route to Frankfurt for a Governing Council meeting when all this was happening. As there was no direct flight from Cyprus, the journey took five and a half hours, including a 45-minute stopover in Vienna. During breakfast the next morning, Wednesday, 21 November, I anxiously texted Takis Phidia, the acting CEO of Laiki, to ask how the deposit flows were going. Seconds later the reply came back. It said:

'Since opening this morning, we are facing a run on deposits. People are coming in and want to break their term-deposits, throughout our branch network, from Paralimni (*on the eastern end of the island*) to Paphos (*on the western coast*)', he said.

We had to take action swiftly. Next to me was Spyros Stavrinakis, the senior director for financial stability at the CBC. Spyros and I realised that this was the most critical moment in our lives (it turned out that there were to be more in the months to come). We agreed on a course of action. First, I had to talk to Phidia. If depositors were to be reassured, the bank needed to be seen to be ready to satisfy their demands. Anything else, like refusing to break term-deposits, which is a typical instinctive reaction by bankers trying to protect their limited liquidity, could produce an even bigger run. Then I would call Anastasiades and try to persuade him to call off the press conference. I then had the final challenge of attempting to convince Christofias that the catastrophe I was warning him about for some time was now imminent.

I carried out the plan. Phidia understood very quickly. Anastasiades wasn't convinced I would be able to persuade Christofias but he, nevertheless, agreed to give me a chance. He would call off the press conference, he said, if Christofias was persuaded to reach agreement with the troika.

Christofias proved the toughest cookie to crack but in the end he was convinced. By that time, he had seen Argyro's document with references to the Great Depression. I explained to him in no uncertain terms that the responsibility for what was likely to follow was his and only his. He went silent for a minute but he said he would soon be making a statement. Later on, someone who witnessed the events in the Cypriot delegation in Brussels—where Christofias was when he took my call—informed me that the President was in tears.

Soon after our phone call, Christofias issued a short statement saying that 'We are very close to an agreement with the troika for an adjustment programme for Cyprus'. The bank run died down soon after that announcement.

A couple of days later, the Commission announced that agreement was reached at a technical level with the Cypriot authorities for a programme of adjustment that would address the sustainability of public finances and the capital shortfalls in the banking system. There was a sigh of relief at the CBC, albeit a temporary one.

Cyprus, in fact, immediately began implementing the fiscal measures agreed with the troika soon after the November agreement was reached. Unfortunately, however, politicians in Europe had different plans. At the Eurogroup meeting in December 2012, Cyprus was not discussed. There were more pressing matters, we were informed. At any rate, the due diligence exercise on the capital needs of the banking system had not, as yet, been completed. At its meeting on 21 January 2013, the Eurogroup discussed Cyprus. It welcomed the progress already made in terms of implementing some of the measures agreed but decided to wait for the presidential elections in February to 'best facilitate national ownership' of the programme.[1] This certainly made sense for them: an agreement with the

---

[1] The Eurogroup terms of reference of 21 January 2013 on Cyprus (see Appendix) also called for the final agreement to 'provide for a close monitoring of the anti-money laundering and tax transparency frameworks and their implementation'.

outgoing government had little value. However, this meant that we were to remain in limbo until 1 March 2013, when the new government of Nicos Anastasiades took office.

Appendix

Terms of Reference of the Eurogroup

We welcome the progress Cyprus has already been making in implementing some of the important measures about which the Troika and the Cypriot authorities are in agreement.

The due diligence exercise on the capital needs of the Cypriot financial sector has progressed. The findings are being reviewed by the Steering Committee. In line with established precedents, the final report is expected to be published as soon as the Memorandum of Understanding would be signed.

We are also assured that Cyprus's short-term financing needs are covered. On this basis, we consider that targeting agreement on a programme after the upcoming presidential elections in Cyprus would best facilitate national ownership. *We expect therefore that final agreement on a programme could be reached as of March* (my italics). It will also provide for a close monitoring of the Anti-Money Laundering and tax transparency frameworks and their implementation. We call on the Troika and the Cypriot authorities to make progress in the interim towards finalising the building blocks of the draft Memorandum of Understanding.

21 January 2013.

9

The Euro at Breaking Point

Incomplete Architecture

The euro was created as an irrevocable currency union. A country can opt in but can never opt out. This design was intended to prevent speculation, which could force it to unravel—the reason why fixed exchange rate regimes and informal currency unions are unlikely to be long-lasting.[1] It was also intended to promote convergence among member states. However, like much else in Europe, the architecture of the euro left a lot to be desired. While member states have a common monetary policy, fiscal policy is left in the hands of national governments. Unlike other currency unions that have fiscal transfer mechanisms to address inevitable internal imbalances, the euro area has fiscal rules that member states have to abide by in order to prevent such imbalances from arising; however, these have proved ineffective in controlling deficits and debt. Even more worryingly, until recently banking supervision remained in the hands of national supervisors, which allowed varying degrees of tolerance to financial fragility across member states: in countries like Cyprus, Ireland and Spain, banking sector weaknesses became the Achilles heel of the Eurozone, more so than fiscal profligacy.

The euro did indeed encourage convergence, but only in borrowing costs. The borrowing costs of countries in the periphery converged downwards to those of Germany. Greek 10-year bond yields declined from nearly 25% in

---

[1]For an excellent analysis of currency unions see Alesina and Barro (2000). For a critical analysis of the euro see Bootle (2015).

© The Author(s) 2017
P. Demetriades, *A Diary of the Euro Crisis in Cyprus*,
DOI 10.1007/978-3-319-62223-1_9

1993 to 6% when the euro was created. They declined further, virtually to the level of the German bund, when Greece managed to join the first group of countries that issued euro bank notes on 1 January 2002. By early 2005, Greek borrowing costs had declined to 3.5%. Not surprisingly, the low-interest rate environment fuelled private and public spending, resulting in high growth rates and higher living standards. It also resulted in large fiscal deficits and created growing imbalances, sowing the seeds of the Greek crisis, which eventually erupted in late 2009.[2]

Grexit

Interest rates throughout the euro area started to diverge soon after the onset of the Greek crisis, when it became clear that excessive debt levels remained very much the responsibility of the governments that created them. Rating agencies and markets turned their attention to Greece's level of public debt. With high and rising borrowing costs and deteriorating competitiveness, Greece already looked like a bankrupt nation: debt levels were pretty unsustainable. In May 2010, following several months of political wrangling, Greece was offered a €110 billion financial assistance package by other euro area countries and the IMF. This was meant to cover the financing and refinancing needs of the Greek government and to recapitalise the Greek banks that were accumulating growing levels of non-performing loans. However, the bailout proved insufficient to address concerns about Greek debt sustainability. It was doubtful whether Greece could deliver on the conditionality attached to the programme which, besides austerity, included wide-ranging reforms to address competitiveness. It was also doubtful if the fiscal targets in the programme were realistic: it was implicitly assumed that a severe fiscal squeeze would have little impact on the real economy and would, therefore, be effective in creating better fiscal outcomes.

The political cacophony that surrounded the negotiations with Greece didn't help either. Europe seemed far from being united. The popular press in Germany and elsewhere portrayed Greeks as lazy and undeserving of hard-working German taxpayers' money, although it didn't explain that Germany may have had fewer exports if Greeks were not lent the money

---

[2]For a discussion of the origins of the Greek crisis and an econometric analysis of the contribution of low interest rates see Gibson, Hall and Tavlas (2011).

to buy German goods.[3] The cracks in the euro's design were beginning to show. It wasn't long before financial journalists, politicians and economists, including Nobel prize winners like Paul Krugman, who were always skeptical about the creation of the euro, started raising the prospect of 'Grexit'—Greece's exit from the euro area.

Initially, the possibility of Grexit was dismissed by euro area politicians. However, all that changed after 31 October 2011, when Prime Minister George Papandreou announced his intention to hold a referendum on a new bailout package that involved additional unpopular austerity measures. By that time, the austerity measures adopted in May 2010 were biting but not delivering in terms of reducing the fiscal deficit. Papandreou was losing popular support as well as support from within his own party. European leaders, including the German Chancellor Angela Merkel and the French President Nicolas Sarkozy, were incensed by Papandreou's intention to hold a referendum. They admitted openly that Grexit was on the cards, following an emergency meeting with Papandreou at the G-20 meeting in Cannes at the beginning of November 2011. Papandreou called off the referendum on 3 November 2011 and stepped down as Prime Minister of Greece soon after that.

The damage that these political developments inflicted on the perception of the euro as an irrevocable currency cannot be overemphasised. Grexit has remained very much on the political agenda since then. Although Grexit risk started dissipating after the election of Antonis Samaras on 20 June 2012, markets started asking questions about other countries. Cyprus was certainly one of them. Its banking system had considerable exposure to Greece and had suffered large losses from the Greek debt write-down of 2011. But Cyprus wasn't the only one. Spain, Portugal, Ireland and even Italy were showing signs of considerable stress. Long-term government bond yields were diverging as investors were flying to safety.

The ECB had to take action. On 26 July 2012, Mario Draghi gave a speech at the Global Investment Conference in London in which he boldly stated that '…the ECB is ready to do whatever it takes to preserve the euro.

---

[3]See, for example, the blog post by Imke Henkel on the LSE's EUROPP (European Politics and Policy blog) 'German public opinion is caught between scapegoating Greeks and love-bombing them', which cites the German tabloid Bild as leading the media campaign that created the stereotype of hard-working Germans and lazy Greeks (and other southerners). According to Henkel, who quotes results from public opinion polls, these myths have had a significant impact on German public opinion. See: http://blogs.lse.ac./europpblog/2015/07/21/german-public-opinion-is-caught-between-scapegoating-greeks-and-love-bombing-them/.

And believe me, it will be enough'.[4] This was perhaps as close as one could get to the ECB officially admitting that the euro was, in fact, in serious trouble.

Cyprus: The Next Weak Link

By the end of 2012, the risk of Grexit had subsided. All the indicators were suggesting that Greece had turned the corner. Also, thanks to the announcement of the Outright Monetary Transactions Programme (OMT) by the ECB in October 2012, which put into action Draghi's earlier pledge 'to do whatever it takes', spreads for Spanish, Portuguese, Irish and Italian bonds had started declining.

The risks to the euro from Cyprus were, however, rising, notwithstanding the agreement between the Cyprus government and the troika in late November 2012. Although the Cypriot side started implementing the austerity measures that were agreed, the Eurogroup started dragging its feet over the much needed political agreement. Germany was showing reluctance to bailout Cyprus, especially in light of the Russian connections. The IMF was becoming increasingly concerned about public debt sustainability, due to the large capital needs of the banks. There was talk that the IMF may not join the Cyprus programme if public debt sustainability wasn't somehow addressed: the Fund didn't want another Greece on its hands. Germany indicated that it would not join if the IMF wasn't part of the programme. At the Eurogroup meeting of 21 January, Wolfgang Schauble, the outspoken German finance minister, started questioning whether Cyprus was 'systemic'.

If Cyprus wasn't deemed systemic, it could easily be kicked out of the Eurozone without consequences for other member states. This may well have been a negotiating tactic, a hardline stance that could justify the take it or leave it offer they would be making to the new Cypriot government. With the benefit of hindsight, however, I suspect that Schauble wasn't bluffing. If in the summer of 2015 he was willing to kick out Greece from the Eurozone, why would he not be willing to consider a Eurozone without tiny Cyprus?[5]

---

[4]See: https://www.ecb.europa.eu/press/key/date/2012/html/sp120726.en.html.

[5]There was, however, a complication in both these cases that would have created additional costs for Germany. If either of the two countries defaulted and left the euro, the Bundesbank stood to lose about 40% of the ELA provision to the respective banking systems of the two countries.

Hostage to Politics

On 10 February 2013, a Bloomberg article appeared in the *Financial Times* entitled 'Radical rescue proposed for Cyprus'. It was authored by Peter Spiegel in Brussels and Quentin Peel in Berlin, and referred to a 'radical new option…that would force losses on uninsured depositors in Cypriot banks, as well as in the country's sovereign bonds'. The article suggested that this was 'one of three options put forward as alternatives to a full-scale bailout'. It pointed out, however, that 'the new plan had not been endorsed by its authors in the European Commission or by individual Eurozone members'. The article went on to say that the proposal was 'intended to produce a more sustainable debt solution for the country' but recognised that risks with this option were significant: they included 'a renewed danger of financial contagion in Eurozone financial markets and premature collapse in the Cypriot banking sector'.[6]

The law and accounting firms that kept reassuring Russian depositors that their money was safe—the 'introducers'—were demanding that I issue a statement saying that deposits in Cyprus were safe. I explained that a statement like that from any Governor could, if anything, be interpreted by depositors and investors as confirming that there was already a bank run going on resulting in the very thing that we wanted to avoid—a rapid and massive outflow of deposits, and ultimately a collapse of the banking sector.

Both Brussels and Frankfurt told us that the leak was from Berlin. Everyone thought that it was terrible. In a telephone conversation I had with troika head Maarten Verwey (European Commission), witnessed by other members of the Governor's office, I was assured that this was just one of many scenarios that the EU was obliged to consider and that it was unlikely to happen. It looked, however, like someone within the German government wanted to force Cyprus out of the euro. There could not have been a more destabilising news story. Not surprisingly, depositors started to flee. Bank of Cyprus started bleeding deposits: within days it ran out of liquidity and had to apply for €1.0 billion of ELA. Laiki's outflows were more modest, possibly because depositors who could, had already fled. However, the bank was very low on unencumbered collateral. We had to ask them to pledge their physical assets, buildings in both Cyprus and London, just to increase their ELA by €100 million. Its reliance on ELA rose to €9.2 billion.

---

[6]See https://www.ft.com/content/1d17a320-736f-11e2-9e92-00144feabdc0.

Yet, we managed. Banks opened, the withdrawals were orderly, there was no panic among depositors, no long queues of the type we associate with bank runs, indeed no bank run. The country could have its presidential elections under normal conditions, although inevitably, the bailout and its conditionality, including the possibility of a 'deposit haircut', were very much at the centre of electoral debates.

Elections

On Sunday, 17 February, only a week after the destabilising news story appeared in the FT, Cypriot voters went to the polls to elect their new president. The three main candidates were Nicos Anastasiades, the leader of the opposition who was widely considered as the front runner, George Lillikas, an independent candidate supported by socialist EDEK and two smaller parties and Stavros Malas, a geneticist who was Christofias' health minister, supported by left wing AKEL. Anastasiades received 45.6% of the vote but was short of the majority needed to be elected. A second round was held the following Sunday, in which Anastasiades competed against Stavros Malas, the AKEL candidate, who came second with 26.9% of the vote in the first round. In the second round, Anastasiades received 57.5% of the vote against Malas' 42.5% and was elected President of the Republic of Cyprus.

The newly elected President found himself in unchartered waters as soon as he took office on 1 March 2013. For Europe and the IMF, Anastasiades was the pro-bailout candidate who was going to help clean up Cyprus's banking system. For Cypriot voters, he was the candidate with the strongest pro-European credentials, the one most likely to extract favourable terms for the bailout. After all, Angela Merkel had publicly proclaimed her support for Anastasiades in a short visit to Cyprus, weeks before the election. The facts, however, indicated that he was very much part of the 'business model', which had considerable responsibility for the banking crisis, by helping to attract very large foreign inflows, particularly from Russia.[7] Influenced by bankers, who were close to him and his political party DISY during the pre-election period, he had been convinced that the capital needs of the banks had been exaggerated. So much so that when the FT story came out, he

---

[7]Anastasiades himself was one of the 'pioneers' in attracting Russian business into Cyprus and his family law firm that bears his name became one of the largest on the island (see, for example, Stavrakis 2012).

pledged that he would never, never accept a deposit haircut. He repeated that pledge in his first few days in office in March 2013. Only an ECB 'blackmail' would get him out of that hole.

Bibliography

Alesina, Alberto and Robert J. Barro. 2000. Currency unions, Working Paper 7927, NBER.

Bootle, Roger. 2015. *The Trouble with Europe: Why the EU isn't working, how it can be reformed, what could take its place.* London: John Murray Press and Boston: Nicholas Brealey Publishing.

Gibson, Heather D., Stephen G. Hall and George S. Tavlas. 2011. The Greek financial crisis: Growing imbalances and sovereign spreads. Economics Working Paper no. 11/25, University of Leicester at Leicester.

Stavrakis, Charilaos. 2012. Economy in politics and politics in the economy (in Greek). Nicosia [n.p.].

10

Illusions

The Russian Deus-Ex-Machina (that Never Was)

On Friday, 15 February 2013, there was a high-level Eurosystem-Bank of Russia seminar in Moscow which I attended. It was an ideal opportunity to find out first-hand what the Russian movers and shakers were thinking about Cyprus. It was also a welcome respite from the pre-election period on the island. The political debates in Cyprus were disheartening. The presidential candidates, instead of focusing on political issues they understood, were trying to impress the electorate with their knowledge of bank stress tests. They were arguing over the need to have an adverse Scenario. Without one, the capital needs would certainly be lower. The bankers' conspiracy theory was certainly gaining ground among presidential candidates. At a superficial level, it was comic. At a deeper level, however, it was extremely depressing to witness all this without being able to say anything.

The day before the high-level seminar in Moscow, I met with Sergei Ignatiev, the then Governor of the Bank of Russia. A very gentle, soft-spoken and pleasant man. He wanted to talk to me about the need to cooperate with regard to suspicious transactions from Russia that were being channelled through Cypriot banks. He seemed as concerned about Cyprus' business model as European governments. I agreed to cooperate. In fact, we were already doing so. I was receiving regular letters from him with dozens of suspicious transactions, which I was passing on to the appropriate officers in the CBC for scrutiny.

© The Author(s) 2017
P. Demetriades, *A Diary of the Euro Crisis in Cyprus*,
DOI 10.1007/978-3-319-62223-1_10

I also informed Ignatiev about the negotiations relating to the bailout. We were at a standstill until the elections were over, I explained. However, we should have an agreement soon after that. I inquired whether he knew anything about the Russian government's intentions to contribute to the bailout. He wasn't able to say.

The next day, Friday, 15 November, soon after the high-level seminar at the Bank of Russia ended, I went to see Anton Siluanov, the Russian finance minister. The meeting had been swiftly arranged by the Cypriot ambassador in Moscow. The ambassador seemed surprised that Siluanov agreed to see me at such short notice. I suspected that previous attempts by others in Cyprus to get appointments with him weren't as successful. A few weeks later, my suspicions were confirmed when Michael Sarris, the new finance minister of Cyprus, was sent to meet his Russian counterpart. Sarris stayed in Moscow for more than a week but never managed to meet with Siluanov. Instead, Sarris met with one of Siluanov's deputies.

I was accompanied by Spyros Stavrinakis, who by then had become Deputy Governor. We sat at one side of a very large table. On the other side, there must have been at least a dozen people—Siluanov, two deputy ministers and a large number of ministry officials.

I explained where the negotiations were. I also mentioned the contents of the leaked letter in the *Financial Times*. What were Russia's intentions? Would it wish to contribute to the bailout? Did they feel that the 'special relationship' between the two countries was being threatened?

We received some very clear, businesslike, answers: there was no beating around the bush. Russia had already helped Cyprus with a €2.5 billion loan at the end of 2011. Russia was concerned about the sustainability of the Cypriot public finances but also about the health of Bank of Cyprus and Laiki, which had large exposure to Greece and had already lost billions from the Greek debt write-down. Russia wanted Cyprus to come to an agreement with Europe and the IMF for an adjustment programme that would restore the sustainability of public finances and address other structural weaknesses. Once that agreement was in place, Russia would be willing to discuss better terms for the €2.5 loan, which was meant to be fully repaid in 2015.

I wondered why our politicians couldn't or didn't want to understand reality. The *deus-ex-machina* from Russia was just an illusion.

An Angry President

On 28 February 2013, I attended the inauguration ceremony of the new President at the Cypriot Parliament. I was allocated a seat at the very back of the room. It was the first sign of things to come.

The next day, Friday, 1 March 2013, his very first day in office, Anastasiades asked for a paper with an up-to-date analysis of the state of the banking system. He wanted it by Monday, 4 March. He also wanted me to brief him in person on the same day. CBC staff worked over the weekend and produced a very thorough ten-page memo with all the important facts and data. It covered the provisions of the November agreement with the troika relating to the banking system, it provided details of the PIMCO diagnostic exercise, including the fact that the adverse Scenario of the stress test was agreed by the steering committee, which, in addition to the Cypriot authorities, included representatives from the IMF, the ECB, the European Commission, the European Banking Authority and the European Stability Mechanism. The memo also included an update on the state of the banking system and stressed the need for rapid restructuring and recapitalisation. It also provided details of the discussions relating to the anti-money laundering framework and concluded with a section on emergency liquidity assistance that included monthly data on ELA provision to Laiki and Bank of Cyprus.

The meeting with Anastasiades was at 11.00am on Monday, 4 March. I was accompanied by the Deputy Governor, Spyros Stavrinakis. We both congratulated Anastasiades on his election. We said we looked forward to a constructive relationship for the benefit of the country.

The niceties, however, didn't last long. Anastasiades was angry. He was angry that I had apparently allowed PIMCO to inflate the banks' capital needs! It was worse than hearing the bankers in replay, who wanted everyone to think that their banks were healthy until PIMCO came along. The bankers were at least trying to defend themselves. The President wasn't just taking the side of the bankers, he was also interfering in the internal affairs of the CBC.

'Why didn't you chair the steering committee?' he asked me. 'Why was this delegated down to a senior officer at the CBC?' The senior officer in charge was Argyro Prokopiou, one of the CBC's most experienced supervisors. She was the CBC's representative at the European Banking Authority (EBA) where bank stress tests methodology was discussed and agreed. I could not think of a more knowledgeable and experienced person for that role. Anastasiades, however, was having none of it. 'Why was it not the head of supervision, Akis Phanopoulos?', he asked.

It was clear that it wasn't just the bankers who fed Anastasiades with misleading information. There was someone from within the CBC who was influencing him. It was very disappointing, although not very surprising. I was aware that there were (at least) two high ranking officials at the CBC—neither of whom had anything to do with the steering committee or indeed banking supervision—who were in regular contact with Averof Neophytou, the deputy leader of DISY. Both were aspiring for high office and wanted to be in the good books of the government.

I explained that Phanopoulos was spending much of his time in Brussels, chairing important EU committees, like the committee on the Bank Recovery and Resolution Directive. I reminded him that this was because Cyprus had the presidency of the EU in the second half of 2012. In any case, Prokopiou was the right person for that role, she was the bank's expert on bank stress tests. I gently reminded him that while I very much wanted to cooperate with him and his government to address the problems of the banking system, the management of the central bank and its staff was my business and not his.

Anastasiades was having none of it. He angrily reminded me that he was elected whereas I was appointed and that he was going to find a way to dismiss me if I didn't support his government's policies. He was so sure that the capital needs were exaggerated that he was going to reject PIMCO's estimates to save the banks and the country. His plan was to use lower estimates of capital needs that were carried out by a company appointed by the bankers. He explained to me that Bank of Cyprus and Hellenic (the third largest bank that belonged to the Church) had appointed another company to carry out stress tests. That was news to me. The bankers went behind the CBC's back and appointed a consultant who would deliver a verdict that suited them. They could then continue to pretend that their banks were healthy and that PIMCO's estimates were part of a conspiracy to destroy the country (nearly everyone accepted that what was bad for the banks was catastrophic for the country). Moreover, they chose to inform the new government about the appointment of this consultant, but concealed their actions from their supervisory authority, the CBC. It seemed that in precrisis Cyprus, it was more important for the banks to have political backing for their actions than their supervisor's consent.

It was glaringly obvious that Anastasiades had been misinformed. Not just by the bankers but also by senior members of staff at the CBC. I shouldn't have been so surprised. His pre-election rhetoric sounded like that, but

I assumed—incorrectly as it turned out—that he would take what the bankers were telling him with a pinch of salt. They certainly had an incentive to distort and to create conspiracy theories. But he should at least have heard the CBC's side of the story before coming to his own conclusions.

Spyros and I explained to the new President that his plan was unlikely to work, which, of course, he didn't like. To start with, the company that the banks appointed was one that had applied for the project that was eventually awarded to PIMCO but had not been shortlisted by the steering committee because it lacked sufficient technical expertise. Second, PIMCO's estimates went through a peer review process that was led by the steering committee. The models, methods and assumptions were challenged by members of the steering committee. PIMCO's final estimates had already been endorsed by everyone on the steering committee. I reminded him that the steering committee included the Cypriot Ministry of Finance and the Ministry of Commerce, in addition to the CBC. I also reminded him that the external members of the steering committee comprised the IMF, the ECB and the European Commission as well as the European Banking Authority and the European Stability Mechanism.

Anastasiades' illusions were quickly shuttered by subsequent developments. It seems that he used the same line of reasoning—that PIMCO exaggerated the capital needs and that another company had come up with much lower capital needs—with European leaders at the European Council meeting ten days later. Soon after his return from Brussels, he implicitly admitted that his attempt to use the other consultant's lower estimates had fallen on deaf ears. In trying to justify why he accepted the 'haircut' on deposits, he revealed that it was Mrs Merkel, the German Chancellor, who, in effect, put an end to the myth about exaggerated capital needs. 'We only know PIMCO', was her response to Anastasiades. That was the end of that illusion. In Cyprus, however, the tale of exaggerated capital needs continued to be repeated in the weeks and months that followed, although four years later most politicians have quietly come to terms with the truth.

11

Taxing the Poor (to Protect the Rich)

At his first Eurogroup meeting, held in Brussels on 4 March 2013, Michael Sarris, the new finance minister of Cyprus, was faced with some tough facts. Besides having to agree to 'an independent evaluation of the anti-money laundering framework in Cypriot financial institutions',[1] he was informed that there was a shortfall of several billion euros between the financing needs of the country and the financial package that Europe and the IMF could jointly make available. This shortfall arose because of IMF rules, which stipulate that the Fund can only take part in bailing out a country if its public debt is sustainable. The IMF's Debt Sustainability Analysis (DSA) revealed that Cyprus' debt could become unsustainable if it borrowed more than €10.0 billion. Of this, €7.5 billion was needed to finance projected fiscal deficits and to rollover maturing (external) debt during the programme period. This left only €2.5 billion to recapitalise the domestic banking system and the credit cooperative sector. However, the capital shortfall of the domestic banking system was €8.1 billion—this was over and above the €1.8 billion capital injection into Laiki made by the state during June 2012. About a quarter of this could be covered by writing down the claims of junior creditors, such as bondholders (this was taken for granted, as junior creditors would have been written off even under state aid rules).[2] On top

---

[1]See Appendix 1.

[2]PIMCO's estimates of the capital shortfall under the adverse scenario was €8.128 million for domestic banks, €149 million for foreign banks and €589 million for participating credit cooperatives. The latter rose to €1.5 billion, when the remaining credit cooperatives were included. The shortfalls did not take into account potential liability management exercises other than those already enacted (i.e. bonds issued by Laiki and Bank of Cyprus reduced the capital shortfall by around €1.8 billion after being written down).

© The Author(s) 2017
P. Demetriades, *A Diary of the Euro Crisis in Cyprus*,
DOI 10.1007/978-3-319-62223-1_11

of that, €1.5 billion was needed to recapitalise the credit cooperatives. Thus, the €2.5 billion set aside for the banking system from the bailout package could cover the needs of the credit cooperatives and Hellenic's (which had a shortfall of €333 million), while also providing a small cushion of just under €0.7 billion. Consequently, Eurogroup and the IMF decided that Cyprus' two largest lenders were too big to save with public funds, given the stretched public finances of the country. Their capital shortfall, following the aforementioned liability management exercise, was €5.8 billion. Sarris was informed that this amount had to be raised by Cyprus itself, in order to ensure that public debt was sustainable.[3] Without that, the IMF could not participate in the bailout and without the IMF, countries like Germany would not participate. It seemed like a very hard constraint.[4]

There was a difference of opinion between the IMF and the European Commission on how the €5.8 billion shortfall could be covered. The IMF's position, which was shared by Germany, was to raise the whole amount by imposing losses on uninsured depositors through the resolution of Bank of Cyprus and Laiki and application of the bail-in measures. The Commission, the ECB and other member states, including France, were not in favour of a full bail-in, largely because of its implications for financial stability but agreed that some form of contribution by uninsured depositors had to be made. It was agreed that the troika was going to sound the Cypriot government before the final decision was made at the next Eurogroup meeting, which was to take place before or after the upcoming European Council meeting on 14 March.

There was also discussion of the critical importance of ring-fencing the Cypriot bank branches in Greece, in order to protect financial stability in both countries and the wider euro area. This proposal came to be known as 'the Greek carve-out' and required Cyprus to sell its bank branches in Greece to a Greek bank, as a prior condition for entering an EU/IMF adjustment programme. This was largely because, Cypriot bank branches

---

[3]While by the standards of other bailouts the shortfall wasn't large, for a country with a GDP of €17.0 billion and a pre-bailout debt-to-GDP ratio of the order of 80%, €5.8 billion represented 34% of GDP, which, if added to total public debt, could make a large difference to the public debt numbers: 172% of GDP compared with 138% of GDP.

[4]To the best of my knowledge, the Cypriot government did not challenge the IMF's Debt Sustainability Analysis, which used a debt-to-GDP ratio of 100% as the debt sustainability threshold. By contrast, in the case of Greece that threshold was set at 120%.

in Greece represented around 11% of banking assets in Greece and were, therefore, considered systemic in both countries (in Cyprus they represented 140% of Cyprus GDP).

I wasn't, of course, privy to the discussions at that Eurogroup meeting, since national central banks do not take part at such meetings. My information came from an informal meeting at the ECB on Wednesday, 6 March 2013, at which my Greek counterpart, George Provopoulos and I were briefed about the political discussions at the Eurogroup and discussed their implications for financial stability and the two national central banks.[5] Just as well, because the new government kept me completely in the dark. When Vassos Shiarly was finance minister, he often briefed me about Eurogroup discussions, at least insofar as there was something of relevance to the CBC, which was immensely helpful. There were also information channels at a technical level between the CBC and ministry officials who attended euro working group meetings, which prepared the agenda of the Eurogroup. Those channels of information suddenly vanished when the new government took office. The CBC was evidently not trusted by the new government.

Troika sources briefed me afterwards that Sarris informed the Eurogroup that he had no authority to agree to anything about the shortfall without first consulting the President. No decision was, therefore, made at that Eurogroup meeting, although a statement on Cyprus was issued that welcomed the new minister and carefully avoided any mention of raising money from depositors.[6]

The next thing I heard was from Laiki a few days later. I received a phone call from the acting CEO of Laiki. Would I mind talking to President Anastasiades as a close relative of his was about to wire several million euros to London out of their bank account? Although this was not illegal, it would certainly send a bad signal, he said, just at a time when depositors were nervous and when the President was reassuring the public that there would be no deposit haircut. I was horrified. I tried to talk to the President but was told that he was not available. I was offered to be passed on to the undersecretary at the presidential palace, Constantinos Petrides, and I agreed. I explained to Petrides what my anxieties were, which were pretty similar to those of the Laiki's CEO. On top of that, I felt that he and I had a duty to

---

[5] I was compelled to make this information public during my tenure in Cyprus.
[6] See Appendix 1.

protect the office of the President, in the eyes of commercial bank officials and the public. He seemed to have understood and said he would convey my message to him. A few hours later I received a text from Laiki's acting CEO which stated: 'It is all fine, the President's relatives are buying property in London'. According to reports in the Greek media—subsequently reproduced by the Cypriot and international press[7]—the President's relatives wired €26.0 million from Laiki to London days after the Eurogroup meeting of 4 March.[8]

The second Eurogroup meeting in March 2013 took place on Friday, 15 March, the day after the EU Council meeting in Brussels. Anastasiades was asked to stay for that, although this was highly unconventional. Once again, my troika sources informed me that Europe was determined to negotiate with someone who had the authority to make decisions; there was no time for toing and froing. I do not know what happened at that meeting. What I know was the outcome, which was made public in the early hours of Saturday, 16 March. At 7.00 am on that day, before anyone from the CBC had called me, I visited the *Cyprus Stockwatch* website, a financial website that somehow managed to avoid capture by big financial interests and which I liked to read every morning before building up the courage to read everything else. The headline news, which still sends shivers down my spine, said something I found hard to believe. The Eurogroup and the Cypriot government had agreed a 'deposit levy' to create the necessary revenue to recapitalise the banks. The proposed levy, which was subject to parliamentary approval, was 9.9% for deposits over €100,000 and 6.75% for deposits under €100,000. I remember telling myself 'Surely it's not true'. I began wondering if I had lost my most reliable news source in Cyprus.[9]

---

[7]The relatives concerned were the parents of Anastasiades' son in law. See, for example 'Leaked DOCUMENTS accuse elite of pulling millions from Cyprus banks before scandal', *The Express*, 2 April 2013. http://www.express.co.uk/news/world/388788/Leaked-documents-accuse-elite-of-pulling-millions-from-Cyprus-banks-before-scandal.

See also 'Cypriot president "warned his friends to move money abroad" before financial crisis hit: leader under fire as he faces just four days to save country from collapse', *The Mail* online, 22 March 2013. http://www.dailymail.co.uk/news/article-2297383/Cyprus-bailout-President-Nikos-Anastasiades-warned-friends-money-abroad.html.

[8]See also David Marsh (2016) p. 61.

[9]Interestingly, the Eurogroup statement on Cyprus of 16 March 2013 makes only a brief mention of the deposit levy, without stating the agreed percentages. It refers to an 'upfront one-off stability levy applicable to resident and non-resident depositors'. See Appendix 2.

Minutes later I received a phone call. It was the Deputy Governor. He informed me that ministry officials had called him at 5.00 am, soon after the Eurogroup meeting had finished, and told him what was agreed, which was exactly what I had read on *Cyprus Stockwatch*. They asked him to shut down the payments system. Deposits had to be frozen until the levy was applied. He explained to me that everything was in place. He had talked to the banks and to the cooperatives and they had shut down everything. ATMs however, remained open, but withdrawals from ATMs could not reduce the revenue from the levy since the levy would be applied on closing balances the night before.

I was still trying to digest the news. It was surreal. How could anyone agree to tax insured deposits? Was it even legally possible, given the government's obligation to protect deposits under €100,000? The levy was beginning to make headlines around the world. The rest of the world was asking the same questions.

Later that day I called Mario Draghi, the ECB's President, and Olli Rehn, the Commission's Vice-President on Economic Affairs. 'How could the ECB and the Commission agree to this?' I asked both of them (separately). They both gave me the same answer. It was the Cypriot government's idea. It was the Cypriot government that insisted on this proposal until the early hours of the morning, notwithstanding all the warnings. By 4.00 am everyone was too tired to resist. Although the Commission and the ECB initially agreed to this, they very soon realised what a dangerous precedent this could be. There could be contagion throughout Europe. Insured deposits would no longer be safe. This decision could—and should—be changed, both Draghi and Rehn independently remarked. There was, in fact, an attempt to change it two days later: a Eurogroup teleconference took place and a statement was issued by the Eurogroup President, Jeroen Dijsselbloem, which, in effect, confirmed that the idea to tax deposits under €100,000 originated from the Cypriot government. The relevant paragraph states:

The Eurogroup continues to be of the view that small depositors should be treated differently from large depositors and reaffirms the importance of fully guaranteeing deposits below EUR 100.000. The Cypriot authorities will introduce more progressivity in the one-off levy compared to what was agreed on 16 March, provided that it continues yielding the targeted reduction of the financing envelope and, hence, not impact the overall amount of financial assistance up to EUR 10bn.

In Cyprus, there was a huge outcry. Not so much about the notion of taxing insured deposits but about the idea of taxing deposits per se, especially those in healthy banks. I received a large and vociferous delegation from the foreign banks based in Cyprus. They were extremely unhappy. Their banks, they stated, were healthy: some had 30% capital ratios and an abundance of liquidity. They had never caused any trouble. 'Why should their depositors pay to bailout banks that took a gamble on Greek government bonds that didn't pay off?' I had no answers. All I could suggest was that they talk to the government. Quite a few of them said they would leave Cyprus if the levy went ahead.

As soon as Anastasiades returned to Cyprus, he started distancing himself from that Eurogroup decision. He said that he agreed to it because he was 'blackmailed' by the ECB. The ECB was going to cut off liquidity to the Cypriot banks if he hadn't agreed, he said. His own party, DISY, distanced itself from Anastasiades. They said they would abstain in Parliament. The rest of the parties said they would vote it down.

That weekend the planes coming to Cyprus were full, not with tourists since it was not the holiday season but with journalists. The levy was a pretty bad idea and it was likely to be turned down. Which meant that Cyprus could be the first country to exit the euro. That would have been the story of the year. Everyone wanted to be there when financial history was being written: the beginning of the unravelling of the euro.

But how did the levy come about? Apparently, when the Cypriot government was asked to raise nearly €6.0 billion from bank deposits, a few trusted Russian 'friends' were contacted. The message that came back was that the Russians would be willing to contribute to help save Cyprus but the contribution should be limited to not more than 10% of their deposits. A 10% levy on uninsured deposits, however, would not generate enough revenue. The shortfall was to be covered by a smaller levy on insured deposits. The 'ingenious' way the government had to 'sell' this idea to the general public was to suggest that this was no more than two years of interest (as deposit rates in Cyprus were very high relative to the euro area). No one, however, mentioned they were taxing the poor to protect not just Russian oligarchs but also the business model from which the elite of Cyprus made its money. Nor that the higher interest rates may have reflected increased risk.

The day of the vote—Tuesday, 19 March 2013—I was invited to Parliament. I was asked by the Chair of the House Finance Committee for my opinion on the levy. I mentioned that if there was going to be one, it

should spare insured deposits both for legal reasons but also f
rebuilding confidence. How could small savers trust the banks
they were subjected to the levy? They could easily spare insured
they raised the levy on uninsured deposits to 16.75%. This wo
the revenue that was needed. I also explained that the modific........ I was
proposing had the backing of the ECB's Governing Council, which in a teleconference we had the day before, was as concerned about the protection of
insured deposits as I was.

Not surprisingly, my suggestions were completely ignored. Some MPs
said they couldn't care less about European directives relating to insured
deposits. Why should they respect them if Europe doesn't respect Cyprus?

The ministry of finance tabled an amended bill in which the first €20,000
was spared but the rate on deposits over €100,000 remained 9.9%. That
didn't go far enough to protect insured deposits, although it was a step in the
right direction. They never explained, however, how the shortfall would be
covered. It was also clear that they still didn't follow the recommendation of
the Eurogroup, which had insisted that they spare deposits under €100,000.

By then, however, whatever the government tabled to Parliament was a
largely theoretical exercise. Parliamentarians had already vowed to vote 'No'
to the deposit levy, with or without amendments, because they considered
it to be unfair. The only problem was that no one seemed to have a plan of
what to do next, although Averof Neophytou (DISY's deputy leader) and
others confided to me afterwards that the contagion that would follow from
the NO vote would force Europe to come back with a better proposal.

I was beginning to understand why so many journalists were convinced
that the euro was about to break up in Cyprus during those days. On the
one hand, there was a new government that was determined to protect the
'business model' that showed little respect for important European norms,
such as deposit insurance. On the other, there was a Europe which was
talking with too many voices, each with its own agenda, that also allowed
important European norms to be breached but was then trying to repair
the damage post hoc, without success. And there was a national Parliament
in which most of its members had little understanding of banking crises or
public debt sustainability, but shared the view that Cyprus was being pun-
ished because of its business and/or political links with Russia. International
journalists could, therefore, be forgiven for thinking that Cyprus' exit from
the euro was an accident waiting to happen. It certainly looked more and
more like that in the days that followed.

ppendix 1

Eurogroup statement on Cyprus 4 March 2013

The Eurogroup welcomed the new Cypriot Finance Minister, Michalis Sarris, and the information he provided on the situation in Cyprus following the presidential elections and on the policy intentions of the new government. The first exchanges with the new Cypriot government have been useful. With the new government now in place in Cyprus, the Eurogroup is confident that a swift conclusion of the negotiations towards a Memorandum of Understanding can be reached.

The Eurogroup welcomes the commitment of President Anastasiades, reiterated by Minister Sarris, to closely cooperate with Cyprus's European partners towards the earliest possible completion of the loan agreement. For its part, the Eurogroup reiterates its readiness to assist Cyprus in its adjustment effort, including of its banking sector, in order to bring the economy to a sustainable growth path with sound public finances and to safeguard financial stability.

The Eurogroup has been informed that the preparatory work for concluding a Memorandum of Understanding is advanced and that the new government has agreed on an independent evaluation of the implementation of the anti-money laundering framework in Cypriot financial institutions.

The Eurogroup called on the international institutions and Cyprus to accelerate their work on the building blocks of a programme and agreed to target political endorsement of the programme around the second half of March.

The Eurogroup will reconvene again in the near term in view of the progress of the discussions between the Cypriot authorities and the international institutions.

Appendix 2

Eurogroup Statement on Cyprus 16 March 2013

The Eurogroup welcomes the political agreement reached with the Cypriot authorities on the cornerstones of the policy conditionality underlying a future macroeconomic adjustment programme. The programme will be based on ambitious measures to ensure the stability of the financial sector, determined action to carry out the required fiscal adjustment and structural reforms to support competitiveness as well as sustainable and balanced growth, allowing for the unwinding of macroeconomic imbalances.

The Eurogroup welcomes the Terms of Reference for an independent evaluation of the implementation of the anti-money laundering framework in Cypriot financial institutions, involving Moneyval alongside a private international audit firm, and is reassured that the launch of the audit is imminent. In the event of problems in the implementation of the framework, problems will be corrected as part of the programme conditionality.

The Eurogroup commends the Cypriot authorities on the steps already taken to adopt fiscal measures agreed with the Commission, in liaison with the ECB and the IMF. This notably concerns the adoption of consolidation measures amounting to 4 1⁄2% of GDP. The Eurogroup welcomes the Cypriot authorities' commitment to step up efforts in the area of privatisation.

The Eurogroup further welcomes the Cypriot authorities' commitment to take further measures mobilising internal resources, in order to limit the size of the financial assistance linked to the adjustment programme. These measures include the introduction of an upfront one-off stability levy applicable to resident and non-resident depositors. Further measures concern the increase of the withholding tax on capital income, a restructuring and recapitalisation of banks, an increase of the statutory corporate income tax rate and a bail-in of junior bondholders. The Eurogroup looks forward to an agreement between Cyprus and the Russian Federation on a financial contribution.

The Eurogroup is confident that these initiatives, as well as a strict implementation of the agreed policy conditionality, will allow Cyprus' public debt, which is projected to reach 100% of GDP in 2020, to remain on a sustainable path and enhance the economy's growth potential. The current fragile situation of the Cypriot financial sector linked to its very large size relative to the country's GDP will be addressed through an appropriate downsizing, with the domestic banking sector reaching the EU average by 2018, thereby ensuring its long-term viability and safeguarding deposits. Moreover, the Eurogroup welcomes that an agreement could be reached on the Greek branches of the Cypriot banks, which protects the stability of both the Greek and the Cypriot banking systems, and does not burden the Greek debt-to-GDP ratio.

Against this background, the Eurogroup considers that—in principle—financial assistance to Cyprus is warranted to safeguard financial stability in Cyprus and the euro area as a whole by providing a financial envelope which has been reduced to up to EUR 10bn. The Eurogroup would welcome a contribution by the IMF to the financing of the programme.

The Eurogroup calls upon the authorities and the Commission, in liaison with the ECB, and the IMF to swiftly finalise the MoU. The Eurogroup will review the programme documentation prepared by the Commission, in liaison with the ECB, and the IMF as well as the ESM once it becomes available. The relevant national procedures required for the approval of the ESM financial assistance facility agreement will be launched.

The Eurogroup expects that the ESM Board of Governors will be in a position to formally approve the proposal for a financial assistance facility agreement by the second half of April 2013 and subject to completion of national procedures.

Appendix 3

18 March 2013 Statement by the Eurogroup President on Cyprus[10]

The Eurogroup held a teleconference this evening to take stock of the situation in Cyprus.

I recall that the political agreement reached on 16 March on the cornerstones of the adjustment programme and the financing envelope for Cyprus reflects the consensus reached by the Cypriot government with the Eurogroup. The implementation of the reform measures included in the draft programme is the best guarantee for a more prosperous future for Cyprus and its citizens, through a viable financial sector, sound public finances and sustainable economic growth.

I reiterate that the stability levy on deposits is a one-off measure. This measure will—together with the international financial support—be used to restore the viability of the Cypriot banking system and hence, safeguard financial stability in Cyprus. In the absence of this measure, Cyprus would have faced scenarios that would have left deposit holders significantly worse off.

The Eurogroup continues to be of the view that small depositors should be treated differently from large depositors and reaffirms the importance of fully guaranteeing deposits below EUR 100.000. The Cypriot authorities will introduce more progressivity in the one-off levy compared to what was agreed on 16 March, provided that it continues yielding the targeted reduction of the financing envelope and, hence, not impact the overall amount of financial assistance up to EUR 10bn.

---

[10]Source: Reuters. See: http://www.reuters.com/article/eurogroup-cyprus-idUSB5E8KL01020130318.

The Eurogroup takes note of the authorities' decision to declare a temporary bank holiday in Cyprus on 19–20 March 2013 to safeguard the stability of the financial sector, and urges a swift decision by the Cypriot authorities and Parliament to rapidly implement the agreed measures.

The euro area Member States stand ready to assist Cyprus in its reform efforts on the basis of the agreed adjustment programme.

Bibliography

Marsh, David. 2016. *Europe's Deadlock: How the Euro Crisis could be Solved and Why it Still Won't Happen, Updated Edition*. New Haven and London: Yale University Press.

12

Heading Towards the Abyss

On Monday, 18 March 2013, when financial markets around the world reopened, there was a noticeable reaction to the news of the deposit levy in Cyprus. *The Guardian*, for example, reported heavy losses in Asia, smaller losses in Europe and a fall on Wall Street by 60 points, all attributed to the news of the unprecedented deposit levy in Cyprus.[1] Bloomberg, which provided more comprehensive coverage, was reporting a fall of the euro and a rise in Spanish and Italian bond yields.[2] The uncertainty that had been created started raising questions about the euro's survival. Without an agreement on Cyprus, the single currency could begin unravelling.

Noticing the reaction from markets and the media, some Parliamentarians in Cyprus started believing that they had a strong bargaining chip. The markets spoke, they thought: Cyprus was systemic.

Europe, however, plays by its own rules. These rules are legal and political. Markets are important but they don't necessarily dictate policy. Cyprus had been asked to raise €5.8 billion from deposits. The lesson that European policy makers drew from the reaction of financial markets was that the deposit levy on insured deposits, which the new Cypriot government was insisting on, wasn't a good idea to start with. However, that didn't mean that Cyprus would be spared the formidable task of having to raise €5.8 billion. The

---

[1] See: http://www.theguardian.com/business/2013/mar/18/eurozone-crisis-cyprus-bailout-savers-markets.

[2] See: http://www.bloomberg.com/news/articles/2013-03-17/europe-braces-for-renewed-turmoil-as-cyprus-deposit-levy-at-risk.

© The Author(s) 2017
P. Demetriades, *A Diary of the Euro Crisis in Cyprus*,
DOI 10.1007/978-3-319-62223-1_12

agreement had to be modified to ensure that deposits below €100,000 were excluded.

A Eurogroup meeting was set for Monday, 25 March—ironically, the day that marks the anniversary of the Greek revolt against the Ottoman Empire in 1821, and a public holiday in both Greece and Cyprus. It would, however, only take place if an agreement at the technical level with the troika—which was still in Cyprus—on how to raise the €5.8 billion could be achieved. That was the message that came through.

Stress levels at the CBC were very high. The staff understood the implications of no agreement. It meant the banks would remain indefinitely closed until an agreement was reached. To reopen them without an agreement, would necessitate introducing a new currency. The lawyers from the ECB were convinced that exiting the euro area would also mean exiting the European Union. It was not possible, they explained, to introduce a new currency and remain within the EU. There was no provision in the Treaty for that. There was, however, a provision for exiting the European Union by activating Article 50 of the Treaty and that was the path that we would have had to follow. The Commission and ECB troika teams would, they said, have to depart from Cyprus in that eventuality, as they could not assist any country that wanted to leave the EU. In that eventuality, the IMF contingency team, that had been encamped at the Cyprus Hilton hotel nearby, would have stepped in to assist us do the unthinkable. The IMF was bound by its own rules, which made financing an insolvent country not possible. All they could do was to offer technical assistance to help us introduce a new currency.[3]

For a country that joined the EU partly, if not largely, in order to safeguard its territorial integrity, that could have translated into a national catastrophe. It wasn't just the economy and the currency at stake. The unobstructed view of the gigantic Turkish flag on Pentadaktylos, the mountain range in the occupied part of Cyprus, from the Governor's office on the fourth floor of the modern CBC building was a daily reminder of those risks.

---

[3]Not surprisingly we were not short of offers to advise us on how to leave the euro. One of them was from a highly respectable think tank based in London.

Waiting for Deus-ex-Machina

I wasn't sure at all if the government and Parliament understood the full implications of failure to come to an agreement with the Eurogroup by 25 March. Their actions, if anything, suggested they didn't appreciate the urgency of the situation.

I tried to talk to the new finance minister, Michael Sarris. It was the same Sarris who, as Chairman of Laiki a few months earlier, had convinced the minister of finance and I—in only my third day in office—to support his plan to have the government underwrite the bank's share issue, which eventually failed and resulted in the bailout of Laiki with €1.8 billion of public funds (just over 10% of Cyprus' GDP). He was, however, appointed as minister of finance on the back of what the local media portrayed as a successful ministerial record during 2005–2008, as he led the country into the single currency on 1 January 2008. Michael was widely credited with the reduction in the fiscal deficit during that period.[4]

Sarris, however, was nowhere to be found. It turned out that he had been sent to Moscow by the president to have another shot at securing a loan from the Russian government. Their thinking, it transpired, was that the Russian government might have a change of heart now that they understood that Europe and the IMF wanted to impose losses on Russian depositors. It wasn't, however, obvious to me how another Russian loan would change the arithmetic of debt sustainability. Even if a loan could be secured, all it would have meant would be a reduction in the amount to be borrowed from Europe and the IMF.

If the terms of the loan were worse—which was quite plausible as the interest rate on the existing Russian loan (4.5% p.a.) was much higher than the rates being discussed for the loan from the European Stability Mechanism, the IMF's debt sustainability analysis would, in all likelihood, have resulted in a lower overall loan amount than the €10.0 billion agreed (because of higher financing costs). This would have implied that the amount Cyprus would receive from Europe and the Fund could have declined by more than the loan secured from Russia. It just didn't make any sense unless Russia was prepared to lend to Cyprus all the

---

[4]With hindsight, the remarkable improvement in the public finances during that period owed a lot to the property bubble that had been fuelled by excessive credit growth. During 2004–2010 total assets in the banking system were growing at an average rate of 24% per annum. Credit growth peaked during Sarris' term of office, as a result of which Cypriot firms and households became the most heavily indebted in the world. For more details see Chap. 17.

amount that was needed, which was highly unlikely. The Russian government wasn't going to throw good money after bad. It wanted, quite understandably, Cyprus to have sustainable public finances before considering whether to soften the terms of the existing loan. How could it lend even more without the assurance that Cyprus' public finances would be on a sustainable trajectory? After all, bilateral loans do not normally carry significant conditionality. Russia wasn't in a position to play the role of the IMF, even before one considers the political ramifications of Russia bailing out a member of the EU.

In Nicosia, the government was busy inventing creative ways of raising money from other sources. It came up with the idea of setting up a 'Solidarity Fund', in which private pension funds would be cajoled into investing all their reserves. This was aired at a meeting of the 'business community' with the government on Wednesday, 20 March, to which I was invited. I didn't, however, notice any businessmen there other than a representative from the Cyprus Chamber of Commerce. The large meeting room at the presidential palace was full to the brim with dozens of bankers, accountants, lawyers, government officials and politicians. They all liked the idea. It would help protect the 'business model'. It would limit damage to their clients. Trouble was there was no one representing the private sector's pension funds, the funds which they were targeting. They agreed that the pension fund managers had to be sounded out.

The acting minister of finance, Harris Georgiades, who was also labour minister, was tasked with discussing the plan with the troika. There was a meeting with troika heads of mission in his office on the same evening. It was held at the ministry of labour, in the minister's office.

I attended that meeting together with the deputy Governor, Spyros Stavrinakis. Harris was holding a chart of the 'Solidarity Fund', which he showed to all of us. It was some sort of flow of funds chart: funds were flowing into the fund from pension funds eventually ending up being invested in banks, with some form of securitisation along the way. The troika chiefs of mission, all of whom were there, weren't at all persuaded, but they were very diplomatic in their responses. Isabelle Von Koppen-Mertez, the ECB's head of mission, suggested it was all very neat financial engineering but that it would take months, if not years, to put in place. There was an urgency to act quickly, she explained. Laiki's cash buffers were being quickly depleted from ATM withdrawals. There was a risk of default. The only way forward now was to resolve the bank and resolve it quickly, the troika chiefs explained.

The resolution bill was finally ready, the troika representatives pointed out. It was time for it to be tabled to Parliament. However, there was no reaction from the government's side at the meeting. They seemed to be taken aback by the suggestion that Laiki would need to be 'resolved'. There were, of course, finance ministry officials at the meeting who knew very well what the term meant, as the drafting of the legislation was, if anything, their responsibility.[5]

The idea of using private pension funds to cover the losses of the banks—which is what the plan of creating a Solidarity Fund boiled down to—was quickly killed by the German government, which was following closely what was happening in Cyprus. The message that came back from Berlin was loud and clear: 'do not take away working people's pension savings to cover bank losses', which was a perfectly valid argument.

On Thursday, 21 March, there was a meeting of the Governing Council in Frankfurt. I sent my apologies. I had to remain in Nicosia to manage the extremely fragile situation. In the morning of that day, I was invited to another meeting at the presidential palace. This time it was with the leaders of all the political parties represented in Parliament. The president, who chaired the meeting, briefed them about the developments. Everyone agreed that it was a good idea to seek another loan from Russia. They felt that Europe and the IMF were being unfair to Cyprus in demanding a 'haircut' on deposits, something that had not been asked of any country that requested a bailout before. No one seemed to appreciate that the deposit levy, for all its ills, protected the taxpayer and future generations from higher taxes and, most importantly, greater austerity.

The then leader of DIKO—Marios Karoyian—thought he had an even better *deus-ex-machina* than the Russian government. 'What if', he said, 'I know someone who has €30 billion that he wants to donate to save Cyprus?' Everyone wanted to know who that someone was. I had been briefed about this just before the meeting. The president had asked me to listen carefully to Karoyian's suggestion and to look seriously into it. The name of that 'generous' person was Artemis Sorras, a Greek American who a few months earlier claimed that he was going to pay off all of Greece's debts. He allegedly was in possession of six US government Treasury Bills that were worth €650

---

[5]The obligation to introduce resolution legislation that was in line with the Bank Recovery and Resolution Directive was part of the November 2012 agreement with the troika. The drafting of the bill required several months of work by the ministry of finance in close collaboration with the CBC, the Commission, the ECB and the IMF. It is worth noting that the bail-in tool was added to the bill in its very final stages.

billion, which had allegedly been deposited in a bank in Canada. The Greek government had considered this offer as a 'bad joke' and had made public statements to that effect.[6]

I could not believe that this was being discussed as a serious proposition at that critical time but the political leaders seemed desperate enough to want to explore every option to avoid what they saw as an unfair EU-IMF programme, even ones that sounded ludicrous. I felt I had to intervene. I explained that a similar 'offer' had been made to the previous Cypriot government. We had looked into this 'offer' as well as the 'benefactor' himself. It was, at best, a joke, in line with reports by the Greek media at the time.

It wasn't, in fact, the only offer that the AKEL-led government had. There were even more ludicrous 'offers'. In one instance, a gentleman whose business was aptly named after the Greek god Zeus, accompanied by a former MP from Larnaca, was offering a plane-full of gold bullion, allegedly having something to do with a deal between the former Shah of Iran and the USSR. A lot of time was wasted before the government sent that gentleman away empty handed.[7] Such offers kept coming in. The con men were always accompanied by some ex-politicians whom they managed to persuade that their offer should at least be looked into.

Karoyian wasn't a happy man. He thought that he had secured a very generous offer and the CBC didn't even want to look into it. He was getting quite a bit of sympathy from around the table. I was horrified. Were they really so naïve? Or was it sheer desperation that was clouding their vision? Being grounded in reality seemed like a sin that day. In their eyes, the CBC and its Governor were becoming a secret ally of the troika that wanted to destroy Cyprus.

Andros Kyprianou, the leader of AKEL, thought that it was good that Sarris was in Russia and that his sources in Moscow had informed him that Russia was going to help Cyprus. He could not understand why I was putting so much pressure on the government to come to an agreement with the troika if we were so near to getting help from Russia. I, on the other hand, couldn't understand his optimism. I explained that this didn't tally at all with my discussions with the Russian finance minister in Moscow a few weeks earlier. Andros nevertheless insisted. He was convinced that

---

[6]See, for example: http://www.greeknewsonline.com/bank-of-montreal-bank-of-montreal-refutes-the-claims-of-ends-trillionaires-that-theydeposited-with-them-600-billion-in-the-name-of-greece.

[7]At some point in the conversation the potential 'benefactor', who visited me in my office at the CBC with the former mayor, revealed that he had fallen from the first floor of his house and had damaged his head but was fine now.

Russia was Cyprus' eternal friend and was going to help. Indeed, he was so convinced that as soon as the meeting ended, he made critical remarks about me to the press, stating that my actions were impeding Sarris' efforts in Russia, who needed more time to conclude his discussions.

Demetris Syllouris, the leader of the European Party, one of the smaller parties in Parliament, said he also had an 'offer' of help that he wanted the CBC to investigate. He mentioned the name of a banker in London that I had never heard of. The offer was very vague but I nevertheless promised to look into it and invited Syllouris back to my office later that day to have a fuller discussion. It turned out that this was an offer of advisory services. We were already up to our neck with advisors in the CBC. We had one of the top four law firms in the UK advising us on bank restructuring, the same firm which advised the UK Treasury on the restructuring of the British banking system during the global financial crisis. We also had a US-based restructuring consultancy with impeccable credentials—they were the firm in charge of the restructuring of Lehman and helped both Spain and Ireland to set up asset management companies during the euro crisis. We also had a blue chip investment bank with considerable political clout advising us on all aspects of the programme negotiations. Syllouris understood and left it at that. Among the many politicians I had met, he appeared to be the one most grounded in reality.

Wake-up Call

The wake-up call came from Frankfurt during that same meeting at the presidential palace. Before the meeting had ended, I received a text from Costas Papadopoulos, the CBC's senior director who was standing in for me at the Governing Council. I hasten to add that Costas did not vote on Governing Council decisions since only the members of the Governing Council can vote at these meetings. His text said that the Governing Council objected to our request to extend ELA to Cypriot banks for another two weeks. In effect, the ECB had decided it was cutting off ELA to Cypriot banks on 25 March, the date of the next Eurogroup meeting.

I went straight out of the meeting into the beautifully landscaped gardens of the palace—a constant reminder of Cyprus' colonial history—and called Costas. I asked him to brief me. He provided a succinct account of the discussion and the decision. He also said that there was going to be an announcement shortly, which was unprecedented. He explained that he had serious misgivings about the announcement, because of the risks to financial stability, which he had expressed to the Governing Council. However, the ECB decided to proceed with the announcement, which stated the following:

'**Governing Council decision on Emergency Liquidity Assistance requested by the Central Bank of Cyprus**
21 March 2013
The Governing Council of the European Central Bank decided to maintain the current level of Emergency Liquidity Assistance (ELA) until Monday, 25 March 2013.
Thereafter, Emergency Liquidity Assistance (ELA) could only be considered if an EU/IMF programme is in place that would ensure the solvency of the concerned banks'.

It was very short but it served its purpose. It was clearly intended to focus minds but it was not a bluff. We had four days, at most, after which all hell was going to break loose. We just didn't know exactly how it would look but we were certainly heading towards the abyss.

All the politicians in the room were, however, incensed. For them, it was yet another ECB blackmail. They were about to find money from other sources. 'We just need time'—was their main argument.

I reminded them that Cyprus had had plenty of time already, since the previous government had already explored all such avenues during the second half of 2012.

I was rapidly becoming *persona non-grata*. I gave my apologies and left the meeting, we had a lot of emergency planning to do back at the CBC.

As soon as I returned to my office I called Mario Draghi, the ECB President. I felt like I was standing between two sides that had little desire to understand each other. I explained that while I understood why the Governing Council had made that decision I could not understand why they had to make that unprecedented announcement, which could cause even more panic among depositors. Draghi calmly explained that they had discussed this and had decided to make an announcement because they feared the ECB decision was bound to leak. And if it leaked it would have been distorted, which would be much worse than being completely transparent about the decision. They had clearly been observing Cyprus very closely.

The announcement meant that it was time to dig out the secret contingency plan. It had been developed in consultation with the troika and the ministry of finance. A very small number of people at the CBC and the ministry were aware of it. By its very nature, if it had leaked out it would have caused panic. Among other things, it involved restricting withdrawals from ATMs to €30 per week from each bank account. In the first draft, the limit was €20 per week. I had objected, explaining €20 per week wasn't enough to buy milk and bread. One IMF official cynically responded: 'Do you think there will be milk and bread in the shops if your country is bankrupt?' I responded sternly that I could envisage situations in which this could make a difference. Situations of life and death, with babies needing milk or sick people needing medicines. No one wanted to take that risk. It was a temporary measure, anyway. It was meant to buy time until our politicians came to an agreement.

There was no Plan B, no plan to leave the euro, other than the 80-strong IMF contingency team based at the Hilton, which would have provided technical assistance. I called a meeting of all the senior directors at the CBC and the deputy Governor. They were fully aware that it took two years to prepare for accession to the euro zone. There was no way we could make all the necessary preparations to leave the euro in a few weeks. Kyriacos Zingas, the senior director in charge of banking operations, explained that even sourcing secure paper on which to print new bank notes would take several weeks. To produce new bank notes would have taken months. Meanwhile, with the banks closed, the economy would grind to a complete halt. It would grind to a halt even if we miraculously managed to produce bank notes. A bankrupt country has no access to imported goods. Cyprus is a very open country. Nearly everything it produces uses imported inputs. A bankrupt country would also have to introduce capital controls to protect its foreign exchange reserves. The deputy Governor had already enlisted assistance from a retired CBC senior director who had headed the CBC's exchange control department back in its heyday during the 1980s.

All the troika chiefs of the mission came to my office soon after the meeting with the CBC senior directors ended. They wanted me to act urgently. Laiki, which they were monitoring very closely, was running very low on bank notes. Its cash reserves would only last for a couple of more days, if not hours. They were concerned that something might trigger a technical default, which could cause an avalanche of other defaults tipping the country over into bankruptcy. The only way to prevent a sovereign default was to bring Laiki under resolution. By doing so, we would be able to ensure the continuation of critical banking services, protect insured depositors and ultimately protect public funds and the solvency of the sovereign. Moreover, consistent with one of the key principles of resolution, we would be able to use resolution tools to protect the value of the bank's assets.

It was certainly time for the government to submit the Resolution Bill to an emergency session of Parliament. However, the government was still hostile to the idea of resolving the banks—they were doing everything possible to avoid that, which included convincing the Eurogroup to impose a tax on insured deposits. I agreed to talk to the President, although I was not sure of what reaction I might receive. After all, it was the same President who only two weeks ago thought I was responsible for the large bailout bill.

It was around 3.00 pm. I called the president's office. The president wasn't available. He was having his afternoon rest, which was not to be interrupted and he would only be available after 5.00 pm. It was suggested to me that I should speak to his young undersecretary, Constantinos Petrides. I talked to Constantinos, who quickly understood the urgency of the situation. But he felt that I first needed to persuade the parliamentary party leaders. 'Did you see what happened with the levy?', he said, reminding me that all the opposition parties had rejected the levy. Even his own party, DISY, didn't vote for the levy, choosing instead to abstain in the parliamentary vote.

Petrides suggested I call a meeting with all the political leaders in my office. He would come and he would also ask the acting minister of finance to attend, as Sarris was still in Moscow. It was highly unconventional but I agreed; these were extraordinary times. I asked my secretary, who, like me, seemed to be spending most of her hours at the CBC during those critical days, to organise a meeting with all the parliamentary party leaders for the same afternoon.

I suspect that never had so many politicians entered the Governor's office. With the help of Harris Georgiades, who was maturing remarkably rapidly into the role of acting minister of finance, I explained to them the need to take urgent action, which necessitated passing the resolution legislation. They were not happy at all but they were willing to study the legislation and debate it in Parliament. That's as much as we could hope for, although it was obvious that some of them were still hoping for a *deus-ex-machina*. The undersecretary of state said he would call an emergency Council of Ministers meeting at the presidential palace for 6.00 pm. The Government had to approve the Bill before sending it straight to Parliament for discussion the same evening.

I was asked to be there so that I could explain it to the president. I took with me several CBC officials and a Greek-speaking member of staff of the ECB, Phoebus Athanasiou, who could explain the technical details of the legislation. When I arrived, I was surprised to see Chris Pavlou, vice-Chairman of Laiki (a soft spoken man with many years of international banking experience outside Cyprus, including at HSBC Hong Kong, who was only appointed to Laiki after its troubles started in late 2011). It was obvious that Chris's presence was meant to verify what we had said about the liquidity position of Laiki. The president stormed into the meeting, wondering who called it. He looked angrily in my direction and asked if it was me. Before waiting for a reply, he shouted that it was not my responsibility to do that and that he was the only one who had the authority to call a meeting of the Council of Ministers. One of his ministers explained that the matter was very urgent and that it pertained to the escalating crisis at Laiki and that, as he wasn't available, the meeting had been called by his own undersecretary. The president sat down and turned to Chris, asking him to explain what the problem was with Laiki. Chris not only verified what we had said but also painted an even more dramatic picture: the bank, he said, was only a few hours away from running out of cash. Moreover, it had all but exhausted its ELA limit. And the ECB decision meant that this could only last until Monday, 25 March, unless an agreement was reached between the Cyprus government and the Eurogroup.

Phoebus, the Greek-speaking lawyer from the ECB, explained the importance of the resolution law. He explained that insured depositors would be protected. CBC staff added that this meant that 95% of depositors would be protected. This statistic proved to be a turning point. In the absence of the lobby group that wanted to protect the business model, protecting 95% of depositors was music to the ears of some politicians. After a very brief discussion, the bill was approved by the Council of Ministers and submitted soon after that to Parliament. It was agreed that I would make a brief statement in Greek to the media. There were literally dozens, if not hundreds, of journalists and camera crews from all over the world, who were waiting eagerly for the news. As soon as the statement was drafted and agreed by both the CBC and the government, I came out of the palace. It was pandemonium. Two members of my security had to push journalists to make space for me to come out in front of the microphones and camera crews. It felt that we were making history. I made the following statement:

The Central Bank of Cyprus has recommended to the Cypriot Government the urgent submission of a legislative framework for the resolution and recovery of the Cypriot banking system to Parliament for an immediate vote. The process of resolution will prevent bank default and protect in their entirety all insured deposits up to the amount of €100,000. In addition, conditions for the recovery of the banking system are created and jobs are protected. The enactment of resolution legislation is an important step towards achieving a bailout agreement that will protect the Republic of Cyprus.

As soon as I had finished, the acting leader of DISY, Averof Neophytou, stepped forward. He also wanted to make a statement, to provide more details. He started by saying that resolution would protect 95% of depositors. I didn't stay to hear the rest. It was late in the evening but there was more work to be done at the CBC.

The next morning, Friday, 22 March, I was invited to a meeting of Parliament's finance committee that was called to discuss the draft resolution bill. The MPs there were very unhappy. The discussions were very heated. Some of them wanted to go back to the deposit levy. They were convinced that resolution meant much bigger losses for depositors compared to the levy. This wasn't, of course, true. The difference was that whereas the levy spread the burden to all depositors and superficially appeared fairer, resolution would only affect uninsured depositors, who would suffer bigger losses. I explained the general principles of the legislation, that it was intended to limit losses and to protect value and that no one would be worse off compared to liquidation. I added that only failing institutions could be brought under resolution, which would mean that depositors at healthy banks would not be affected. Phoebus Athanasiou, the lawyer from the ECB, provided many more details and helped me to answer questions.[8] We stayed there for over two hours fielding questions. However, some MPs were complaining inside the room and to the media outside that they didn't have enough time to study the bill. True, the legislation was 68 pages long but it had been submitted to Parliament the evening before and it was an emergency situation. The luxury of time was simply not available. We were not just running out of time, we were literally running out of euros to replenish the cash in ATMs. Two planes full of euro bank notes destined for Cyprus, which we had ordered in anticipation of the increased demand for cash during the crisis, were sitting on the tarmac at Frankfurt airport waiting for the ECB's authorisation to take off.

The bill was passed in the late hours of the same day, following a very lengthy and heated full session of Parliament, during which there were calls for my resignation from centrist DIKO, socialist EDEK and the Greens; it certainly didn't help speaking out the truth about the 'benefactors' and the impossibility of a loan from Russia the day before.

Passing that legislation was a very important step forward, but on its own was not enough to avert the disaster that still loomed large. Although

---

[8]MP's subsequently criticised the CBC for including a member of the troika in the technical delegation that briefed Parliament about the legislation.

various modern resolution tools were now available to the CBC in its new role as Resolution Authority, there was still a big divide between the troika and the government on the key resolution actions that needed to be taken. Without the government's consent, the process of resolution and restructuring could not start. The main point of contention was over the resolution of the Bank of Cyprus. This was the bank closest to the government. The president, in particular, who was very close to several members of the bank's board of directors, seemed determined to do everything possible to 'protect' it from resolution.

Cyprus remained on a knife-edge until late on Sunday, 24 March, although the passing of much-needed bank resolution legislation was an important step in the right direction. All that was now needed was political agreement at the European level.

13

"Take It or Leave It"

The days and nights that followed the passing of the resolution legislation on 22 March 2013 felt like we were about to enter hell. To start with, as of the morning of Saturday, 23 March, there was the divide between the government and the troika on the resolution actions to be taken. Even if an agreement was reached, it would have to be ratified by the Eurogroup and various 'hardline' national parliaments (e.g. Germany, Finland and Slovakia), which was by no means certain. If there was no agreement at the political level on the main ingredients of the programme, the ECB could be left with no option but to demand repayment of ELA on 26 March. Such a development would have triggered a series of defaults, including a sovereign default, leading to economic meltdown with all the implied social consequences.

A different version of hell was waiting for us even if an agreement was reached at the political level. In that case, we would need to take resolution actions that would inflict considerable pain on investors, including retail investors who often, understandably, see themselves as victims when things go wrong with their investments. The political environment was already a very hostile one. We had a new government that still behaved as if the bankers did nothing wrong and that the crisis had more to do with the 'inflated' capital needs of the banking system than any wrongdoing by the bankers. On top of that, I was also held responsible for providing the ECB with their alleged weapon of 'blackmail'—ELA. It wasn't just the government that held these views. Other politicians also shared them and were trying to influence public opinion accordingly. There was little objective coverage in the media. Communication mattered enormously but the CBC had very limited

© The Author(s) 2017
P. Demetriades, *A Diary of the Euro Crisis in Cyprus*,
DOI 10.1007/978-3-319-62223-1_13

resources to counteract the myths created by politicians that were propagated uncritically by much of the media.[1]

In the real battles ahead, we were very dependent on the troika's rapport with their superiors in Brussels, Frankfurt and Washington. We understood very well the necessity of those breaks in the meetings when there were critical sticking points, which allowed the troika chiefs to make phone calls to their head offices. We were also dependent on the Commission's behind the scenes work with the various hardline governments. Although we were aware that this was happening—and that it was happening for good reason since the agreement would need to satisfy sceptical parliaments—we had no way of knowing how good those channels were until the votes in those national parliaments took place.

Whatever the nature of the agreement that would finally be reached, there was no escaping from the fact that it would involve an unprecedented amount of restructuring and resolution actions that would need to be carried out in a very short space of time, and which would cause a great deal of discomfort for many of the stakeholders. Those actions needed to be backed by sound legal work since they were bound to be challenged in courts of law. Our own legal team was small and had no experience in bank resolution or restructuring, although they were familiar with the principles of resolution through their involvement in the drafting of the Resolution Law (in collaboration with the ministry of finance, the Commission and the ECB) and the discussions of the Bank Recovery and Resolution Directive that were ongoing during 2012. Our Cypriot external counsel had even less familiarity in these matters, as they were mainly engaged in human resource disputes. There were lawyers from the Commission and the ECB who had more experience but we could hardly rely on them to offer us independent advice. It was, therefore, vital to have our own top-notch external legal advisors, ideally lawyers who had recent bank restructuring and resolution experience in Europe. Fortunately, the background work that was needed to appoint external lawyers had already been done in the months prior to March 2013. Those lawyers—the prestigious London firm Slaughter and May, who had considerable experience from the restructuring of the British banking system—were already on the ground. The British lawyers were an important source of optimism that salvation from hell was possible. If their work was

---

[1]My own attempts to strengthen the CBC in those areas were frustrated by the legal constraints we faced to hire new staff due to the freeze in public sector hires that parliament imposed (which included the CBC) and the CBC board's reluctance to legally challenge that decision.

good—which seemed to be the case—the actions we took would stand up the test of the courts and the test of time. Sooner or later, I thought to myself, the government and their political supporters would understand that what we did was to salvage as much as could be salvaged, in very difficult circumstances. Even the investors who lost money from our actions might, in the fullness of time, come to recognise that they would have lost even more had those actions not been taken.

Working Towards Agreement

On Saturday, 23 March, the fourth floor of the CBC, where the Governor's office and two board meeting rooms were located, seemed like a beehive. In addition to being the favourite location for technical meetings between dozens of troika members, CBC supervisors, lawyers and our army of consultants, a delegation from Pireaus Bank complete with a full panoply of Greek lawyers had just arrived at the CBC to agree the legal terms of the sale of the Greek branches of Cypriot banks.[2]

The Pireaus delegation decamped in the Governor's dining room on the fourth floor of the CBC. There was a large dining table in the room that could comfortably sit 14–16 people. However, at times there must have been as many as 80 people in that room, as there was hardly room to stand. I don't think I have ever experienced such a high concentration of lawyers. There were two sets of lawyers from Greece (ours and Pireaus'), there were Cypriot lawyers from the banks and the CBC, lawyers from the Commission and the ECB and lawyers from the UK. On top of the lawyers, there were CBC supervision staff and ministry of finance staff, as well as troika technocrats and our restructuring advisors. The meeting seemed to have continued non-stop until Tuesday, 26 March, when the final agreement was reached, although it wasn't at all plain sailing. There were many heated arguments and the deal—which could make or break Cyprus and the euro—remained very close and also very far during those critical hours.

On one occasion, the Pireaus delegation walked out and said they were going back to Greece without signing the deal. On another occasion,

---

[2]The Greek carve-out had already been marked by the Eurogroup as a prior action that needed to be taken to protect financial stability in the euro area. Pireaus had been chosen by the Greek authorities as the buyer of the Greek branches of Cypriot banks. The financial terms of the agreement were also agreed at the Eurogroup meeting and comprised a 26% discount on assets, in line with the expected losses under the PIMCO adverse scenario.

I received a call from George Provopoulos, the Greek central bank Governor, who was complaining about the 'inflexibility' of our lead British lawyer. On talking to our British lawyers I discovered that what the Greek lawyers were insisting on was simply unacceptable. Pireaus wanted to have an opt-out clause, which they could exercise following a fair valuation of the assets they would acquire. This would, in essence, mean that the Greek carve-out could be reversed a few months later, which would certainly not have been consistent with the Eurogroup agreement as it could unleash financial contagion between the two countries later on. This point was also forcefully made by the troika: we could not sign such an agreement. Eventually, Pireaus agreed not to include an opt-out clause but they demanded a premium of several hundred million euros to compensate them for the 'risk of the unknown' that they were taking on. That was a major sticking point that was only resolved at the highest political level between Cyprus's President, Nicos Anastasiades, and the Greek Prime Minister, Antonis Samaras, who between them agreed to a more reasonable premium than was initially demanded.

On his return from Moscow empty handed and rather subdued, Michael Sarris became another inhabitant on the fourth floor of the CBC, and took considerable interest in the negotiations that were going on between Pireaus bank and our side, which was extremely helpful as he knew better than anyone else what exactly had been agreed at the Eurogroup about the sale of the Greek branches. On several occasions when there were sticking points, he talked to his counterpart in Greece, Yiannis Stournaras, who also took an interest from Athens.

In the CBC board meeting room, which was adjacent to the Governor's office, there were back-to-back meetings between various groups of CBC staff, ministry officials, advisors and sections of the troika, often with direct telephone participation from the Competition Directorate—known as DG Comp—in Brussels. The discussions encompassed the future of the entire banking system, including the credit cooperative sector, which consisted of 94 regional coops. The major sticking point was, however, what was to be done with Bank of Cyprus and Laiki, the banks that had the largest capital needs. DG Comp very much dictated what was to happen to them, since, in effect, they had the authority to veto any proposal from our side.[3]

---

[3]They did, however, take a more flexible stance on the restructuring of the credit cooperative sector, which allowed the coops themselves to have a say in their future, through the work of our restructuring specialists. DG Comp wanted to merge all the coops together into one legal entity. However, the coops themselves wanted to retain their regional identities. In the end, it was agreed that the 94 regional coops be merged and reduced to 18 and that they would all come under the umbrella of the Cooperative Central Bank.

Their idea was to split Laiki into a 'good bank' and 'bad bank' and to merge the good part of Laiki with Bank of Cyprus, which would be recapitalised by bailing in shareholders, bondholders and uninsured depositors. At a superficial level, this sounded like major surgery that would, if anything, reduce competition in the banking sector, as it would create a mega monopoly bank. However, DG Comp provided a rationale behind their suggestion. They were convinced that this was the only viable way forward. There were efficiency gains that could be created through the merger, which would help facilitate the downsizing of the Cypriot banking system. It was also one of the other key objectives that was agreed by the Eurogroup. Bank of Cyprus, DG Comp argued, was also the only bank that could take on such a large balance sheet of assets and liabilities: trying to merge Laiki with a smaller bank would be like driving an ocean liner into a dinghy. If Laiki was merged with a smaller bank, the large ELA liability could tip it over, unless it had a large volume of unencumbered assets.[4]

Not surprisingly, the idea of merging Laiki with Bank of Cyprus encountered strong political resistance. Bank of Cyprus board members didn't want to hear and expended all of their remaining political capital trying to oppose it. That was enough to ensure that Anastasiades remained vehemently opposed to the merger, until the bitter end. The bankers were convinced that Laiki's ELA would prove to be a big 'burden' for Bank of Cyprus and was a threat to its survival. They felt that it was only a matter of time before the bank would run out of liquidity. To this day, I fail to see the logic of that argument, notwithstanding the fragile conditions of the time. If Bank of Cyprus needed extra liquidity it had a sufficiently large volume of high quality unencumbered assets that it could use to obtain it. Moreover, the whole point of the programme was to increase capital buffers and restructure the bank, in order to increase depositors' confidence. Unless they also thought that the ECB was going to 'blackmail' them (which, given what they had been told by the president, is not impossible), ELA was, if anything, a blessing for them. For a start, the cost of ELA was less than half the average, let alone marginal, cost of deposits (deposit rates were over 4% at the time). In a crisis, ELA is a more stable source of funding than deposits that can flee overnight. Although ELA is renewed every two weeks, it could not be withdrawn unless the bank became insolvent, something which was

---

[4]A small bank was unlikely to be able to provide a large volume of unencumbered assets, which could be used as additional collateral in case of downgrades of existing collateral due to deteriorating economic circumstances. Moreover, collateral was needed in case additional liquidity from the ECB was needed, which was likely if depositors' confidence remained fragile and outflows continued.

effectively ruled out by the economic adjustment programme. If the programme failed, the sovereign would have defaulted and the entire banking system would also have failed with disastrous consequences for the economy and the Cypriot people. Why would it matter who they owed money to in the event that the bank failed?

With their actions, the Bank of Cyprus board members and their political supporters created additional fragility because they managed to demonise ELA. Most of the media thought that ELA was a big burden that would need to be repaid by taxpayers. As a result, depositors' confidence took longer to return than was necessary.[5]

Anticipating the likely resistance to the merger, our consultants worked hard to provide an alternative scenario. They proposed to keep the two banks largely separate, and to recapitalise them both through converting uninsured deposits into equity. The government was much more sympathetic to this scenario that was presented to the president himself in the late hours of Saturday, 23 March. There were, however, reservations over whether the numbers could work, without there being a need for Laiki to somehow 'lean' on Bank of Cyprus for collateral or on the government itself for additional guarantees, which had already been ruled out by the Eurogroup. Thus, in the end, this alternative scenario remained a paper exercise that was turned down by the technocrats of the troika.

The Final Hours

In the evening of Sunday, 24 March, I was invited to a meeting at the presidential palace with Michael Sarris, the minister of finance, who continued to look subdued, and the troika. President Anastasiades insisted on keeping the two banks separate, because of the perceived ELA 'burden', which he could not, however, rationalise. He wanted to invite the bankers to explain it better, which the troika was refusing. After a lot of discussion that was going nowhere, the heads of the troika asked for a break to call their superiors. On their return, Maarten Verway, the head of the troika, issued an ultimatum: 'Mr President', he said, 'this is the only option you have, you can take it or

---

[5]In subsequent interviews, I explained that Bank of Cyprus received assets from Laiki, not just liabilities. The assets it received exceeded in fair value the liabilities, including the ELA. Moreover, I explained that as a result of ELA the bank had a stable and inexpensive source of funding, compared to deposits. Finally, I also pointed out that 80% of the profits made by the CBC from ELA went into the government coffers and helped to reduce the public deficit by hundreds of millions of euros.

leave it'. The president responded by insisting that we should at least invite the bankers to hear their views.

Maarten seemed very frustrated—as did the other chiefs of staff. He was, nevertheless, very polite in his response. He said:

> Mr President, you can invite anyone you like here, but we are leaving now. In any case, what do you expect to hear from the bankers whose banks are about to be resolved?

Once the troika chiefs left, the president did invite the bankers who vehemently opposed the idea. Some of them said they would prefer to leave the euro than have their bank resolved and subsequently fail. I tried to counter their arguments but they were simply not listening. They thought the president would protect them. They were certainly used to enjoying political protection and were not prepared to consider the arguments of a central bank Governor who was very much an outsider.

The bankers left and the leaders of the parliamentary political parties arrived soon after that. The president was already softening his position, as both Sarris and I made it very clear to him what would happen otherwise. However, he wasn't going to take any decision without consulting them. It was beginning to look like an exercise in damage limitation, which was more promising, although nothing was certain.

The president certainly needed help with the political leaders. Andros Kyprianou, leader of AKEL, came out the strongest against what was on the table. He stated that we should consider leaving the euro instead of accepting the troika's proposals. He also mentioned that AKEL already had a paper prepared by a Greek academic who worked at the University of London on how to achieve this. I was aware of who the academic was. However, although there was no shortage of economists proposing how to leave the euro, I had not seen any plans that looked remotely workable. Even if one agreed that it was a bad idea that a country joined the euro in the first place, it was a much worse idea to abandon it without fully understanding the mechanics, let alone the catastrophic consequences. I explained that it would be like trying to exit a plane in mid-air when one realised they were on the wrong flight. I suggested that they take what was on offer and reconsider their choices at a later stage, if the programme wasn't working.

At the end of that meeting, Anastasiades seemed ready to take whatever was on the table. I felt I had done my duty, advising frankly the government and the political leadership of the risks arising from their choices, rather than telling them what they wanted to hear. Because of that, however, my own political capital, if I ever had any, was being rapidly depleted.

14

Resolution and Capital Controls

Once the agreement with the troika was reached on the evening of Sunday, 24 March, Anastasiades and Sarris headed for Larnaca airport. A plane dispatched by the Belgian government was waiting to fly them to the Eurogroup meeting. Anastasiades asked me if I could join them but I politely declined. I explained that I had to stay behind to 'press the buttons' once the Eurogroup decision was made. My physical presence and signature were both needed for the resolution actions that were about to take place. Moreover, the presence of a central bank Governor at a Eurogroup meeting—which is a political meeting—would have raised many eyebrows given that central banks are supposed to be independent. I didn't say that to Anastasiades. The independence of the CBC was already a taboo subject for him. He never missed an opportunity to remind me that he was elected (and hence represented the wishes of the Cypriot people), while I was appointed and thus only represented myself.

We had no time to waste. The banks had remained shut for a whole week already and we wanted to be able to reopen them on Tuesday, 26 March, if at all possible. It was a race against time. I explained all that to him. I asked him to call me himself as soon as they had an agreement at the Eurogroup meeting and he readily agreed.

I went back to my office at the CBC. The beehive of activity on the fourth floor was continuing, although there were now fewer people. The lawyers were busying themselves producing drafts of the resolution decrees. The discussions between Pireaus and our lawyers were progressing.

© The Author(s) 2017
P. Demetriades, *A Diary of the Euro Crisis in Cyprus*,
DOI 10.1007/978-3-319-62223-1_14

Anastasiades' phone call came in the early hours of Monday, 25 March at around 2.30 am Cyprus time. It was brief. 'You may now press the buttons', he said, 'we have an agreement'.

The agreement had already been posted on the Eurogroup website, which I had been checking every few minutes. We knew exactly what was to happen. The details of the resolution and restructuring actions that were agreed were included in the annex of an unusually long Eurogroup statement. The annex stated the following:

'Following the presentation by the Cyprus authorities of their policy plans, which were broadly welcomed by the Eurogroup, the following was agreed:

1. Laiki will be resolved immediately—with full contribution of equity shareholders, bond holders and uninsured depositors—based on a decision by the Central Bank of Cyprus, using the newly adopted Bank Resolution Framework.
2. Laiki will be split into a good bank and a bad bank. The bad bank will be run down over time.
3. The good bank will be folded into Bank of Cyprus (BoC), using the Bank Resolution Framework, after having heard the Boards of Directors of BoC and Laiki. It will take 9 bn Euros of ELA with it. Only uninsured deposits in BoC will remain frozen until recapitalisation has been effected, and may subsequently be subject to appropriate conditions.
4. The Governing Council of the ECB will provide liquidity to the BoC in line with applicable rules.
5. BoC will be recapitalised through a deposit/equity conversion of uninsured deposits with full contribution of equity shareholders and bond holders.
6. The conversion will be such that a capital ratio of 9% is secured by the end of the programme.
7. All insured depositors in all banks will be fully protected in accordance with the relevant EU legislation.
8. The programme money (up to 10bn Euros) will not be used to recapitalise Laiki and Bank of Cyprus.

The Eurogroup is convinced that this solution is the best way forward for ensuring the overall viability and stability of the Cyprus financial system and its capability to finance the Cyprus economy'.

The agreement didn't explicitly state that Bank of Cyprus would be brought under resolution, but this was certainly implied by points 3 and 5, which alluded to the use of the resolution framework and the conversion of uninsured deposits into equity, respectively. The latter could only be carried out using the bail-in resolution tool. The same was true of the freezing of deposits in Bank of Cyprus: it could only be done under resolution. However, unless one was familiar with the resolution legislation, the lack of explicit mention that Bank of Cyprus was to be brought under resolution could create the erroneous impression that it was only Laiki that was being resolved. Such opacity was rather unfortunate: it left room for politicians to manipulate public opinion by suggesting that it was the CBC's initiative to resolve the Bank of Cyprus.

We had already noticed that point 3 suggested that resolution actions would take place 'after having heard the Boards of Directors' of the two banks. This sounded extremely odd unless one knew the discussions the previous evening between the troika and Anastasiades, during which the president insisted that the troika had to listen to the bankers.

I interpreted it as a political concession from the Eurogroup to Anastasiades, one that would allow him to save face in front of his banker friends. The troika did, however, avoid seeing the bankers. In my absence, they clearly had decided that it was I who had to listen to them, in my new role as, in effect, the Resolution Authority. As if I hadn't already listened to the bankers who brought the country to its knees before that. As if I didn't already know their views. Thank you, Eurogroup, for that, I thought.

I could not fully understand, however, why the statement didn't explicitly state that Bank of Cyprus would be brought under resolution. I wanted to make sure that Anastasiades understood that. I, therefore, fired a straight question:

'You do recognise, Mr President, that both banks will be brought under resolution, don't you?' I asked.

I was astounded by his reply: 'I will pass you on to Averof', he said.

Averof Neophytou, acting leader of DISY, had evidently accompanied him to the Eurogroup meeting; I wasn't even aware of that until that moment. Averof seemed to be present at all the critical meetings during the programme discussions, although his presence wasn't always publicised.

I then heard the familiar high pitch voice of Averof:

Panico, we know that but we are not saying it yet.

I was startled. Before I had a chance to respond, he hung up. It all sounded extremely odd. The agreement was in black and white, how could they avoid saying that Bank of Cyprus would be brought under resolution? It turned out later that day that they were already preparing the ground for the start of the political blame game. They certainly didn't want to take responsibility for having to resolve Bank of Cyprus. But who were they going to blame for it? And for how long was their economical version of events going to last?

As soon as that telephone conversation finished, I called Harris Georgiades who was acting as finance minister, as Sarris was in Brussels. I invited him to come to the CBC to sign the two resolution decrees, one for each bank. Harris wasn't thrilled, it was 2.00 am and I probably woke him up, but he agreed. He said very little but he agreed that he would be at the CBC at 5.00 am, by which time the decrees would be ready for signing. The resolution law stipulated very clearly that bringing a bank under resolution required the consent of the minister of finance.

I tried to sleep for a couple of hours on the sofa in the Governor's office but it was difficult. I must have dozed off at some point because I remember Eleni, my secretary, coming in at around 5.00 am to wake me up. I got up from the sofa and tried to freshen myself up before Harris arrived. When he arrived the decrees were not ready. He had to wait a few minutes. He was silent. I tried to make polite conversation but without much success. By about 6.00 am we had finished signing the two decrees—one for each bank. He asked me if we had finished. I said yes, there is nothing else we wanted from him at that point. He got up and left. I thought he must have still been in sleep mode and that he was going back to bed after that, that's why he wasn't talkative. I was wrong. I heard from colleagues at the CBC later that day that Harris was giving interviews to the media soon after he left the CBC. They reported to me that he—and other DISY party politicians—were creating the impression that the resolution of Bank of Cyprus was my idea. I am not entirely sure exactly what was said during these interviews and I made no effort to find those interviews afterwards. There was simply no time for that. My priority was to save what could be saved by implementing promptly and in a legally sound manner all the actions that were agreed at the Eurogroup meeting. It was the only way to ensure the economy did not collapse.

I focused my mind and my efforts on what we had to do and pushed everything else aside. First and foremost we had to appoint administrators for each of the two banks to oversee their restructuring. We also had to 'listen' to their boards, before dismissing them. Actions also needed to be taken to protect branches and subsidiaries overseas and decisions on those could only be taken by coordinating with regulators outside Cyprus, including the Bank of England and the Bank of Romania. In the UK, Laiki had a branch and Bank of Cyprus had a subsidiary. In Romania, it was exactly the opposite. Laiki had a subsidiary and Bank of Cyprus had a branch. The subsidiary could stand alone, even if the parent had failed, thanks to the actions already taken by their respective regulators that ring-fenced them from their parent. However, it was less obvious what needed to be done with branches which, in principle, could have been allowed to fail. On top of all that, there was still no agreement with Pireaus.

Ignoring political and media criticism and focusing on one's duties doesn't, however, come without consequences. During the morning of Tuesday, 26 March I heard a lot of noise coming from outside. It was a crowd demonstrating and they were heading out from the Bank of Cyprus building, just opposite the CBC, towards the CBC premises. They were the employees of the Bank of Cyprus and they were shouting for my resignation. They were also holding placards saying 'Δημητριάδη [my surname in Greek] go home'. The BBC's Tim Wilcox reported that one protester told him that the CBC Governor's actions were 'causing the closing of the Bank of Cyprus'.[1, 2] The political propaganda was clearly working.

It was certainly very disheartening to be attacked and undermined like that, when all we were trying to do was to ensure the stability of the country and, ultimately, protect as many jobs as we could. We were putting in 24-hour shifts to implement what the government had agreed with the Eurogroup. There was to be major surgery to the banking system and the CBC had to do all the work for that. The least we expected from government politicians was to explain to the public what was happening and why. Resolving the banks wasn't a pleasant task, but it was necessary because anything else would have been far worse for everyone concerned, even for the depositors who lost money.

---

[1] 'Bank of Cyprus workers protest outside central bank': http://www.bbc.co.uk/news/world-europe-21947481.

[2] I was told a few days later that the demonstrators were organised through text messages sent by a member of the bank's senior management.

Capital Controls

In the afternoon of 25 March, there was a teleconference of the Governing Council of the ECB. In light of the Eurogroup agreement, ELA to Cypriot banks could now be renewed. Point 4 in the annex of the Eurogroup agreement explicitly stated that 'The Governing Council of the ECB will provide liquidity to the BoC in line with applicable rules'. This was—not surprisingly—vague and, in some sense, redundant as the ECB would have to do that anyway. But it still served a useful purpose in that it signalled that the Cypriot banking system would not be starved of liquidity. It contrasted with what was stated by the ECB on 21 March, which was that beyond 25 March 'ELA could only be considered if an EU/IMF programme is in place that would ensure the solvency of the concerned banks'. Strictly speaking, while an agreement was reached with the Eurogroup, the EU/IMF programme could not be put in place until it was ratified by various national Parliaments in Europe and until agreements were signed with the IMF and the European Stability Mechanism. That was to take several more weeks, and it was, therefore, useful to send a signal to the markets that the ECB would be providing liquidity before these formalities had been completed.

Conditions were, however, volatile and fragile and depositors' confidence had been shaken not just because of the resolution measures, which people were trying to make sense of, but more importantly by the earlier Eurogroup decision to impose a levy on all deposits, even those on healthy international banks that had nothing to do with the crisis. It was likely that we were going to face very large withdrawals if not an outright bank run after the banks reopened. The ELA request had to take this into account. It also needed to take into account whether the banks would reopen with some form of capital controls.

The possibility of capital controls being introduced was mooted in the main body of the Eurogroup statement that morning. A paragraph stated:

> The Eurogroup takes note of the authorities' decision to introduce administrative measures, appropriate in view of the present unique and exceptional situation of Cyprus' financial sector and to allow for a swift reopening of the banks. The Eurogroup stresses that these administrative measures will be temporary, proportionate and non-discriminatory, and subject to strict monitoring in terms of scope and duration in line with the Treaty.

This was another surprising Eurogroup initiative. If 'authorities' was intended to include the CBC alongside the government, we at the CBC certainly had not made any such decision. There was hardly any serious discussion at all of this possibility, other than in the context of the contingency plan that had been put together for the eventuality that an agreement wasn't reached. The possibility of capital controls being introduced, following an agreement with Eurogroup, was not discussed at all with the president or the finance minister before they set off for the Eurogroup meeting.

I was informed by Isabelle Von Koppen Mertez, the ECB troika chief of mission, just before the teleconference with the ECB Governing Council that the European Commission came out strongly in favour of capital controls while the ECB was against the idea while the IMF sat on the fence. It was obvious that if we were to reopen the banks without capital controls, we needed to have the agreement of the Governing Council that the ECB would stand ready to supply whatever liquidity was needed to cover those outflows. Anything else would create more panic.

The ECB agreed in principle to our request to supply as much liquidity as was necessary to prevent capital controls from being imposed. Thus, there was no need, whatsoever, to introduce capital controls. With the two banks remaining under resolution, with much of their deposits frozen, what needed to be done was to stand ready to supply liquidity to the rest of the banking system. Our judgment at the CBC was that we would have witnessed very large outflows from the rest of the banking system but it would have been a matter of days before they slowed down, as the public began to understand what had happened and that only the two big banks would have their deposits bailed-in.

We felt that the introduction of capital controls would be another blow to confidence that could be avoided, just like the ill-designed deposit levy. The banking system had already been closed for one week. Every day that it remained closed constituted another blow. On the back of the supportive ECB decision, we decided to reopen banks the following morning, except for Bank of Cyprus and Laiki that would be undergoing restructuring and merger. We were about to make an announcement to that effect. The announcement was to also say that all banks, other than Laiki and Bank of Cyprus that would have remained closed for another two days, would be operating normally. The banks were informed accordingly and the announcement was being typed.

Within minutes, I received a phone call from Kirill Zimarin, the chairman of the Association of International Banks in Cyprus who congratulated me for that decision. It was the right decision, he said. He assured me that all the international banks were sufficiently liquid and they could face any level of deposit withdrawals without requesting ELA.

Immediately after that, I received a phone call from the presidential palace. The President wanted to see me urgently. A meeting had already been scheduled at the CBC with the Board of Directors who wanted to be briefed on developments. They were all there but I asked them to wait so I could go to the presidential palace. They were disappointed, if not annoyed, that they were not going to be briefed about what was happening. The matter which the president wanted to discuss—our imminent announcement that the banks would reopen the following day—had to take priority. I asked the CBC staff to hold fire on the announcement and left for the presidential palace with the Deputy Governor, Spyros Stavrinakis.

Michael Sarris, the finance minister, the undersecretary of state, Constantinos Petrides and Averof Neophytou, the leader of DISY were already in the president's office, all sitting next to each other on the same side of the large conference table. Averof didn't wait for the president to start the meeting. He asked us why we wanted to reopen the banks the next day. Spyros explained that in our judgment the longer the banks stayed closed, the greater the blow to confidence. Averof responded by asking with a sarcastic smile 'Is that Spyros' judgement?'

The President then came and sat down. He informed us that he had talked to Jose Manuel Barroso, the President of the European Commission, who explained to him that the view of the Commission was that we should only reopen the banks after introducing capital controls. The same view, he continued, was held by the Belgian Prime Minister, with whom the president had also talked. I explained that our views, which concurred with those of the ECB, differed. Moreover, the ECB was prepared to supply as much liquidity as was needed to reopen the banks the next day, with the exception of Bank of Cyprus and Laiki that had to undergo resolution. I also added that capital controls are easy to impose but very difficult to lift. While they are in place, international investors would take notice and avoid investing on the island. I explained that capital controls would have negative real effects and we could face a longer recession as a result.

Sarris and Averof did not agree because, they argued, there would be a stigma attached to the Bank of Cyprus and they wanted to avoid that. It was astonishing. This was the bank that had failed spectacularly and was threatening the entire economy. There was already a stigma attached to it. Keeping it closed for two more days to perform the operation that would save it would surely not add any more stigma than it already had. Did the rest of the banking system not count at all? Was there not going to be a stigma attached to the entire banking system if all the banks remained closed for another two days? Was it better to impose restrictive measures that would be difficult to lift? Indeed, days after the capital controls were imposed, the government came under pressure to lift them, as businesses started protesting about the restrictive measures impacting on their activities. Their immediate reaction was to start exerting pressure on the CBC to lift them. Yet another example of time inconsistency in government policy.

The President wanted the final word. His television interview had already been videotaped. In it, he had mentioned that the banks would reopen in a few days with some mild restrictions in place that would only last for a very short period. He wasn't going to change that so we'd better go back and make another announcement.

I left the room and I went into the gardens of the palace. I called Mario Draghi on his mobile. I explained the position of the government. Draghi thought that we could still go ahead with the plan to reopen the banks that was backed by the ECB. We could explain that in our statement, he suggested. We could also mention that introducing capital controls was the Commission's idea, which the CBC and ECB did not share. This was easier said in Frankfurt than done in Nicosia.

We went back to the CBC and issued another statement. All banks were to reopen on Thursday under administrative controls that would be announced later. I felt dispirited and demoralised. I quickly briefed the board of the CBC on what had just happened and apologised for the wait. We could still not hold the formal board meeting because my presence— along with the minister's—was urgently needed in the dining room where the negotiations with Pireaus were getting stuck. Tensions were rising again over some fine legal detail. It was make or break time. Without that agreement, we would go back to facing the abyss, as it was a prior action for the programme. Sarris was already there. I am not sure if either of us made a substantive contribution to the legal deliberations but our presence seemed to have helped to calm the nerves down. Both Sarris and I explained how important this was for both countries. This was no ordinary business deal. It was a deal that would ring-fence the two banking systems from potential financial contagion from each other.

I came out of that room at around midnight, as soon as the final agreement was reached. I felt a strong sense of relief. It was a poignant way to end Greek national independence day—without another national catastrophe. I looked for the members of the board but I was told they had already left.

International Reaction[3]

The Eurogroup agreement on Cyprus made headline news worldwide. Those who were expecting the euro to unravel in Cyprus were clearly disappointed. The Euroskeptics, however, argued that the deal was so bad that it was only a matter of time before it failed: they predicted that Cyprus was going to become a 'zombie' economy. It didn't help, of course, that the Cypriot government itself was in two minds about the agreement. On the one hand, it wanted to distance itself from the resolution of Bank of Cyprus and the losses imposed on Russians. On the other hand, it wanted to remain in the good books of Europe and the IMF (after all, the role of 'bad pupil' had been played by Greece). The official EU-IMF view, which was expressed by Dutch finance minister and Eurogroup chairman, Jeroen Dijsselbloem and Christine Lagarde, the IMF's Managing Director, was quite positive. Many were also surprised by Russian President Putin's response, who welcomed the new EU-IMF deal on Cyprus and announced that Russia would, as a result, agree to improve the terms of the €2.5 billion loan to Cyprus.[4]

At the Eurogroup press conference held soon after the agreement was reached, Dijsselbloem boldly announced that '*We've put an end to the uncertainty that has affected Cyprus and the euro in recent days*', although he also admitted that 'It was a difficult road to get here'. Christine Lagarde was even more optimistic and described the deal as '*a durable and fully financed solution to the underlying problems facing Cyprus and places it on a sustainable path to recovery*'. Jose Manuel Barroso, President of the European Commission, who issued a press statement later that morning, recognised 'the challenges for 'Cyprus are immense', but added that, Cyprus could [now] count on the European Union for support'.[5]

The German government also put a positive spin on the deal. Angela Merkel, in particular, was quoted as saying: '*I am very pleased that a solution was found and that we have been able to avoid an insolvency. I believe the agreement that was reached is the right one*'. The German finance minister, Wolfgang Schauble, in his usual blunt fashion, stated that 'this deal is better

---

[3]This section draws on an article in the *Daily Telegraph* 'Cyprus bailout: as it happened', 25 March 2013. See: http://www.telegraph.co.uk/finance/debt-crisis-live/9951727/Cyprus-bailout-live.html.

[4]I was certainly not among those who were surprised because Putin's announcement was completely in line with what I had been told by Anton Siluanov, the Russian finance minister, during my visit to Moscow a month earlier.

[5]Barroso's statement on Cyprus is included in Appendix 2.

for Germany than the previous one' and expressed optimism that it would be approved by all national Parliaments by 17 April.

The Cypriot finance ministry's perspective was put forward by Michael Sarris, who stated: *'It's not that we won a battle, but we really have avoided a disastrous exit from the Eurozone'*. Sarris added that the *'Russians were understandably disappointed by this turn of events. They have had a long, successful and happy history and association with Cyprus. This has come partly as a shock despite the fact that many of these things have been rumoured'*. There were conflicting reports about the stance of Anastasiades, with Barroso being quoted by *The Guardian* as saying that Anastasiades fully supported the deal, while Cyprus EU Twitter sources were quoted as saying that Anastasiades fought tooth and nail on bank closure, restructuring and downsizing.[6]

The Russian Prime Minister, Dmitry Medvedev, was reported by western media as more than just disappointed. He was described as reacting furiously to the bailout deal. Medvedev was quoted as saying: *'In my view, the stealing of what has already been stolen continues in Cyprus'*.[7] The western press was initially perplexed as Medvedev's comments seemed out of line with those made by President Putin, who, despite the heavy blow on Russian businesses on the island, expressed support for the EU-IMF rescue deal. The restructuring of the €2.5 billion Russian loan to Cyprus involved extending its payback deadline beyond 2016, which was very much in line with the IMF's debt sustainability analysis. Putin's positive stance on the new deal between Cyprus and the EU-IMF contrasted sharply with remarks he made a week earlier on the deposit levy, which he had described as 'unjust, unprofessional and dangerous'. It was obvious that Sarris didn't have the Russian Government in mind when he said that 'the Russians were disappointed'.

Both the USA and UK governments also welcomed the deal. The UK's Prime Minister, David Cameron, added that *'the first proposals of taxing people with bank accounts under £100,000 was a complete mistake and I am glad that has been avoided'*. Cameron also seized the opportunity to remind

---

[6]I have no reason to dispute either of the two sources. Anastasiades came to terms with the deal, albeit reluctantly, before going to the Eurogroup, while domestically he continued to maintain that he had been blackmailed.

[7]It became clear later that Medvedev's comments were lost in translation. Medvedev had paraphrased a famous phrase by Lenin, who when asked about the expropriation of money that belonged to the capitalists by the Bolsheviks replied that this was money that had already been stolen from the workers by the capitalists. Medvedev was clearly hinting that the provinence of Russian money in Cyprus had been illegal. This seems to suggest that the Russian government cared little about the losses imposed on wealthy Russians, possibly because they may have evaded government taxes in Russia.

people that Britain was right not to join the euro and that there was no alternative to getting public spending under control.

UK commentators weren't, however, persuaded by the deal and some were predicting that the demise of Cyprus and the euro would be a matter of time. The Euroskeptics were having a field day. The *Telegraph's* Jeremy Warner, for example, questioned Christine Lagarde's view that the solution would be durable.

> How can this be durable when it offers no way out of the economic ruin that the single currency has visited on the island? ....Under this deal, Cyprus is, in effect, kissing goodbye to one of the mainstays of its prosperity and growth – finance. It's a bit like saying that closing down the City of London would put the UK on a sustainable path to recovery. Many might welcome the death of finance, but the impact on output, tax revenues, employment and public services would be devastating. The same is likely to be true in miniature of Cyprus.

Warner also predicted that '*No national banking system can survive such a restructuring. Thousands will lose their jobs, not just in the banks but in legal, accountancy and business services industries that the banks have supported. An immediate collapse of 10pc to 20pc in national income is in prospect, with unemployment soaring to more than a quarter of the population*'.

Euroskeptics found an unlikely ally in Christopher Pissarides, Professor of Economics at the LSE, recipient of the Nobel Memorial Prize in Economics and chairman of the Council of the National Economy for the Republic of Cyprus, who discussed the deal on Radio Four's *Today Programme*. Chris, who had been reported as being dismayed by the deal, was quoted as saying: '*You might say the Cyprus government does not have the money [to provide deposit insurance] but that's why Cyprus joined the Eurozone in the first place. That's why we are heading towards monetary union, to pool risks. A German finance minister thinks 'I do not like your economy, your economic development over the last 60 years. The way I am going to change it is to bankrupt two main banks then you sort out the mess afterwards'. It was not a "no" with every other country which asked for help. Greece has a corrupt, non-functional economy. It got €140bn. Cyprus needs [another] €8 or €9bn. How could they [the Eurozone] say that's too much money?*'

Banks Reopen

Banks reopened on Thursday, 28 March 2013. By then the merger between 'good' Laiki and Bank of Cyprus had been completed, which by itself was a small miracle. All Laiki branches reopened, although they were now legally under the control of Bank of Cyprus. The employees of Laiki were all 'moved' to Bank of Cyprus, though physically nothing had changed. Insured depositors had access to their cash. The banks had replenished their cash buffers and ATMs with new euro banknotes that had just arrived from Frankfurt.

The boards of the two banks were dismissed, and while Laiki's board came in quietly and tendered their resignation, the same could not be said of Bank of Cyprus, which continued to behave as if nothing had changed. They were having a board meeting at the bank's headquarters in Ayia Paraskevi (exactly opposite the CBC building) and sent a message to us that they would be arriving later. In the end, few of them decided to turn up. The Chairman, Andreas Artemis, and the CEO, Yiannis Kypri, to their credit, came in and tendered their resignation without much fuss. However, there were fireworks when three other members of the board entered the CBC and came into my office. They were extremely unhappy and chose not to hide their anger and frustration. They said in loud tones that it was all my fault. Their bank was healthy and I had failed to protect it. 'Thank you, Eurogroup, for agreeing that I had to listen to the bankers whose banks were going to be resolved', I thought to myself.

A lot of preparation work had to be done before reopening the banks as the entire banking system, which comprised 41 banks and 94 credit cooperatives, had to reopen under a long list of restrictive measures that not only prohibited capital outflows but also imposed a long list of restrictions on domestic transactions. It was not business as usual, and thousands of bank and coop employees had to be trained to operate in the new and much more complex framework, in which the banks had delegated authority for some transactions but not others. A committee was set up at the CBC that also included ministry officials to which large or exceptional transactions had to be referred to.

There was very little time for preparation of the banking system to operate in this brave new world as the restrictive measures had only been agreed two days before the banks were to reopen. There were tense discussions between the troika, the ministry of finance and the CBC, that had also to take into account the views of the banks as to what was practical to implement and what wasn't. The starting point for the restrictive measures was the contingency plan, although this included some very draconian restrictions. The troika, led by the Commission in this instance, had the view that it was better to start with something close to the draconian measures in the contingency plan and to review them every two weeks, relaxing them where appropriate. They certainly had a point. Given that the Commission and the government were committed to proceeding with capital controls, it wouldn't make any sense to start loose and tighten up later, as that would deliver a further blow to confidence. By contrast regular relaxations, no matter how small, could help to rebuild confidence. We all agreed on that but the starting point was still a matter of choice.

It took many hours and many meetings before striking the right balance between restrictions that would protect the liquidity of the weakest banks in the system and ones that wouldn't bring the economy to a standstill. They included restrictions on daily withdrawals, a ban on premature termination of time and savings deposits and a ban on the opening of new current accounts.

The banks did reopen on Thursday for a shorter day than was normal. We announced in advance the restrictive measures and launched a media campaign to explain them in simple language. This proved to be our most successful media campaign—we had no political opponents on this one. When the banks reopened on Thursday, 25 March 2013, everything went smoothly. It was another mini miracle, thanks to the hard work of the CBC staff and excellent support from our restructuring advisors. We started feeling more optimistic, although it may not have shown in our faces after a long week and several sleepless nights.

Appendix: Eurogroup Statement on Cyprus

25 March 2013

The Eurogroup has reached an agreement with the Cypriot authorities on the key elements necessary for a future macroeconomic adjustment programme. This agreement is supported by all euro area Member States as well as the three institutions. The Eurogroup fully supports the Cypriot people in these difficult circumstances.

The programme will address the exceptional challenges that Cyprus is facing and restore the viability of the financial sector, with the view of restoring sustainable growth and sound public finances over the coming years.

The Eurogroup welcomes the plans for restructuring the financial sector as specified in the annex. These measures will form the basis for restoring the viability of the financial sector. In particular, they safeguard all deposits below EUR 100.000 in accordance with EU principles.

The programme will contain a decisive approach to addressing financial sector imbalances. There will be an appropriate downsizing of the financial sector, with the domestic banking sector reaching the EU average by 2018. In addition, the Cypriot authorities have reaffirmed their commitment to step up efforts in the areas of fiscal consolidation, structural reforms and privatisation.

The Eurogroup welcomes the Terms of Reference for an independent evaluation of the implementation of the anti-money laundering framework in Cypriot financial institutions, involving Moneyval alongside a private international audit firm, and is reassured that the launch of the audit is imminent. In the event of problems in the implementation of the framework, problems will be corrected as part of the programme conditionality.

The Eurogroup further welcomes the Cypriot authorities' commitment to take further measures. These measures include the increase of the withholding tax on capital income and of the statutory corporate income tax rate. The Eurogroup looks forward to an agreement between Cyprus and the Russian Federation on a financial contribution.

The Eurogroup urges the immediate implementation of the agreement between Cyprus and Greece on the Greek branches of the Cypriot banks, which protects the stability of both the Greek and Cypriot banking systems.

The Eurogroup requests the Cypriot authorities and the Commission, in liaison with the ECB, and the IMF to finalise the MoU at staff level in early April.

The Eurogroup notes the intention of the Cypriot authorities to compensate potential individual victims of fraudulent practices, in line with established legal and judicial procedures, outside the programme.

The Eurogroup takes note of the authorities' decision to introduce administrative measures, appropriate in view of the present unique and exceptional situation of Cyprus' financial sector and to allow for a swift reopening of the banks. The Eurogroup stresses that these administrative measures will be temporary, proportionate and non-discriminatory, and subject to strict monitoring in terms of scope and duration in line with the Treaty.

Against this background, the Eurogroup reconfirms, as stated already on 16 March, that—in principle—financial assistance to Cyprus is warranted to safeguard financial stability in Cyprus and the euro area as a whole by providing financial assistance for an amount of up to EUR 10bn. The

Eurogroup would welcome a contribution by the IMF to the financing of the programme. Together with the decisions taken by Cyprus, this results in a fully financed programme which will allow Cyprus' public debt to remain on a sustainable path.

The Eurogroup expects that the ESM Board of Governors will be in a position to formally approve the proposal for a financial assistance facility agreement by the third week of April 2013 subject to the completion of national procedures.

Annex

Following the presentation by the Cyprus authorities of their policy plans, which were broadly welcomed by the Eurogroup, the following was agreed:

1. Laiki will be resolved immediately—with full contribution of equity shareholders, bondholders and uninsured depositors—based on a decision by the Central Bank of Cyprus, using the newly adopted Bank Resolution Framework.
2. Laiki will be split into a good bank and a bad bank. The bad bank will be run down over time.
3. The good bank will be folded into Bank of Cyprus (BoC), using the Bank Resolution Framework, after having heard the Boards of Directors of BoC and Laiki. It will take 9 bn Euros of ELA with it. Only uninsured deposits in BoC will remain frozen until recapitalisation has been effected and may subsequently be subject to appropriate conditions.
4. The Governing Council of the ECB will provide liquidity to the BoC in line with applicable rules.
5. BoC will be recapitalised through a deposit/equity conversion of uninsured deposits with full contribution of equity shareholders and bondholders.
6. The conversion will be such that a capital ratio of 9% is secured by the end of the programme.
7. All insured depositors in all banks will be fully protected in accordance with the relevant EU legislation.
8. The programme money (up to 10bn Euros) will not be used to recapitalise Laiki and Bank of Cyprus.

The Eurogroup is convinced that this solution is the best way forward for ensuring the overall viability and stability of the Cyprus financial system and its capability to finance the Cyprus economy.

Press conference/Brussels

25 March 2013

Good afternoon ladies and gentlemen,

After talks at the highest level with the President of Cyprus, the Eurogroup yesterday reached an agreement on a programme for the Republic of Cyprus that, if properly implemented, we believe will restore the viability of the Cypriot economy.

The European Commission has worked intensively to make this deal possible. We have had the interests of the people of Cyprus in mind throughout this process, since we started talks on a possible programme already in 2011. We had to find a solution together for a business model that was not viable and could not offer lasting prosperity to the people of Cyprus.

The challenges for Cyprus are immense, but Cyprus can count on the European Union to support it. As I have underlined yesterday in the talks that preceded the Eurogroup discussion, we should think not only about financial stability. It is about restarting the real economy. Last night, we agreed on a 10 Billion Euro package worth 55% of the GDP of Cyprus. And we need to look at how we can mobilise all the means at our disposal. That is why I have decided to set up a Task Force for Cyprus to provide technical assistance to the Cypriot authorities.

We want to alleviate the social consequences of the economic shock by mobilising funds from European Union instruments and by supporting the Cypriot authorities' efforts to restore financial, economic and social stability. We will bring in further expertise to facilitate the emergence of new sources of economic activity. The Commission stands by the Cypriot people.

The Task Force will be based in Brussels, with a support team in Nicosia. It will work closely with the Cypriot authorities to support and supplement the EU-IMF programme. Its work will have a strong focus on employment, competitiveness and growth. The Task Force will provide quarterly progress reports to the Cypriot authorities and the Commission. General coordination of the Task Force, which is also coordinating closely with the Task Force for Greece, will be ensured by Commission Vice President Olli Rehn.

As we have shown in the past, Europe faces its challenges together. We do not leave Member States facing a financial crisis alone. With responsibility on the part of Cyprus, we will ensure that solidarity is provided by the euro area.

I call on Cyprus to show unity and responsibility in the implementation of the agreements reached. And I call on all Member States of the European Union to show solidarity with the country that is facing extraordinary challenges and that needs this solidarity in very concrete terms.

15

Toxic Fallout

Legal Challenges

We were certainly expecting the resolution actions to be challenged in court, but not so soon. On Wednesday, 27 March, in the early afternoon, I was informed by our lawyers that the Greek Orthodox Church of Cyprus—which happened to be the largest single shareholder of Bank of Cyprus—had obtained an interim court injunction stopping the application of the bail-in tool to the shares of the bank. The order was valid for two weeks during which we could not proceed with writing down the existing shareholders.

It was made clear to me by our lawyers that ignoring it would be tantamount to contempt of court, which could lead to my immediate arrest by the police—this would certainly have made a lot of people in Cyprus very happy. In effect, the court order meant we could not open the banking system for at least another two weeks, which would have been disastrous. We had already announced the banks were to reopen on Thursday. To go back on that would have been another severe blow to confidence. There was only one way out of this and it involved persuading the Church to change its mind over the injunction. The lawyers of the Church had already asked to see me. One of them was Alecos Markides, an eminent lawyer who had served as Attorney General between 1995 and 2003. The other was Costas Velaris, a lawyer who I knew little about, other than that he was close to the Archbishop. They asked to see me together with the Attorney General, Petros Clerides, who was representing the Republic. It was an ideal oppor-

© The Author(s) 2017
P. Demetriades, *A Diary of the Euro Crisis in Cyprus*,
DOI 10.1007/978-3-319-62223-1_15

tunity to explain to the Church—through its lawyers—how much was at stake.

I readily agreed to meet the Archbishop's lawyers. Petros Clerides, however, was less willing. I was advised that he had reservations about one of the Archbishop's lawyers. I picked up the phone and talked to him. In the few months, I was in office, I had already met him several times on various other issues and I had developed a good rapport with him. I pointed out how important it was to open the banks the following day and how disastrous it would be for the country if the banks remained closed for another two weeks. I managed to change his mind. He agreed to come to the meeting, although he said he would leave if there were any unpleasantries.

The meeting started at around 8.00 pm that evening. The main point put forward by the lawyers of the Church was that our actions were unconstitutional. Resolution, they argued, was expropriation of private property, the rights to which are protected by the constitution.

We responded by explaining that when a public company fails, its shareholders lose their capital. There is nothing unconstitutional about that, as there is nothing unconstitutional with the liquidation of an insolvent company. In the case of a systemic bank that is failing, resolution, compared to liquidation, helps protect value and prevent financial meltdown. Moreover, a bank under resolution can continue to be operational, unlike liquidation. Through resolution and bail-in, Bank of Cyprus would, in fact, be saved, although the bank would have new shareholders, as the old shareholders would see their shares written off. The fate of shareholders. would be no different if the bank was liquidated. Even if the bank was bailed out by the taxpayer, EU state aid rules stipulate that the value of existing shares is written off before public money goes into a bank. Thus, the bank's shareholders had no ground to stand on if the bank had failed.

Not surprisingly, the second line of defense was the one that many bankers had put forward, which had also been endorsed by the government in its early days. The Bank of Cyprus, they argued, was a healthy bank until the troika came along. They intended to challenge the results of the diagnostic exercise and the capital shortfalls estimated by PIMCO. We couldn't, therefore, possibly take resolution action against Bank of Cyprus while that was happening, they argued.

Markides certainly came across as a very charismatic figure in putting their case across. He was also prepared to listen. I explained to them that their action meant that we couldn't proceed with implementing the Eurogroup agreement. Cyprus would have to leave the euro and Bank of Cyprus would become insolvent. I explained that liquidation is worse than resolution for other stakeholders, including depositors and the state, which might also become insolvent if it wasn't able to pay out billions in deposit insurance claims.

The discussion moved to numbers. They were convinced that the capital needs were exaggerated and that the bank was not insolvent. We moved to the meeting room next door to the Governor's office, which is used for board meetings. Our consultants and supervision staff came in with all the numbers, including PIMCO's results.[1] Bank of Cyprus had a capital shortfall of €2.8 billion under the base scenario and €3.9 billion under the adverse scenario. Its expected losses under the base scenario were €5.2 billion, while its loss absorption capacity (which included forecasted pre-provision profits) was €4.2 billion. It had negative capital under the base scenario, instead of the €1.9 billion implied by the required 9% Tier I ratio. Moreover, the sale of its assets in Greece, which necessitated immediate recognition of the losses from their Greek portfolio, meant that the bank had negative capital in accounting (static) terms. The expected losses would need to be recognised anyway. Without an injection of new capital, the bank was insolvent.

The lawyers remained unconvinced, although we were clearly beginning to shift them from their original positions. Whatever the legal arguments, the numbers spoke for themselves. They responded that the banks had different numbers, which were produced by their own diagnostic tests. We explained to them that the company that had carried them out for the banks—behind our backs was among those that had applied to carry out the diagnostic work but was ruled out because it did not possess the required expertise. I also explained that without the Eurogroup agreement, the Church would stand to lose a lot more than just its shares in Bank of Cyprus.

At about midnight, the Church's lawyers showed willingness to reach a compromise. They said that they were prepared to see the shares diluted but not completely written off. If they could only have a small fraction of the new shares, they would be prepared to withdraw their application for a court injunction. They stood up and left, leaving the onus on us to find a solution with the troika, our consultants and the Republic's legal service. The troika, and especially the Commission, were very unhappy with the idea of

---

[1]See pages 85–86 in PIMCO (2013) 'Independent Due Diligence of the Banking System of Cyprus'. Downloadable from: http://www.centralbank.gov.cy/media/pdf/cyprusindependentduediligencereport_18april.pdf.

not wiping out existing shareholders. It would violate creditor hierarchy and could create legal complications later on. However, no one had an alternative solution. Keeping the banks closed for two more weeks while the court heard both sides wasn't really an option. Everyone agreed that we had to make every effort to reopen the banks in the morning. By 4.00 am we all agreed that we had no choice but to give the Church a very small shareholding. It would be meaningless and messy and could allow them to make claims afterwards but it was the lesser of two evils.

I went to sleep for a couple of hours after that. Our lawyers, however, stayed up until the morning to amend the relevant decrees, which looked pretty messy as we now had various classes of shares. I signed the decrees at 7.00 am. The Church withdrew its application later on that morning. Miraculously, we managed to reopen the banks in the morning of that day.

Scapegoat

The Archbishop wasn't a happy man. He had risked the property of the Church on bank shares and had lost out. It wasn't just financial losses. It was also loss of power. Not only did he lose influence over Bank of Cyprus but he also lost control of Cyprus' third largest bank, Hellenic. The Church had a much bigger shareholding in Hellenic than in Bank of Cyprus, around 25% compared to around 5% in Bank of Cyprus. Although Hellenic wasn't resolved, it also had a large capital shortfall that it managed to cover through a rights issue a few months later. At the end of that, however, existing shareholders were diluted. By the end of summer 2013, the Church no longer had any influence on the banking system.

The Church wasn't the only institution that lost out from the banking crisis. However, it was certainly one that had considerable leverage over the new government and influence over the media (the Church part-owned Mega TV and had financial interests in the leading daily newspaper Phileleftheros). The Archbishop, Chrysostomos II, who had openly supported Anastasiades during his pre-election campaign, seized the opportunity to behave like the 'ethnarch' of yesteryear, urging the government to exit the Eurozone rather than relinquish the country's dignity. Speaking to the media on the morning of 25 March 2013, soon after his meeting with Anastasiades, who had just returned from Brussels, Chrysostomos said:

'If the troika is going to lead us into bankruptcy, it is better not to do any agreement and go directly to bankruptcy. At least we will save our dignity'.[2]

Included among the long list of institutions and individuals who lost out were private sector pension and provident funds, particularly those of bank employees, which had invested heavily in both shares and deposits in the two banks. Shareholding in Bank of Cyprus was very diverse. Its shareholders ranged from a Russian tycoon and the ruling elite of the island to small savers and retail investors, who had considered the Bank of Cyprus as a safe investment. George Vasiliou, president of the Republic during 1998–1993 and Afxentis Afxentiou, Governor of the CBC during 1982–2002, came to see me independently to protest about what they saw as my failure to protect [their investments in] Bank of Cyprus. Many others, I suspect, protested directly to the government and party political leaders.

Then there were the lawyers representing wealthy clients from Russia, Ukraine and other countries, some of whom had lost hundreds of millions of euros, who were also up in arms. Some of them had been reassuring their clients that their money was safe in Cyprus, notwithstanding the reports in the international media that a bail-in of deposits was being considered. One of them, a former classmate of mine from secondary school, confided to me that he couldn't sleep at night. He was terrified by what some of his clients, who had lost millions, could do to him or his family. I had often wondered why lawyers such as him sought clients with dubious backgrounds like that but I never asked him. I didn't want to upset him more than he was already.

Bondholders organised themselves into an association and took to the streets. They saw themselves as being the victims of the crisis, which to some extent they were. They claimed that during 2010 and 2011 they had been mis-sold hybrid instruments, including COCOs (contingent convertible bonds) that resembled deposits but were convertible into equity when a bank's capital ratio fell below a certain threshold. The alleged miss-selling had happened before I took office at the CBC. Thus, they didn't have issues with me on the mis-selling. They were, however, angry with me that despite ordering an investigation into the practices of the banks during that period, which confirmed that the banks had indeed engaged in mis-selling, I couldn't offer them any redress for their losses. I could only advise them to apply to the courts.

[2]Rachel Cooper, 'Cyprus archbishop urges Eurozone exit', *The Telegraph*, 25 March 2013. See: http://www.telegraph.co.uk/finance/financialcrisis/9951813/Cyprus-archbishop-urges-eurozone-exit.html.

The government desperately needed a scapegoat. The CBC, in general, and I, in particular, were an ideal target. With little, if any, political protection, the attack could start even before the signing of the Eurogroup agreement. In any case, this was consistent with the pre-election rhetoric of Anastasiades, which largely reflected the views of the bankers whose banks were being resolved. To the conspiracy theories about the inflated capital needs, the government could now add the alleged weapon of 'blackmail'—the ELA to Laiki. It was the same ELA about which Anastasiades, as leader of the opposition, had threatened me in writing with criminal charges if it had been discontinued back in November 2012. The same ELA had now become 'illegal' because Laiki was folded, *ex post*. What would have happened had I not provided ELA to Laiki in that hypothetical nightmare scenario, which is what Anastasiades correctly warned about in his letter to me dated 16 November 2012, no longer mattered. I should, of course, have anticipated that politicians in government can be fickle. The idea of central bank independence itself was borne out of that inconsistency.

The conspiracy theories were repeated *ad infinitum* in Parliament, on television, in radio programmes and in newspapers. The acting leader of DISY, Averof Neophytou, went as far as to say in public that the Republic should sue Mario Draghi for providing ELA to Laiki. By the end of March 2013, ELA became fully demonised. In the minds of many ordinary people, who had been listening to the politicians repeat the same accusations *ad nauseam*, ELA became synonymous with a crime. This was the crime that brought down the economy and I was the chief criminal who had provided it, with the consent of the ECB. I should have been put behind bars without a trial. It was so self-evident. The fact that ELA was the very mechanism that kept the country in the euro area was no longer relevant.

Against that climate of misinformation and hostility, it was not surprising that, as a result of the blame game that was in full swing, I started receiving public death threats.[3] While I treated them rather lightly, I couldn't do the same when such threats were made against my family and when my young children started feeling uncomfortable at the school they joined only a few months ago. It was time to move them back to the UK.

Parliament started debating my dismissal during their discussions of the resolution bill but the troika asked them to postpone that discussion until

---

[3]See, for example, Jeff Black 'How Trading Blame led to Death Threats for ECB's Cypriot Banker', Bloomberg, 29 May 2013. https://www.bloomberg.com/news/articles/2013-05-29/how-trading-blame-led-to-death-threats-for-ecb-s-cypriot-banker.

we were out of the danger zone. If I could have been readily dismissed, I would have been kicked out within days, if not hours from the moment my dismissal started being debated in Parliament. The ruling party, DISY, together with the centrist DIKO, which supported Anastasiades and participated in his government, had overall majority in Parliament. They were well aware, of course, that the independence of the Governor was protected by the EU Treaty and that dismissal wasn't that straightforward. They were, nevertheless, determined to exert pressure on me by passing a motion demanding my resignation. After all, they were all representatives elected by the voters while I was appointed. How could I, an appointed central bank Governor, stand in the way of a democratically elected Parliament?

On 10 April 2013, Draghi decided to intervene. It was long overdue, as he confessed to me when I next met him in Frankfurt. Draghi wrote a strongly worded letter to President Anastasiades and to Yiannakis Omirou, the President of the House of Representatives, reminding them that the 'independence of central banks is a key pillar in the economic and institutional set-up of the European Union'. He also reminded them that '…a decision to remove a Governor from office is subject to the judicial control of the Court of Justice of the European Union'.[4] It was enough to get them off my back but not for very long.

That was just a tactical retreat in the war of attrition that I found myself inadvertently engaged in. That retreat wasn't even a truce. The next day the hostilities continued on a different front. It was the second act of war. Deputy Governor Stavrinakis, who had been my right hand during the crisis, received a letter from Anastasiades. It was the letter of *his* dismissal. Strictly speaking, it was a presidential act that 'annulled' his original appointment, which the president deemed was invalid. The pretext was that he wasn't a Turkish Cypriot, as specified in the 1960 constitution that became defunct in 1963. The same was true of various other posts in the Republic, for example, that of Deputy Attorney General was reserved for a Turkish Cypriot. However, it was filled by a Greek Cypriot like all the other positions intended for Turkish Cypriots by appealing to the law of necessity. There was a necessity for the Republic to be able to function. There was even greater necessity for a central bank to have a deputy Governor during a banking crisis. Without one, in my absence, many things had to wait for my return. That was why Spyros was legitimately appointed to the post of Deputy Governor.

---

[4]See Appendix 1.

The Attorney General—who is the government legal adviser—distanced himself from Anastasiades' letter to annul the Deputy Governor's appointment. He stated that the appointment was legally sound, although was perhaps politically insensitive, as it happened during the pre-election period. Anastasiades was indeed incensed when it had happened and made a pledge to dismiss Spyros if he came to power.[5]

The letter of the deputy Governor's dismissal arrived in the middle of a CBC board meeting. The deputy Governor was actually briefing the board about how we had handled the crisis and was about to go through the contracts of various consultants that had been appointed. Board members greeted the news of Spyros' dismissal with shock, horror and disbelief. One of them suggested that we should reappoint Spyros to his previous position, that of Senior Director of the CBC. Some wanted to challenge the president's decision in the courts, but others were less enthusiastic. They all wanted some guidance from the ECB on this matter, in light of its implications for central bank independence. It was clear that if they were to stand up to the president, they at least needed some form of backing from the ECB. I agreed that I would call another meeting of the board as soon as I had obtained an initial response from the ECB. The next day, all but one of the board members resigned. In their letters of resignation they thanked me for our cooperation. The situation was clearly getting too much for them. They didn't want to be in the middle of a war of attrition between the government and the CBC. Their own independence wasn't protected by the law, anyway. They had very little to gain if they had stayed and very much to lose, especially if they tried to help me defend the CBC's independence. I cannot for a minute blame them for that decision. However, as of that day, the CBC could not convene its board, a situation that lasted for several months and which paralysed some of its decision-making. The CBC's personnel committee, for example, which comprises members of the board and the Governor could not convene; as a result personnel matters, including, promotions and recruitment of much needed temporary staff to help with the management of the crisis, wasn't possible.

---

[5]This was probably because he had wanted to fill it himself. However, by annulling the appointment, because of its alleged unconstitutionality, he was unable to replace Stavrinakis with someone else.

Dragoman of the Troika

New board members were appointed by the government in the beginning of June. I was pleasantly surprised that some of the new members of the board seemed to be acting independently of the government. My initial relief, however, did not last for very long. The next battle occurred during the troika's visit in late July 2013, which coincided with the fair valuation of the two balance sheets that were being merged. It was the time to decide the final bail-in at the Bank of Cyprus. That decision legally belonged to the Resolution Authority, although the decision had to adhere to the Eurogroup agreement of 25 March 2013, which stated the following:

> 5. 'BoC will be recapitalised through a deposit/equity conversion of uninsured deposits with full contribution of equity shareholders and bond holders.
> 6. The conversion will be such that a capital ratio of 9% is secured by the end of the programme'.

The initial bail-in, which allowed the bank to reopen with a positive capital ratio, was 25%. A large chunk of uninsured deposits had been frozen to allow for the final bail-in, which we had anticipated would be an additional 25%. When the valuations came in they were analysed and used in combination with PIMCO's projected future losses to arrive at an estimate of the amount of capital needed upfront to ensure that at the end of the three-year programme, the bank would have a capital ratio of 9%. Our consultants estimated that a 22.5% bail-in, which would have resulted in 47.5% total bail-in, would be sufficient to satisfy the Eurogroup's constraint. This in itself made sense as the bank wasn't going to receive programme money, in case it needed additional capital. It had to have enough to last until the end of the programme, without resorting to the taxpayer. Our calculations were reviewed by the troika. The 22.5% bail-in allowed for a very small margin of error, with which the troika was just about comfortable. Isabelle Von Koppen-Mertez, the ECB's chief of mission, who had been in close contact with the executive board of the ECB, explained that 47.5% was the minimum bail-in required for the ECB executive board to be able to support the request for reinstatement of Bank of Cyprus as a counterparty for monetary policy operations. Without the backing of the executive board, the Governing Council was unlikely to approve it. Reinstating the bank as an ECB counterparty would certainly have been an important first step towards normalisation. The bank could start repaying ELA by borrowing more cheaply through monetary policy operations. It was going to be an important signal to the markets.

Two of the new members of the CBC board—Mike Spanos and Stelios Kiliaris—were fully involved in the bail-in discussions in Nicosia. They were convinced that 47.5% was the magic number. However, the government wasn't convinced. They wanted to go for 45%. They argued that it would have made a difference to confidence if the bail-in was lower than expected. I suspect that they probably felt that it would also have been politically easier to sell to the electorate, the uninsured depositors and the media. I—and others at the CBC—tried to explain to them that the only way in which the new shareholders of Bank of Cyprus—the uninsured depositors—could recover some of their losses was if the bank was put on a sound basis. That included a strong capital ratio that would see it through until the end of the programme. It also included regaining counterparty status with the ECB sooner rather than later.

I had several telephone conversations over this with Anastasiades. I remember going to visit my father in Limassol, who was in his last few days dying from cancer and having a very heated discussion with the president just before arriving.

Anastasiades was unyielding, although he had exactly the same message from one of the newly appointed board members of the CBC—Mike Spanos—whom he knew well and presumably trusted. When the final decision was made on 28 July 2013 the finance minister, Harris Georgiades, said that the government disagreed with it but understood that it was the CBC's decision. I have no doubt that Harris understood that it was a necessary first step to stabilise the bank. I was, once again, a convenient scapegoat.

The next day, *Phileleftheros*—the biggest circulation daily newspaper on the island—ran an editorial entitled 'Dragoman of the troika'. I was the dragoman. The article made no attempt to explain the rationale behind that decision. All that mattered was that I was siding with the enemy. Instead of protecting my country, it argued, I was advocating the positions of the troika.

I had little time to deal with such criticism, although I was very angry. As soon as I signed the decree for the final bail-in, I signed a second one taking the bank out of resolution and left for the next Governing Council meeting of the ECB. It was the first and only one in August. If I didn't manage to convince the Governing Council to restore the Bank of Cyprus as a counterparty for monetary policy operations, we would have to wait another month before reapplying. I cannot report the details of the discussions, although I can state that the outcome was a positive one. Soon after that, the *Financial Times*, which had been following developments in Cyprus, ran an article explaining why the government was wrong not to understand that a higher bail-in was beneficial for the bank.

Death Knell of the CBC's Independence

While I was fully preoccupied with trying to return the banking system to a modicum of normality, the ruling political party (DISY)—not the government—tabled two bills in Parliament. One was to modify the Resolution Authority by creating a tripartite body to run it and the other one was to change the governance of the CBC, which included the enlargement of the CBC's board through the creation of two new director posts. Both bills were, in effect, designed to reduce my powers, which the leader of DISY, Averof Neophytou, considered as being excessive. He argued publicly that there was too much concentration of power in one person. Both bills were voted in with the help of DIKO and failed to take on board relevant ECB legal opinion. The troika wasn't happy.

The proposed changes to the resolution legislation turned the CBC into a minority party in resolution matters. The minister of finance had the upper hand as the third person appointed was the Chairwoman of the Cyprus Securities and Exchange Commission (CSEC), an organisation that has a very limited degree of independence from the government.[6] This change effectively enabled the government to use 'bad' Laiki's 18% shareholding in Bank of Cyprus to appoint the new board of the bank soon after it exited resolution. Mike Spanos, who—regrettably—had resigned from his position at the CBC to become a candidate for the Bank of Cyprus board was not supported by the government and failed to get elected. While the changes made the decision-making of the Resolution Authority more cumbersome, I had no particular desire to have resolution powers in the first place. Although I was quietly relieved that the burden of responsibility had shifted from the CBC, it wasn't at all obvious that placing the resolution powers into the hands of politicians constituted an improvement for the country.

However, the proposed changes to the governance of the CBC were much more worrying since they were intended to shift power from the Governor, whose independence is protected by the EU Treaty, to the board, that does not have the same degree of independence. As a result, the CBC could become more susceptible to political influence, which was, in all likelihood, the hidden agenda behind the proposal. Specifically, there was to be: (a) an increase in the number of board directors from five to seven through the

---

[6]Unlike the central bank, the Cyprus Securities and Exchange Commission's budget has to be approved by the Ministry of Finance and Parliament. Moreover, the Chair of the CySEC can be removed from office by the government much more easily than the central bank Governor, whose independence is protected by the constitution and the EU Treaty.

creation of two new executive director positions; (b) the duties of the executive directors were to be decided by the board and not by the Governor; (c) the remuneration of board members was to be set by Council of Ministers at the time of their appointment; (d) the number of mandatory meetings of the board was to increase from six to twelve per annum; (e) decisions about bank licensing and amendments to existing licenses would require the consent of the board and (f) an audit committee was to be established comprising non-executive directors.

ECB legal Opinion CON/2013/41, published on 3 June 2013, raised some very serious concerns about the impact of the proposed changes to the CBC's independence and the CBC's decision-making ability. It objected specifically to the idea that the two executive directors would have their duties assigned by the board. The Opinion stated: '…the independence of the Governor of the CBC should be reinforced by ensuring that the assistance provided by the executive directors to the Governor should be conducted under the supervision of the Governor. Without clarity in these respects, *the ECB is concerned that the CBC's decision-making processes will be undermined* (my italics)….. Central bank independence needs a stable legal framework for the central bank's functioning. Frequent changes to the legal framework may adversely affect the organisational and governance stability of an NCB and could, therefore, affect its institutional independence….'

I was invited to Parliament's finance committee to express my views on the proposed legislation, as is customary. I urged them to make a serious attempt to address the concerns raised by the ECB. I wasn't, of course, expecting them to do that. If anything, the ECB's response must have convinced them that the proposed changes were serving the purpose for which they were intended: to increase their ability to exert political influence over the CBC by shifting powers from the independent Governor to the board.

The game they were playing was becoming obvious. The proposals were voted in on 26 July 2013, without even a feeble attempt to address the ECB's concerns.[7] Soon after that, the government used its new powers to increase the remuneration of non-executive board members from €1700 per annum to €30,000 per annum. This was an extraordinary increase of 1700%

---

[7]The ECB returned to the matter in letters to the government but also in a new legal opinion—ECB. (CON/ 2013/78)—issued in 22 November 2013 on further proposed changes to the CBC law relating to bank licensing (to extend the scope of decisions controlled by the board): 'The ECB refers to its Opinion CON/2013/41 on changes to the governance of the CBC, which concerns previous amendments to the Law on the CBC. A number of observations made in that Opinion were not taken into account and the ECB invites the relevant Cypriot authorities to address them in this draft law'.

at a time when public sector salaries, including those of the CBC staff, were being cut. This increase in board members' remuneration was done without any prior consultation with the CBC, notwithstanding the ECB's legal opinion of 3 June 2013, which recommended that:

> the Cypriot authorities have an obligation to ensure that any amendment to the legislative provisions on the remuneration of the CBC's Board members is decided in cooperation with the CBC, *taking due account of the CBC's views.*

The ECB's legal opinion, which the legislators ignored, proved prophetic. It was precisely DISY's legislative changes that eventually determined the winner of the war of attrition, by signalling the death knell of the CBC's independence.

Appendix

Opinion of the European Central Bank of 5 June 2013 on changes to the governance of the Central Bank of Cyprus (CON/2013/41).

EUROPEAN CENTRAL BANK

EUROSYSTEM

OPINION OF THE EUROPEAN CENTRAL BANK
of 5 June 2013
on changes to the governance of the Central Bank of Cyprus
(CON/2013/41)

Introduction and legal basis

On 18 April 2013, the European Central Bank (ECB) received a request from the President of the House of Representatives of the Republic of Cyprus (hereinafter 'the consulting authority') for an opinion on a proposed amendment to the Central Bank of Cyprus Laws of 2002 to 2007[1]. On 16 May 2013, the ECB received a revised version and, on 31 May 2013, a further revised version of the proposed amendment (hereinafter the 'draft law'), and it is this last version which forms the basis for this opinion.

The ECB's competence to deliver an opinion is based on Articles 127(4) and 282(5) of the Treaty on the Functioning of the European Union (hereinafter the 'Treaty') and the third indent of Article 2(1) of Council Decision 98/415/EC of 29 June 1998 on the consultation of the European Central Bank by national authorities regarding draft legislative provisions[2], as the draft law relates to the Central Bank of Cyprus (CBC). In accordance with the first sentence of Article 17.5 of the Rules of Procedure of the European Central Bank, the Governing Council has adopted this opinion.

1.   Purpose of the draft law

The draft law provides for the following:

1.1   The composition of the CBC's Board of Directors (hereinafter the 'Board') is modified by providing for seven directors instead of five, in addition to the Governor and the Deputy Governor. Two of the directors will be executive directors, while the remaining five will be non-executive directors.

1.2   Remuneration and other terms of tenure of the executive directors and the remuneration of the non-executive directors are to be set by the Council of Ministers at the time of the directors' appointment.

1.3   The number of annual mandatory meetings of the Board is increased from six to twelve.

1.4   The quorum for meetings of the Board is increased from four to five members.

---

1   Law 138(I)/2002 as amended and currently in force.
2   OJ L 189, 3.7.1998, p. 42.

ECB-PUBLIC

1.5 Decisions relating to the CBC's policy, including licensing of banking institutions and amendments to existing banking licences, are to be adopted by the Governor with the approval of the Board.

1.6 The Board will assign specific duties to the executive directors who, in turn, will assist the Governor in the management, supervision and control of the CBC's operations. Executive directors will be employed on a full-time basis.

1.7 The composition of the CBC's Personnel Committee is augmented by the inclusion of the two executive directors, and the quorum for meetings of the Personnel Committee is increased from three to four members.

1.8 An Audit Committee comprised of three members of the Board, appointed by the Board and who will have no executive powers, is to be established and its functions will be to audit compliance with the corporate governance code, supervise the carrying out of internal administrative audits and report to the Board. The Audit Committee may also use the services of an internal auditor.

2. ECB observations on the draft law

2.1 The ECB notes the consulting authority's aim to facilitate the smooth functioning of the CBC's decision-making bodies. It nevertheless makes the following observations to the consulting authority, for its consideration.

2.2 As a general remark, unless the executive directors and board members of a national central bank (NCB) are subject to the same legal requirements, and enjoy the same independence safeguards as the Governor of the NCB concerned, any provision assigning ESCB-related tasks of the Governor to an executive director, or requiring the approval of that NCB's Board for decisions of the Governor, raises concerns about the Governor's ability to independently carry out the ESCB-related tasks assigned to the Governor. This would not be compatible with Article 130 of the Treaty and Article 7 of the Statute of the European System of Central Banks and of the European Central Bank (hereinafter the 'Statute of the ESCB'). The Governor should not be influenced by an executive director or the members of the Board in the performance of ESCB-related tasks which, under national law, are assigned exclusively to the Governor.

2.3 The ECB considers that the draft law is unclear with regard to the nature of the executive directors' powers and the division of competences between the Board and the Governor. In the case of Cyprus, the ECB understands that the competences of the CBC's Governor stem both from primary Union law – in particular the Statute of the ESCB – and from the Constitution of the Republic of Cyprus[3]. Although the draft law purports to vest two members of the Board with executive powers, in addition to the Governor, it does not specify the corporate governance arrangements applicable to the CBC once the draft law has entered into force. In the ECB's view, the draft law should

---

3   It follows from Article 119 of the Constitution of the Republic of Cyprus that the Governor and Deputy Governor are independent State officials, with clearly circumscribed powers and tasks. The same provision also provides that the Governor shall be in charge of the management of the CBC and shall exercise all powers and perform all functions and duties within the scope of the CBC's competences.

provide clarity in terms of: (a) the precise scope of the powers and tasks to be assigned to the executive directors, (b) the limits of the competence of the executive directors when assisting the Governor, in particular as regards whether the executive directors will have decision-making powers[4], and (c) the position of the proposed executive directors in the CBC's organisational structure, for instance, whether or not CBC staff members will report directly to the executive directors. In particular, the independence of the Governor of the CBC should be reinforced by ensuring that the assistance provided by the executive directors to the Governor should be conducted under the supervision of the Governor. Without clarity in these respects, the ECB is concerned that the CBC's decision-making processes will be undermined.

2.4   Clarification of the division of competences between the Board and the Governor is also necessary in order to ensure that the draft law does not interfere with central bank independence requirements. The ECB notes that, under Sections 15 and 17 of the Central Bank of Cyprus Law, (a) the Board has no competence in relation to matters which fall within the fields of competence of the European System of Central Banks (ESCB); and (b) the Board, when exercising its duties and tasks, should take due account of the Governor's role as a member of the Governing Council and the General Council of the ECB. Sections 17 and 17A as amended or introduced by the draft law provide that the proposed amendments are without prejudice to the powers of the ESCB and the ECB, and to the Treaty and the Statute of the ESCB. Notwithstanding this, the ECB invites the consulting authority to clarify the interplay between the powers newly granted to two of the members of the Board and the proposed governance structure's compliance with the requirements of central bank independence.

2.5   The ECB would like to point to the fact that there are currently a number of vacancies on the Board. Against this background, it is unclear why the number of Board members is being increased, taking into account: (a) the appointment of executive directors; and (b) the requirement for the approval of the Board as regards decision-making in implementing the CBC's policy. Central bank independence needs a stable legal framework for the central bank's functioning. Frequent changes to the legal framework may adversely affect the organisational and governance stability of an NCB and could therefore affect its institutional independence.

2.6   The ECB also has concerns about measures which might affect the personal independence of the Board members. To protect the CBC's autonomy in staff matters, which is part of the principle of central bank independence under Article 130 of the Treaty, the Cypriot authorities have an obligation to ensure that any amendment to the legislative provisions on the remuneration of the CBC's Board members is decided in cooperation with the CBC, taking due account of the CBC's views[5]. Furthermore, in order to comply with the Treaty requirements for the personal independence of the members of an NCB's decision-making bodies who are involved in the

---

4   For instance, Article 17, as amended, requires the Board's approval for decisions laying down *and* applying the CBC's policy.

5   See, paragraph 3.4 of ECB Opinion CON/2010/56. All ECB opinions are published on the ECB's website at www.ecb.europa.eu.

ECB-PUBLIC

performance of ESCB-related tasks, any adjustments to salaries should not affect the terms under which the members concerned were appointed[6].

2.7   In light of the above concerns, the ECB urges the consulting authority to take appropriate steps in order to preserve the independence of the CBC and the members of its decision-making bodies involved in the performance of ESCB-related tasks.

This opinion will be published on the ECB's website.

Done at Frankfurt am Main, 5 June 2013.

[signed]

The President of the ECB
Mario DRAGHI

---

6   See, for example, paragraph 3.5 of ECB Opinion CON/2010/56.

4

Bibliography

PIMCO (2013) Independent Due Dilegence of the Banking System of Cyprus, February. Available from: http://www.centralbank.gov.cy/media/pdf/cyprusindep endentduediligencereport_18april.pdf.

16

The Final Act

Colourful Language

'Governor, the President wants to talk to you. Please use my office', Harris Georgiades, the minister of finance, said to me politely.

Given how keen the government had been to change the resolution legislation before the Bank of Cyprus Annual General Meeting (AGM), which was scheduled to take place in the evening of that day (Tuesday, 10 September 2013), I had a good idea of what the President might want to talk to me about. He clearly knew that I was at the ministry where we had just concluded the second meeting of the freshly reconstituted Resolution Authority, in which the government had the upper hand.

I entered the minister's office and closed the door behind me.

'Is that the Governor?', asked a cheerful female voice at the end of the line. 'Yes', I replied. 'I am connecting you to the President', she continued. In no time president Anastasiades was on the line. I was surprised by the tone of his voice, and by how he chose to start the conversation:

'Που χωρκογυρίζεις ρε αθεόφοβε;' he asked [in Greek], which, roughly translated, means 'Where have you been wondering in the villages you Godless man?'

It was his way of expressing disapproval of my absences from Cyprus. I felt like a school child being told off by his teacher but I maintained my calm. I said that I was only doing my job and that every other week I had to be in

© The Author(s) 2017
P. Demetriades, *A Diary of the Euro Crisis in Cyprus*,
DOI 10.1007/978-3-319-62223-1_16

Frankfurt for ECB Governing Council meetings. On top of that, there are other meetings in Europe as well as the bi-annual IMF World Bank meetings that central bank Governors are expected to attend.

'[While you are away] your staff are not working hard enough', he protested. 'They haven't yet finished processing the candidates for the Bank of Cyprus board... you should have them disciplined', he continued.

I thought his remarks were very unfair to the CBC staff, whose professionalism and hard work during the crisis saved the country from bankruptcy. Some of them were doing 24-hour shifts and had little, if any, sleep for over a week at the peak of the crisis. They had been working relentlessly since then. In fact, I have vivid images of some of them looking exhausted on the day we reopened the banks.

'With due respect, Mr President', I replied, 'the bank's AGM has not taken place yet and we do not even have the forms of all the candidates, but the staff have already started sifting through the applications'. I explained that the central bank had no obligation to assess the fitness and probity of prospective bank directors in advance of the AGM, only of those elected and that could only happen when they had submitted all the necessary paperwork to the CBC. There were, in fact, 48 candidates and just 16 positions on the board.

The thought crossed my mind that I should perhaps mention that he had no right to be interfering in the affairs of an independent central bank, but before I could even think of his likely anger at that he continued with his demands:

'I hope you will not turn down the candidates put forward by the Resolution Authority, who will almost certainly be elected by the AGM', he said.

It was almost certain that whoever was nominated by the Resolution Authority that controlled the 18% equity share of legacy Laiki in the Bank of Cyprus would be elected to the board of directors. This was so important to the government that in the month before Parliament came back early from its traditional August recess to enact the change in the composition of the Resolution Authority that had been proposed by DISY, the ruling political party. As a result of this legislative change, the government, in effect, gained control of the Resolution Authority. The CBC, while remaining part of the Resolution Authority, became a minority partner.

At the meeting of the Resolution Authority that had just been completed, the minister, with some support from the Securities and Exchange Commission, more or less dictated most, if not all, the 16 members to be nominated. I had expressed the CBC's non-objection to ten of the individuals that were being put forward by the minister. However, I could not express an informed opinion about the other six candidates, given that they had not completed the application forms and hence we had nothing to go on. I was, however, alerted by the CBC staff that there was a (Reuters) story in that day's *Financial Times* about a Russian oligarch who was about to become the vice president of Bank of Cyprus. The article was saying that he was a former KGB agent and close ally of the Russian president, Vladimir Putin.[1] The only additional information my staff had about this individual was that he was one of the largest new shareholders of Bank of Cyprus, and that he was represented by the law firm that was co-owned by the President's immediate family.

Both the minister and the president were aware that the CBC could still turn down elected members of the board, following the necessary fitness and probity checks that the CBC had to carry out in its supervisory capacity. The list of 16 became known as 'Averof's list', because Averof Neophytou, who by that time had become leader of the ruling party, DISY, had reportedly put it together following discussions with the Archbishop, two other political parties, two trade unions representing provident funds and several large law firms, whose clients' deposits had been bailed in. Although the Bank of Cyprus had not been bailed out with taxpayers' money, the politicians were determined to find a way to appoint their own people to its board of directors.

Against this background, it was easy to understand why the President of the Republic took such a keen interest in the Bank of Cyprus. It didn't make my job any easier, however. The next words he uttered will remain with me for the rest of my life:

'Είμαι η μεγαλύτερη πουτάνα της πολιτικής', he said, which, literally translates into: 'I am the biggest whore in politics'.

He continued with even more colourful language:

'Δεν θα με ξεγελάσεις εσύ, κανένας δεν το κατάφερε. Δεν είμαι μόνο η μεγαλύτερη πουτάνα της πολιτικής, είμαι και η μεγαλύτερη πατρώνα', which literally translated means:

---

[1]"Russians, including Putin ally, join bailed-in board of Bank of Cyprus" 10 September 2013. See http://www.reuters.com/article/bankofcyprus-idUSL5N0H63FF20130910.

'You will never deceive me. No one has managed that. I am not just the biggest whore in politics. I am also the biggest pimp', he said proudly.

There is no doubt that some of the meaning of what he said is lost in translation. This kind of colourful language is often used by some, though certainly not all, Greek-speaking people to convey pride or achievement in their line of business.

He continued by explaining to me why he felt deceived:

> ...You tricked me with the election of Sophocles Michaelides to the chairmanship of the bank. I will not allow this to happen again. This country has no room for both of us.

I was shocked. It was as if he considered me as his political opponent. I had no idea. Later on, a friendly journalist alerted me to some political columns in the press that were making the point that by standing up to him on key banking sector decisions that the public had an interest in (e.g. the percentage of the final bail-in) I was making him look like a weak leader in the eyes of some political commentators. The same journalist explained to me that Anastasiades read all the papers religiously every day and found criticism very hard to swallow. He would often call the journalists who dared to criticise him to protest. Whoever wrote the columns knew the effect it would have on Anastasiades. There were certainly enough people behind the scenes, affected by the CBC's actions during the crisis, who wanted my head and, thus, knew that such articles would goad him into taking action against me.

I managed to keep my composure and calmly replied:

> With due respect Mr President, I will do my job. I can also assure you that the central bank staff will do their job professionally and objectively.

That infuriated him even more. He said:

> 'Watch it, because I will make public statements about you. I will not stop, no one wins against me', he fumed. 'I am the biggest whore in politics', he repeated, just in case it didn't sink in the first time.

I summoned up all my strength and explained to him that at the time Sophocles Michaelides was elected by the interim board as its chairman, the Bank of Cyprus was still under resolution and that at the same time the CBC was the Resolution Authority. As such, the CBC had every legal right, as well as responsibility for which it was accountable to Parliament, to ensure a properly functioning interim board. I also explained to him that Sophocles was a former senior director of the CBC and thus was trusted to carry out that important role at that critical time when the Bank of Cyprus had first and foremost to be protected and stabilised.

The interim board, which served for a relatively short period—from 24 April until 10 September 2013—was all about saving the bank and safeguarding it from those who, through their actions or negligence, brought it to its knees. It was about making sure that the bank wasn't looted by insiders during the first stages of its recovery, which is a real possibility in those kinds of situations. It was all about stabilising the bank and organising an orderly AGM so its new shareholders could take over. All the indicators suggested that they had done a good job. On its exit from resolution, the bank was well capitalised, it had a new interim management and had made progress with its restructuring plan.

Anastasiades calmed down after that. I am not sure if it was because of what I had said or because he had vented all his anger. However, at the end of that conversation, I had the impression—wrong as it turned out two weeks later—that he no longer had any issues with me. He even became affectionate calling me 'Panico mou' ('my Panicos') and used 'please' and 'thank you' in abundance. Perhaps he was just sweet-talking me into doing what he wanted. Or perhaps he was reassured that I had said that I would do my utmost to expedite the process, although I kept reminding him that we were reliant on the elected candidates supplying the requisite information.

On that evening, at the first AGM of the new Bank of Cyprus, 15 of the 16 candidates proposed by the finance ministry's director general on behalf of the Resolution Authority, were elected to the board. Immediately afterwards, the new board had a meeting and elected a new chairman and vice-chairman, without waiting for CBC approval of fitness and probity. There were several bailed-in Russians on the board and one of them, the one whom the FT described as an ally of Putin, was elected vice president.

In the days that followed, the CBC compelled them to provide all the necessary information and interviewed nearly all of them, before confirming their fitness and probity using the guidelines issued by the European Banking Authority. However, during that period, large sections of the press, including the leading daily *Phileleftheros*, continued to criticise me and the CBC for alleged delays.

Official Declaration of War

On Wednesday, 18 September I was on the 36th floor of the Eurotower, the ECB headquarters in the middle of Frankfurt, taking part in a Governing Council meeting when I received a text message from a friendly journalist that said:

> The president is about to give a live TV interview in which he will declare that he wants to dismiss you. You should try to stop it.

I went out of the room and made some phone calls. Indeed, this was about to happen. It was going to be an official declaration of war from which everyone would lose, including the country. But how could I stop it? I talked to the CBC's external counsel who had been minister of justice under a previous DISY government and had good relations with the current government. He offered to talk to the presidential palace. Soon after that, he called me back to say that there was no way the president would change his mind.

During his interview the president stated the following[2]:

> I am investigating and documenting all the things that make up the weaknesses or the inadequacy in the performance of his duties and, accordingly, in line with the constitution, I will decide the prospect of the referral to the highest legal council.

He continued by saying that: 'My patience is at a stage at which I can no longer allow inaction to threaten our country'.

He went on to state that I 'should have evaluated all of the candidates who had put forward their names to be members of the board ahead of the AGM' and said that he had called me and advised me 'to be careful because we had already suffered a lot of delays and it would be unthinkable that any of those elected to the board of directors would depend on what he [I] decided'.

He added that: 'The economy's and the country's needs will not depend on the whims of anyone. We are not student organisations that play games' and that 'Someone who holds such an important position will not

---

[2]See: "My patience has reached its limits: Anastasiades mulls legal action over the CBC Governor's 'inadequacies'", by George Christou, *Cyprus Mail*, 19 September 2013.

be allowed to spend such long periods abroad instead of carrying out his duties'.

On Monday, 23 September I had a visit from Mr Afxentis Afxentiou, former Governor of the CBC during 1982–2002. He asked me what I was intending to do about the president's statement. Nothing, I replied. I will just continue to do my work. He disapproved. He said he was someone with 20 years service as Governor of the CBC and he wouldn't have remained for one day as Governor if he didn't have the backing of the president. 'After all, the president is the highest office in the land and he is elected by the people, but you are appointed'. I tried to explain to Afxentiou that times had changed. Cyprus was now in the EU and the independence of central banks was enshrined in the EU Treaty.

The president no longer had the right to dismiss the Governor at will. I tried to explain the importance of central bank independence in terms of delivering better economic outcomes. He reminded me that he and his family had lost millions from the bail-in. So did many other people. I should have protected the banks from the troika, he said. That is the role of the central bank Governor, he added. He then stood up and left.

Two days later there was a board meeting at the CBC. The most elderly member of the board, who happened to be a close friend of the president, suggested we meet informally before the meeting. He asked me, in front of all the other board members, what were my intentions. He didn't mention the president. I replied by repeating more or less what I had said to Mr Afxentiou two days earlier. I reminded the board members that they had a duty to protect the independence of the CBC. They didn't seem persuaded.

Coup D' Etat

Two days before the president openly declared war, board members started behaving as if they were taking over the daily management of the CBC. On 16 September 2013, the board decided, notwithstanding my strong objections, to assign wide-ranging duties to the executive directors, which boiled down to them overseeing nearly all the operations of the CBC. Predictably, assigning such duties to executive members of the board, who did not report to the Governor but to the board itself, created confusion and divided loyalties among the staff. It eroded the internal hierarchy of the CBC and undermined its decision-making processes. It most certainly impacted on my own ability to manage the CBC. My warnings that this board 'decision' was a clear violation of the Constitution, which did not make reference to any other person entitled to legally intervene between him and the staff of the CBC, besides the Deputy Governor who 'assists' the Governor, were pushed aside.[3]

From that day onwards, they were de facto shifting power to themselves, through the executive directors, even more so during my absences. Staff who remained loyal to me started reporting that they were being harassed. It was nothing short of a constitutional *coup d'etat*.

On 21 October 2013, the board 'decided' to withdraw the CBC's recourse against President Anastasiades' executive order to terminate the appointment of the Deputy Governor. They argued that this was in the interests of improving relations with the President. The fact that the President had dismissed the Deputy Governor on shaky legal grounds and openly declared war on the Governor was of no interest to them. My refusal to act on that 'decision' led to more hostilities and was described by sections of the press as another example of unreasonable behaviour by me.

In the weeks that followed the hostilities escalated. I started being bombarded with countless emails about anything and everything on a daily basis about events that happened, events that they imagined happened or events they thought could happen, not only at the CBC but also in the rest of the banking system.[4] I felt like I was being harassed every minute of the day. As if that wasn't enough, the board started putting pressure on me to sell the CBC's gold reserves in order to 'help the government' meet its public finance targets, although the law was very clear on this: it wasn't something over which they had a say. My continued refusal to do so resulted in yet more serious rounds of hostility.

Confidential CBC documents were then leaked to the press which allegedly suggested that I colluded with the PIMCO to 'inflate the capital needs of the banking system' so that the bail-in would be higher. The bankers, who made similarly ludicrous claims in the past, had suddenly found allies from within the CBC. The newly established audit committee of the CBC took it upon themselves to conduct an 'investigation' behind my back and without prior authority by the board. Although the law stipulated that audits should

---

[3]Article 118.2 states that the Governor of the CBC has the power of managing the CBC according to Article 119.1.

[4]One example of such imaginary events was my alleged installation of 94 security cameras to monitor the CBC staff in their offices, which turned out to be four cameras that were installed outside elevators following prior data protection clearance (which was obtained during the tenure of the previous Governor, Athanasios Orphanides), which I was not even aware of. The story made headlines in various local TV stations and daily newspapers, who found the opportunity to describe me as 'big brother'.

be carried out by the CBC's internal or external auditors, this 'investigation' was conducted by the three non-executive members of the board who made up the audit committee, violating the principle of independence in audits. Their 'report', when I finally got to see it, was full of factual errors and all kinds of unfounded allegations about me, yet I was not even given the opportunity to respond to them before they started leaking their 'findings' to the press (and to the presidential palace).[5] The audit committee was the investigator, the judge and the jury.

Under Siege

I was under siege but I continued fighting. By the end of the year, I was, however, getting tired and stressed. My health started deteriorating. In Frankfurt, fellow members of the Governing Council offered considerable moral support. Most of them encouraged me to keep fighting and to stay on. One of the members of the executive board of the ECB asked me if I had the financial muscle to defend myself in court, as the CBC board was unlikely to approve budgets for legal support. I certainly didn't have the resources to pay for lawyers, let alone expensive ones. I had been only an academic before becoming a Governor. And as Governor my financial position, if anything had deteriorated, especially since I sent my family back to the UK for safety reasons, which meant I had to maintain two homes. I was convinced that it wouldn't come to that, as long as the European Commission, which has the legal obligation to protect central bank independence, acted swiftly.

Indeed the Commission was quick to react privately to the statements made by the President on 18 September. On 24 September 2013, Olli Rehn, the Vice President of the European Commission and Commissioner for Economic and Monetary Affairs, sent a letter of warning to the minister of finance. The letter alluded to the negative public statements made by the government on my performance and reminded the minister of the government's obligations to conform with 'The European Union Treaties and the provisions therein on Central Bank Independence'. However, the letter did not contain any indication of what action the Commission could—and arguably should—have taken in case the government continued its efforts to exert pressure on me by other means.

---

[5]The report was sent to Makarios Droushiotis, a close aide of the President with whom the board had regular email correspondence.

The extent of the Commission's effectiveness can be judged by the fact that nine days later, on 3 October 2013, Anastasiades exerted new pressure on me to resign through public statements he made during an interview with the lunchtime programme of Antenna TV. Specifically, he said that the findings of the judicial enquiry about the crisis, as well as other findings relating to my behaviour and professional conduct, would be sent to the Attorney General to establish whether a case could be made for my dismissal. When he was asked whether he wanted me to resign, he replied that 'this is an option if he thinks it is appropriate'.[6]

The president's remarks didn't go unnoticed by the international media. When asked about them at a conference in Washington, DC, ECB President Mario Draghi responded: 'We would have a dim view of an attempt to constrain, or to threaten, or to undermine the independence of the central bank'.

Anastasiades was, however, untouched by Draghi's remarks. On 17 October, he made new statements calling for my resignation.[7] In this instance, he stated: 'I will not let the country get hurt because there is a different mentality on behalf of the Governor'. He criticised me for providing ELA to Laiki, which by that time had become demonised. 'Can you tell me how someone persuaded (the ECB) so that an insolvent bank was given €9.5 billion without all these commitments?', he asked, suggesting that I was responsible—he seemed to have conveniently forgotten that it was him who had written a letter to me and his predecessor, Christofias, in November 2012 warning both of us of possible criminal charges if the ECB stopped providing liquidity to Laiki.

The narrative was changing as if he were indirectly trying to garner support from the ECB. I was 'serving other expediencies instead of his [my] country's interest', he said. Large sections of the media endorsed Anastasiades' views. The *Cyprus Mail*, the only English daily newspaper on the island, ran an editorial entitled 'President right to press on with removal of CB Governor'. The editorial alluded to the comments made by Mario Draghi and the letter sent by Olli Rehn but stated that 'None of Demetriades' defenders recognised the President's right to question the adequacy of the Governor, as if the latter is some infallible official, who has the right to lead the country to destruction, because the central bank's inde-

---

[6]Relevant excerpts of the president's interview (in Greek) can be found in an article on Cyprus Stockwatch, 3 October 2013 entitled "Ο πρόεδρος ρίχνει το γάντι στον διοικητή της ΚΤ".

[7]See "President: CBC Governor must go", by George Psyllides, *Cyprus Mail*, 18 October 2013.

pendence must be preserved'. Similar editorials were run by Greek-language newspapers, radio and TV stations on a daily basis. My elderly mother was becoming ill from the stress of listening to the lies the politicians were propagating about me on the TV news every night.

With the hostilities escalating, the ECB finally took the action that it needed to take. On 1 November 2013, Mario Draghi wrote a strongly worded letter to Jose Manuel Barroso, President of the European Commission, informing him of the serious concerns of the Governing Council. The letter did not mince its words. It concluded by asking the Commission to 'take all the actions necessary to ensure compliance in practice with the letter and the spirit of the Treaty and regards central bank independence in the Republic of Cyprus'.

My sources in the Commission informed me that the Commission started preparing to take appropriate legal action against the Republic of Cyprus. However, the action—known as the infringement procedure—was never taken. Instead, I was informed by a member of staff of the European Commission that Jose Manuel Barroso, the then President of the European Commission, had talked to Anastasiades and asked him to stop making negative public statements about me. The person who informed me about Barroso's action asked me to refrain from making negative comments about the President (which I had never made anyway).

Enemy of the State?

There was no shortage of investigations—or more precisely 'fishing expeditions'—to which I was subjected during 2013. On 13 August, I gave evidence to the judicial inquiry that was set up by Anastasiades to supposedly investigate the causes of the crisis. The inquiry effectively discredited itself by finding little evidence of wrongdoing by the bankers and, instead, apportioned most of the blame on the fiscal policies of the previous government. Throughout 2013, I provided evidence and documents to the Ethics Committee in parliament that was carrying out its own investigation. In 2013, the police started investigating the provision of ELA to Laiki, without any clear idea of what exactly it was they were looking for. The Governing Council of the ECB gave its consent to excerpts of secret minutes to be provided relating to the decision points about ELA to Laiki. The Auditor General of the Republic—the current Governor—started to investigate the contracts of consultants hired by the CBC to assist with the management of the crisis.

When the leaks were made by the CBC's audit committee, there was such a public uproar that I felt I needed to issue a public statement to defend myself from the unfounded allegations. My statement explained that the leaking of confidential documents to the press was a criminal offence and that I had the intention of reporting it to the police. In no time, the police arrived in my office. They were ordered to do so by the then Deputy Attorney General, Rikkos Erotocritou, a lawyer-politician from Limassol who was a close aide of Anastasiades during his pre-election campaign.[8] The leader of the police investigation team visited me in my office and assured me that the leaking of documents was illegal and that they were going to investigate it. Within a week the police investigation team was replaced. The new team said that they found no evidence of leaks but that they now had orders to investigate my relationship with the restructuring consultants (a US-based firm with impeccable credentials in corporate restructurings that was involved in the restructuring of Lehman, and the setting up of asset management companies in Ireland and Spain). That investigation lasted for several months, although I provided all the evidence they needed (including being questioned over three consecutive days) to their satisfaction. The (new) Attorney General, who was regularly asked many times by journalists how long it would take for me to be dismissed, eventually stated to the press that no evidence had been found for the pressing of charges against me.

I spent Christmas 2013 and the New Year at my home in Leicestershire with my family. The board wanted to have a meeting on 31 December to discuss the sale of the gold reserves (yet again). I refused. However, it was clear that the situation in Cyprus was becoming more challenging, if not altogether dangerous, in light of the Commission's unwillingness to take the appropriate legal action that would safeguard my independence. My personal circumstances, with my wife and two young children in the UK getting increasingly anxious about the attacks against me in Cyprus, were pointing in the same direction: it was time to start thinking seriously about the exit option. In the days and weeks that followed, I assessed everything carefully. The banking sector was beginning to show signs of stabilisation: deposits were returning, NPLs were beginning to be restructured, albeit slowly. The restructuring and recapitalisation of the credit cooperatives were nearing completion and capital controls were being lifted earlier than

---

[8]In 2016 Erotocritou was dismissed from that position by the Supreme Court on grounds of misconduct. In February 2017, he was found guilty of corruption and collusion by a criminal court. He is currently serving a three and a half year prison sentence.

expected. At the same time, my position within the CBC was becoming precarious thanks to the actions of the board and the interjections between the staff and the executive directors that were creating divided loyalties. I thought my resignation might also help to expedite the return of normalcy within the banking system. It was a good time to go.

In my letter of resignation that I sent to President Anastasiades on 10 March 2014, I stated personal reasons and difficulties working with the board as the reasons for my resignation. The recovery was still too fragile for me to mention in my letter that I felt as if the CBC under my leadership had, thanks to an unrelenting and unprecedented propaganda campaign, become perceived as an enemy of the state. In his letter of acceptance, Anastasiades thanked me for my efforts to stabilise the banking system. He could afford to be magnanimous. He had got what he wanted.

17

The Key Ingredients of the Crisis

The boom that sowed the seeds of the crisis was to a large extent driven by a business model that was heavily dependent on the financial sector, with domestic banks and politically connected law firms playing a major role. The set-up, in which law firms acted as introducers of wealthy foreign clients, helped to attract very large inflows of foreign deposits, facilitated by interest rates that were, on average, substantially higher than those prevailing in the rest of the euro area.[1] This led to a massive expansion of bank balance sheets which created a major contingent liability for the taxpayer that remained largely ignored. Specifically, between December 2014 and June 2010, total banking sector[2] and domestic banks[3] assets more than doubled to 953% and 601% of GDP, respectively.[4]

This chapter draws on a document submitted by the Central Bank of Cyprus to the judicial enquiry on the economy, chaired by retired judge George Piki, in August 2013. and PIMCO (2013). Data sources include: ECB, CBC, PIMCO (2013) and World Bank.

---

[1]The law firms had a distinct advantage over other firms because they could help their clients register companies and could act as their nominees. They could also provide a range of other services, including, for example, international tax planning and naturalisation (e.g. the scheme for obtaining EU citizenship by investment).

[2]Including the Cooperative Central Bank but excluding the cooperative credit institutions.

[3]Bank of Cyprus, Laiki Bank, Hellenic Bank, Cooperative Central Bank, Housing Finance Corporation, Cyprus Development Bank.

[4]See also, Lascelles (2013) and Demetriades (2015).

© The Author(s) 2017
P. Demetriades, *A Diary of the Euro Crisis in Cyprus*,
DOI 10.1007/978-3-319-62223-1_17

Imprudent lending practices by domestic banks reflecting inadequate risk management and, more generally, lax corporate governance, channelled the capital inflows into domestic credit, which, in turn, fuelled a boom in the real estate sector. A lax provisioning methodology meant that the quality of the banks' loan portfolio started to deteriorate rapidly with the eruption of the global financial crisis, which affected Cyprus through a reduction in demand for new holiday homes and retirement properties by foreign nationals. The rapid expansion of bank lending resulted in high levels of household and non-financial corporate debt, thus, making the private sector highly vulnerable to potential shocks. At the same time, high real borrowing rates contributed to a deterioration of the financial position of firms and households and affected their ability to service their loan commitments.

Another key ingredient of the crisis was the significant presence of Cypriot banks in Greece, where their exposure was of the order of 140% of Cyprus' GDP. With Greece experiencing a deep and lengthy recession, asset quality in Greece deteriorated rapidly reflecting the accumulation of non-performing loans (NPLs). The increased provisions due to the deterioration in the quality of banks' loan portfolio and the Greek PSI, which involved a deep 'haircut' of Greek government bonds (GGBs), led to record losses for banks in the period 2011–2012, and exerted strong pressure on their liquidity and capital base.

As the Greek economy was deteriorating, successive downgrades in the credit rating of the Republic of Cyprus and Cypriot banks by international credit rating agencies led to their exclusion from international money and capital markets. Because of steady deposit outflows and rising NPLs, which impacted adversely on their cash inflows, the liquidity buffers in the banking system were gradually eroded. Banks initially resorted to the refinancing operations of the Eurosystem to cover their short-term funding. However, following the downgrades of Greek and Cyprus bonds to junk status, which quickly depleted most, if not all, their eligible collateral, banks turned increasingly to Emergency Liquidity Assistance (ELA) to satisfy their liquidity needs.

At the same time, there was a build up of significant external and internal imbalances outside the banking sector, including an enlarged current account deficit, substantial losses in competitiveness, a growing budget deficit and increasing public debt. These, together with the large contingent liability represented by the bloated domestic banking sector, were behind the successive credit rating downgrades of the sovereign. As a result, by the summer of 2011, the government lost access to international financial markets, which meant it could only rely on domestic sources to finance the fiscal

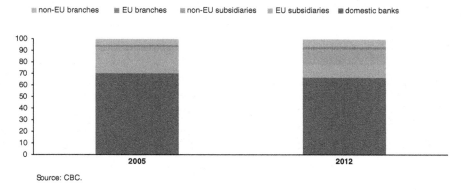

Fig. 17.1   Market share of banks (% of total consolidated assets). *Source* CBC

deficit and refinance maturing debt. Thus, when Laiki and Bank of Cyprus requested state aid in May and June 2012, respectively, the Cypriot government had no choice but to apply for financial assistance from the European Financial Stability Facility (EFSF) /European Stability Mechanism (ESM) and the International Monetary Fund. The request was submitted on 25 June 2012.

The Banking Sector Before the Crisis

At the end of December 2012, there were 41 banks operating in Cyprus, comprising seven domestically controlled banks and 35 foreign banks, of which 8 were subsidiaries and 27 branches. In contrast to other small countries with large banking sectors (e.g. Luxembourg), Cyprus' banking landscape had been traditionally dominated by domestic banks.[5] At the end of 2012, domestic banks accounted for nearly 67% of total consolidated banking system assets, compared to around 70% in 2005. Over the same period, non-EU subsidiaries and branches grew their market share from just under 13% of total banking sector assets to nearly 19%. Over the same period, the share of EU subsidiaries and branches declined from around 17% to 14% (Fig. 17.1).

---

[5]The comparison with Luxemburg allowed policy makers in Cyprus to deflect criticism of the large size of the banking system relative to GDP before the crisis. However, the important point that was omitted was that Luxemburg's banking sector is dominated by foreign banks and hence none of them present a systemic risk to the country.

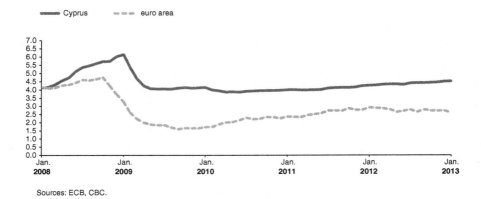

Sources: ECB, CBC.

Fig. 17.2 MFI interest rates on new deposits in Cyprus from euro area households (%). *Sources* ECB, CBC

Cypriot banks offered relatively high-interest rates on deposits to households and non-financial corporations (NFCs), compared to their peers in Europe, thus, attracting substantial inflows of foreign deposits. Soon after Cyprus joined the euro area in January 2008, average-interest rates on new deposits from euro area households, shown in Fig. 17.2, started rising sharply from around 4.0% to over 6.0% by the end of the year. As a result, the spread between interest rates in Cyprus and the euro area average widened considerably, as euro area rates rose more modestly during 2008. Deposit rates in the euro area started declining sharply from October 2008 to less than 2.0% by mid-2009. Although interest rates in Cyprus also started declining, they fell less sharply compared to the rest of the euro area and stabilised at around 4.0%. As a result, the deposit rate spread increased to around 2.5% by mid-2009. The spread narrowed somewhat during 2010 but it remained at around 2.0% until the end of 2012. A similar pattern of behaviour was observed with respect to deposit rates to euro area NFCs (Fig. 17.3).

During 2006–2012 deposits of non-residents, shown in Fig. 17.4, more than doubled. By the end of that period, they accounted for over 38.0% of the total deposits in the banking system.

Cypriot banks used their abundant liquidity to fund their lending within Cyprus and Greece and to acquire stakes in banks and other risky assets in Russia, Ukraine and other parts of Eastern Europe. Figure 17.5 provides snapshots of the asset allocation of the three largest Cypriot banks (Bank of Cyprus, Cyprus Popular Bank and Hellenic Bank) in these countries/regions. By December 2008, a year before the onset of the Greek crisis,

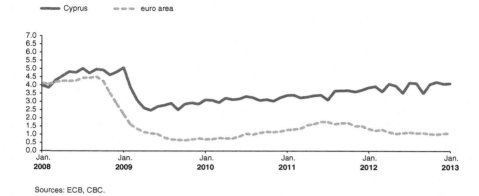

Sources: ECB, CBC.

Fig. 17.3 MFI interest rates on new euro-denominated deposits in Cyprus from euro area NFCs (%). *Sources* ECB, CBC

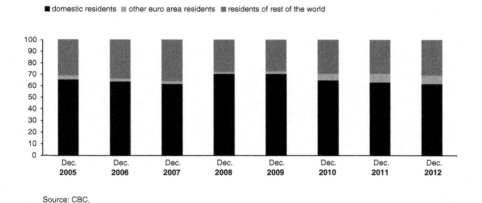

Source: CBC.

Fig. 17.4 Analysis of bank deposits by geographical area (% of total bank deposits). *Source* CBC

the operations of the three largest Cypriot banks in Greece had grown to 43.0% of the total consolidated assets of these banking groups, compared to just under 32.0% in December 2005. As a result of their expansion outside Cyprus, by 2008 their domestic operations accounted for less than 50% of their business. By 2012, however, domestic operations bounced back to 61%, largely reflecting the decline of the Greek market due to the deep and protracted recession in Greece.

The aggressive expansionary strategy followed by Cypriot banks was reflected in rapid asset growth, over and above that of deposits. In the period

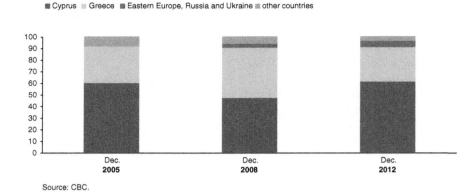

Source: CBC.

Fig. 17.5 Asset allocation of the three Cypriot banking groups by country (%). *Source* CBC

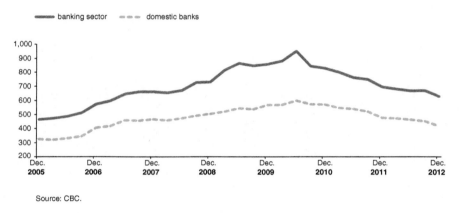

Source: CBC.

Fig. 17.6 Total consolidated assets of the banking sector as a percentage of GDP. *Source* CBC

December 2005–June 2010, the assets of domestic banks grew at an average rate of nearly 24%, compared with an average annual growth rate of deposits of just over 13%. As a result, banking sector assets (on a consolidated basis) increased from 388% of GDP at the end of 2004, respectively, to a peak level of 953% of GDP by June 2010. Over the same period, the assets of domestic banks (on a consolidated basis) increased from 286% of GDP to 601%. The evolution of banking sector assets during this period is shown in Fig. 17.6.[6]

---

[6]These figures include the assets of the Co-operative Central Bank but exclude the assets of the credit cooperatives.

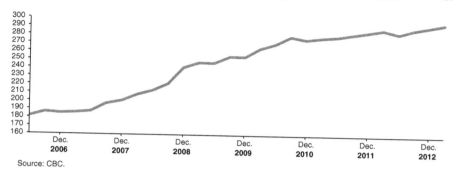

Fig. 17.7 Bank credit to the private sector as a % of GDP. *Source* CBC

Underlying the growth in assets was the expansion of credit to the private sector,[7] the evolution of which is shown in Fig. 17.7. By December 2012 private credit reached 296% of GDP compared to 181% of GDP at the end of March 2006. Comparable data published by the World Bank suggest that Cyprus as of 2007 overtook Spain as the country with the highest ratio of domestic credit to the private sector in the European Union (as well as worldwide).

Much of the increase in private credit from during this period was channelled to households and construction, both helping to create a bubble in real estate prices. As a result of the excessive growth in lending to domestic households which occurred from 2005 to 2010, the ratio of household debt[8] to GDP increased from 99% at the end of December 2005 to nearly 114% at the end of December 2008 and 136% at the end of December 2012—becoming more than double the euro area average. These developments, which resulted in the over-indebtedness of the private sector that was one of the key ingredients of the Cyprus crisis, are illustrated in Fig. 17.8.

Similarly, credit to domestic non-financial corporations, shown in Fig. 17.9, grew rapidly until September 2008. Although it decelerated sharply after that, the excessive growth in loans to domestic non-financial corporations during the previous 5 years resulted in the ratio of non-financial

---

[7]Private credit includes loans to Cyprus residents (excluding MFIs and general government) and investments in bonds and other debt securities issued by Cyprus residents (excluding MFIs and general government) provided by banks and credit cooperatives.

[8]Based on data from the quarterly financial accounts. It includes loans to households and non-profit institutions serving households.

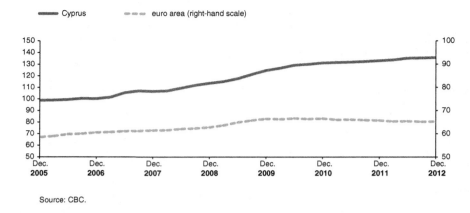

Source: CBC.

Fig. 17.8 Total household debt as a % of GDP. *Source* CBC

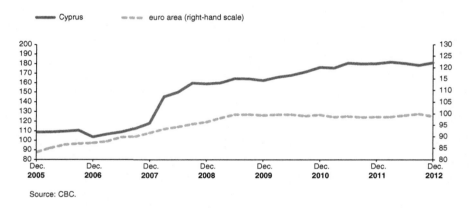

Source: CBC.

Fig. 17.9 Total non-financial corporate debt as a % of GDP. *Source* CBC

corporate debt to GDP reaching 181% of GDP at the end of 2012, compared with 109% in December 2005.[9] By comparison, the debt of non-financial corporations in the rest of the euro area was around 99% of GDP in December 2012.

The cost of financing for non-financial corporations by domestic MFIs in Cyprus, shown in Fig. 17.10, remained, however, very high, compared to the lending rates prevailing in the rest of the euro area. The difference, if anything, widened from 2008 onwards, as a result of the steady decline of euro area lending rates and an opposite trend in Cyprus. Lending rates in Cyprus

---

[9]Based on data from the quarterly financial accounts. It includes loans and debt securities of non-financial corporations. It should be noted that the data include organisations or businesses of residents without a physical presence in Cyprus.

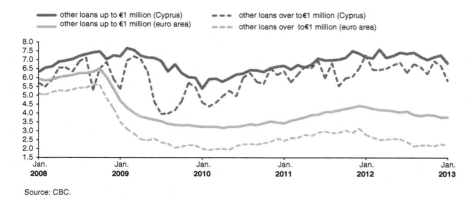

Fig. 17.10   MFI interest rates on new euro-denominated loans in Cyprus and the rest of the euro area to non-financial corporations in the euro area (% annually, period averages). *Source* CBC

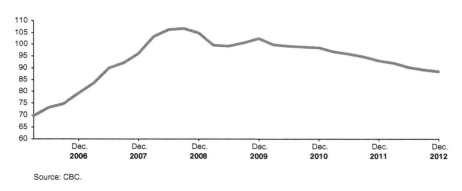

Fig. 17.11   Residential property price index (December 2010 = 100). *Source* CBC

increased from 6.0% in March 2010 to 7.6% in March 2012, reflecting growing risks and tighter liquidity conditions in the banking system.

During 2005 and 2008, the exuberant lending by domestic banks for the purchase of real estate fuelled an increase in prices to unprecedented levels by 2008 and a subsequent downward trend since 2009, depicted in Fig. 17.11. Specifically, in March 2008 the largest-ever annual percentage increase in the general house price index[10] was recorded, which amounted to 23.7%. From March 2009 onwards what was clearly a real estate price bubble started deflating steadily, with the exception of two quarters.

---

[10]CBC residential property price index.

Along with their domestic operations, Cypriot banking groups expanded significantly in Greece. The growth in the loan portfolio of the Cypriot banks continued amid the first phase of the prolonged recession of the Greek economy, with exposures to Greek households and businesses reaching €22.3 billion in December 2012, following a decline of 7.6% from their peak level in 2010. Loans to non-financial corporations accounted for about two-thirds of total loans in Greece in December 2012, with the remaining credit being accounted for by loans to Greek households.

The Greek sovereign debt crisis and the subsequent deterioration of the macroeconomic environment in the country negatively affected the quality of the loan portfolio of Cypriot banks. From December 2008 until December 2012, NPLs from the activities of Cypriot banks in Greece increased dramatically, constituting 38.1%[11] of total loans in December 2012 from just 4.1% in December 2007. At the same time, the worsening of the macroeconomic conditions in Cyprus resulted in a rise in NPLs from domestic operations, reaching a peak of 21% in December 2012, compared with 5.9% in December 2009.

Deteriorating Balance Sheets

Deficiencies in banks' lending practices as well as in the legal and regulatory framework, contributed to the rapid increase in NPLs. A key feature of risk assessment practices in banks prior to the crisis was the over-reliance on collateral and guarantees, often with little attention to the repayment ability of borrowers. The quality of credit was masked by complex collateral arrangements that involved a high degree of cross-collateralisation, which intensified as problem loans increased. For example, the same property (or even multiple properties) could serve as collateral for multiple loans, while large borrower groups had complex structures involving numerous entities with extensive cross shareholdings, cross pledges, cross guarantees and floating charges of various priorities.[12] The decline in real estate prices adversely affected the value of collateral, having a negative impact on the quality of banks' loan portfolio.

---

[11]Preliminary data for the end of December 2012 for the Bank of Cyprus and Laiki Bank.
[12]See PIMCO (2013).

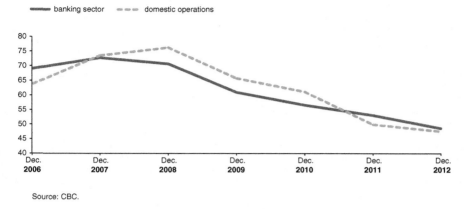

Fig. 17.12 Provisions as a percentage of non-performing loans (coverage ratio).
Source CBC

Moreover, the lengthy process of foreclosure and repossession of immovable property as well as the limitations of the legal framework, whereby banks were not given the right to take possession of the mortgage but could only force the sale of the property, created incentives for strategic default. The lax legal framework on foreclosures discouraged borrowers from repaying their loans and banks from taking legal action against them; thus, adversely affecting recoveries. Both these factors contributed to the accumulation of NPLs in the banking system.

Weaknesses were also present in Cypriot banks' provisioning methodologies and impairment practices, which differed significantly from European norms (e.g. see PIMCO 2013, p.12). Specifically, banks calculated provisions as the difference between the current principal amount of the loan and the undiscounted recovery value of a 'forced sale'—where the latter was defined as 25% below the most recent valuation of collateral. For provisioning purposes, banks adopted the NPL definition outlined in the CBC 'Directive to banks for the classification of non-performing loans', thus, excluding loans that were over 90 delinquent loans that were fully secured by tangible collateral. This definition fell significantly short of international best practices that define all loans that are past due more than 90 days as non-performing. In addition, banks often engaged in loan modifications to accommodate problem borrowers, which allowed them to continue classing problem loans as performing. Moreover, banks recognised unpaid but accrued interest on problem loans in interest income, which led to unusually high amounts of unpaid capitalised interest in banks' income statements.

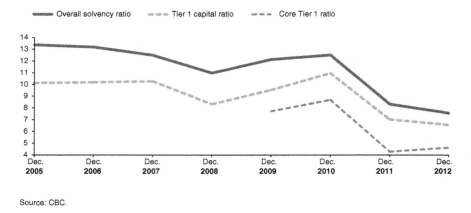

Fig. 17.13 Capital adequacy ratios (%). *Source* CBC

These deficiencies led to substantial under-provisioning, which was also compounded by rapidly declining collateral values.[13]

Evidence of under-provisioning, which vividly illustrates the gradual weakening of bank balance sheets during 2007–2011, is shown in Fig. 17.12. As can be seen from the chart, the coverage ratio (loan loss provisions as a percentage of NPLs) exhibited a continuous downward trend from December 2007 onwards, dropping to just under 50.0% by the end of December 2012. Banks, however, started making increased provisions for doubtful debts arising from their domestic operations in the second half of 2012, which helped to stabilise the coverage ratio in the face of increasing recognition of NPLs during the same period.

The deteriorating quality of the loan portfolio and increased provisions for doubtful debts adversely affected their capital buffers. During 2011 and 2012, the losses incurred due to the 'haircut' on Greek government bonds and increased provisions resulted in deteriorating capital adequacy. As shown in Fig. 17.13, the capital adequacy ratios of the banking sector recorded a steep decline during 2011. By the end of 2012, the total capital adequacy ratio and the Tier 1 capital ratio decreased further to 7.6% and 6.6%, respectively, while the core principal Core Tier 1 capital ratio increased to 4.6%.

---

[13]The definition of NPLS was brought in line with international norms soon after the change of CBC Governor in 2012.

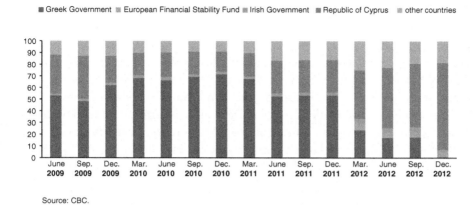

Source: CBC.

Fig. 17.14 Exposure of domestic banks in government securities by country (nominal value) (%). *Source* CBC

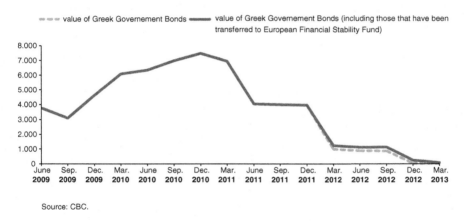

Source: CBC.

Fig. 17.15 Exposure of domestic banks in Greek Government Bonds (nominal value, € million). *Source* CBC

The Gamble with Greek Government Bonds (GGBs)

Cypriot banks, especially the two largest domestic ones, , invested excessively in GGBs during the first half of 2009 and 2010.[14] Figures 17.14 and 17.15

---

[14]Banks started reporting their exposure to government bonds to the CBC in June 2009 on a quarterly basis.

show the exposures of domestic banks in government securities by country and their exposure in GGBs, respectively. Figure 17.14 reveals the extraordinary risk concentration in GGBs and the surprisingly modest exposure to Cyprus government bonds before 2012, contrary to what might have been expected. The losses from the Greek PSI for each of the three systemic banks amounted to €1.9 billion and €2.4 billion or 10.4% and 13.4% of GDP, respectively, for Bank of Cyprus and Laiki. By contrast, Hellenic Bank made much smaller losses, amounting to €77.0 million or 0.4% of GDP. In total, however, the three largest banks made losses amounting to 24.2% of GDP, which was reported in their 2011 accounts and became the trigger for the crisis.

Capital Shortfalls

PIMCO's independent, bottom-up, loan level due diligence exercise covered 22 participating institutions (PIs) representing domestic banks (including their branch operations in Greece, Russia and elsewhere), subsidiaries of Greek banks operating in Cyprus and cooperative credit institutions. The PI's covered 83% of Cyprus' domestic institutions' assets.

The reference date used was 30 June 2012 and the forecast period extended from 30 June 2012 to 30 June 2015. The capital shortfalls or surpluses were estimated as of 30 June 2015 taking into account projected loan losses and offsetting pre-provision earnings. The capital shortfalls estimated were in addition to the injections of public capital into the banking system that took place before 30 June 2012. They, therefore, excluded the €1.8 billion already injected into Laiki during June 2012.

For the preparation of its report, PIMCO evaluated the credit portfolios of PIs, including provisions, and provided estimates of portfolios' expected losses over a 3-year period under a base and an adverse macro-economic scenario that were agreed by the steering committee.[15] It performed evaluations of each PI's ability to generate pre-provision profits through the forecast period and determined the capital needs of each PI. PIMCO's work was overseen by a steering committee comprising representatives from the Ministry of Finance, the CBC, the Ministry of Commerce (that was responsible for supervising credit cooperatives), the IMF, the European Commission, the European Central Bank, the European Stability

---

[15]See the book website.

Mechanism and the European Banking Authority. PIMCO's modelling approach, methodology and assumptions were tested and challenged by the steering committee as part of an in depth peer review process.

The total assets covered by the due diligence exercise amounted to around €100.1 billion, of which €77.0 billion were accounted for by domestic banks, €12.7 billion by credit cooperatives and the rest by foreign banks. PIMCO's estimates of capital shortfalls amounted to €6.0 billion under the base scenario (at 9% required Core Tier 1 Capital) and €8.9 billion under the adverse scenario (at 6% required Core Tier 1 Capital). These corresponded to expected losses of €14.0 billion and €18.5 billion, respectively, over a 3-year period. Bank of Cyprus and Laiki had capital shortfalls of €2.8 billion each under the base scenario and €4.0 billion and €3.8 billion, respectively, under the adverse scenario. Between them, they accounted for 94% of the capital shortfall under the base scenario and 87% under the adverse scenario. The credit cooperatives accounted for €364 million or 6.0% of the shortfall under the base scenario and €589 million or 6.6% of the total shortfall under the adverse scenario.

PIMCO's estimated capital shortfalls were so large that they were initially greeted with disbelief and denial by the bankers and their politician friends, followed by anger directed towards the CBC. To this end, the bankers and their backers claimed that the macroeconomic scenarios that were provided to PIMCO by the CBC were too pessimistic. The criticism was totally unfounded not least because the macroeconomic scenarios were discussed and agreed by the steering committee, in which the CBC was only one of eight institutional members. Moreover, the critics never seemed to appreciate that bank stress tests have little, if any market credibility, if they are perceived as too lenient. While the base scenario provides the best estimate of what is likely to happen, the adverse scenario is, by construction, intended to gauge the ability of banks to withstand shocks—defined by the European Banking Authority as 'extreme but plausible events'.

The adverse scenario turned out to be not so extreme after all. Specifically, the actual cumulative change of the rate of unemployment in Cyprus during 2012–2015 turned out to be 3.0% compared to 2.5% under the adverse scenario and 1.0% in the base scenario. GDP at constant prices during the same period declined by 5.8% compared to 2.8% in the base scenario and 7.3% in the adverse scenario. The outturn for the change in GDP at constant prices was worse than expected under the adverse scenario for 2013 (−6.0% compared to 5.2%) and roughly halfway between the base and adverse scenarios for 2014 (−1.5% compared to −0.6 and −2.3%, respectively). For 2015, the outturn for GDP growth was +1.7%, which was better than both the adverse and base scenarios (0.0% and 0.8%, respectively). Thus, the recession in Cyprus was deeper than predicted but its duration was shorter than anticipated.[16]

Critics failed to recognise that the shortfalls largely emanated from the rapid growth in the size of bank balance sheets that took place during 2005–2010, outlined in earlier sections of this chapter. The shortfalls could, of course, have been much smaller had banking risks been managed more prudently. For that to have happened, better regulation and more effective supervision was needed during that period. While it is convenient ex post to blame the CBC for those failures, the fact remains that parliament failed to exercise proper scrutiny over the CBC. Had the CBC been made accountable for the growing banking risks—as it should have been—the Cyprus crisis may never have happened.

Bibliography

Demetriades, Panicos. 2015. Political economy of a euro area banking crisis, London School of Economics, Financial markets group, Special paper series, No. 245, *The Cambridge Journal of Economics*, forthcoming. doi: 10.1093/cje/bex001.

Lascelles, David. 2013. *Independent commission on the future of the Cyprus banking sector,* Final report, 31 October 2013. http://www.centralbank.gov.cy/media/pdf/ LSE_ICFCBS_Final_Report_10_13.pdf.

PIMCO. 2013. Independent due dilegence of the banking system of Cyprus, February. Available from: http://www.centralbank.gov.cy/media/pdf/cyprusindep endentduediligencereport_18april.pdf.

---

[16]The deeper recession in 2013 probably reflects the shock to confidence and the introduction of capital controls. The quicker than anticipated recovery can probably be ascribed to the fact that the bail-in spared the economy from additional austerity measures that are often recessionary.

18

Lessons for Europe and Beyond

Soon after the crisis erupted, I felt it was important for the CBC to draw lessons from the crisis and put forward proposals to make the Cypriot banking industry stronger, more resilient and better suited to meet the country's banking needs. To this end, in November 2012, the CBC appointed an Independent Commission to make recommendations on the long-term recovery of the Cypriot banking industry. The Commission was asked to take into account international best practice as well as the institutional set up of Cyprus as a euro area member state. In April 2013, the Commission's terms of reference were revised to take into account the banking sector reforms that were already agreed as part of the EU-IMF economic adjustment programme.

The Commission was led by David Lascelles, former banking editor of the *Financial Times* and Senior Research Fellow of the Centre for the Study of Financial Innovation.[1] In June 2013, the Commission published its Interim Report, which laid out its proposed recommendations for public consultation. The Commission received 50 responses from individuals and institutions, not only from within Cyprus but also from overseas. The Final Report was published in October 2013 and was well received within Cyprus.

---

[1] The Commission's other members were: (i) George Charalambous who was a key figure in the Cypriot financial sector and served as chairman of the Cyprus Securities and Exchange Commission; (ii) David Green, a leading international expert on financial stability matters with considerable experience in banking regulation and supervision at the Bank of England and the Financial Services Authority and (iii) Pierre de Weck, a senior Swiss banker with over 35 years experience in international banking, which included positions in Europe, North America and the middle east with Citibank, UBS and Deutsche Bank, where he was Global Head of the private wealth management division.

© The Author(s) 2017
P. Demetriades, *A Diary of the Euro Crisis in Cyprus,*
DOI 10.1007/978-3-319-62223-1_18

So much so that the government publicly endorsed its recommendations (although they took no action to implement them). The Commission came to seven conclusions in relation to the causes behind Cyprus' banking crisis, which are (verbatim) as follows:

1. That over the period 2004–2010, Cyprus' banks grew dangerously large through a combination of aggressive management and weak governance, compounded by a failure by the public authorities to appreciate the risks that the banks were running, and therefore to take effective measures to rein them in. At its height in 2009, the banking sector was equivalent to nine times the country's GDP, one of the highest levels in the EU.

2. That the banks engaged in imprudent lending both domestically and through their rapid expansion abroad, mainly in Greece and East Europe because of failures in their risk management systems and poor lending practices. This included taking on an inappropriate and ultimately fatal €5.7bn exposure to Greek Government Bonds (GGBs). Poor lending practices also occurred at the cooperative banks because of weak governance and internal controls, causing them to suffer extremely large loan losses. In 2012, private sector indebtedness in Cyprus reached 271% of GDP, the highest level in the EU, with most of this secured on property that was declining in value.

3. That while Cyprus' international financial centre, based on foreign deposits and tax-driven business, was remarkably stable in the circumstances, it nonetheless channelled large amounts of liquidity into the domestic market and contributed strongly to the problem of excessive credit growth which the authorities did not do enough to control.

4. That the government's failure to correct Cyprus' deteriorating financial position in the 2009–2012 period concealed underlying weakness and precipitated a fiscal crisis which caused it to be excluded from the international capital markets, and which left it without the resources to support its banks when they entered their critical phase in 2012. The government's reluctance in 2011–12 to seek outside support from the EU and the IMF, followed by long delays in agreeing rescue terms, made matters considerably worse.

5. That Cyprus' failure to take adequate precautionary action against the combined threats of a real estate bubble on the domestic market and increasingly turbulent conditions on the international financial markets showed a lack of awareness as to the country's potential vulnerabilities on the banking front.

6. That there were supervisory failures at many levels, including poor coordination between the Central Bank of Cyprus and the Ministry of Finance over the mounting risks to the system, and the ineffectiveness of the supervisory agencies when it came to controlling the banks and the coops, due mainly to lack of firm leadership, influenced by a prevailing attitude in political circles and the international agencies that all was sufficiently under control.

7. That there were also external factors, notably Cyprus' entry into the EU (2004) and the euro (2008) which liberalised the banking system very rapidly and gave it access to new sources of funds while also removing Cyprus' ability to control credit expansion by monetary means. Although the subsequent global financial crisis did not much affect Cyprus directly, it had a large indirect impact through its banks' involvement with Greece and through the collapse in foreign demand for residential real estate on the island. Turbulence in the euro area placed further stresses on the Cyprus economy and banking system, and also greatly complicated Cyprus' later efforts to obtain financial support. Lascelles (2013, pp 21–23)

Most of the above conclusions accord well with what I have laid out in the previous chapter as the key ingredients of the crisis. It is important, however, to delve deeper into the causes of the crisis. For example, it is critical to understand what can explain the *'prevailing attitude in political circles…that all was sufficiently under control'*. Was it just ignorance? Or were there political economy factors that encouraged them to turn a blind eye to the growing banking risks? I argue below that close examination of what happened suggests that it was the latter.

In addition to the lessons that can be learned from the deeper causes of the crisis, it is also important to draw lessons from the management of the crisis and its aftermath, both of which were outside the remit of the Independent Commission.

Lesson 1: Prevention is Better than Cure (TBTF and TBTS)

The first major lesson is, without doubt, the importance of prevention. By 2010, Bank of Cyprus and Laiki had grown to a combined balance sheet size that was over four times the country's GDP. They were more than just systemic. If either of them failed in the absence of an orderly resolution framework, the entire economy would have ground to a halt for years until their assets were liquidated and depositors would not have had access to their liquidity. The sovereign was not in a position to compensate insured depositors. As a result, the failure of one or both banks would, in all likelihood, have led to a disorderly sovereign default and euro exit.

The banks were certainly (far) too big to fail (TBTF). A bailout, however, was out of the question. The IMF and the international lenders—especially Germany—concluded that Bank of Cyprus and Laiki were too big to save

(TBTS). The argument—which as far as I know was never challenged by the government—was that if they were bailed out by the taxpayer, the public debt would have spiralled out of control, leading to sovereign default.[2]

Lesson 2: Beware of Capture (TBTR)

Better macro-prudential regulation could have prevented the banks from becoming TBTF and TBTS, by containing systemic risk and the excessive growth in balance sheets. Stricter micro-prudential regulation would have ensured better corporate governance that would have resulted in better management of credit risk through more appropriate lending standards, which should have focused more on the borrowers' ability to repay rather than their ability to provide collateral. It would also have deterred other forms of excessive risk taking, such as the unacceptably large investments in Greek government bonds and the acquisition of risky foreign banks. A stricter implementation of the AML framework could also have deterred some of the capital inflows that led to the bloated balance sheets.

If better regulation could have averted the crisis, why didn't Cyprus have it? Was it because the authorities were simply not aware of the risks, as suggested by Lascelles (2013)? Or was it because of interest group politics? While I do not doubt that many stakeholders under-estimated the risks, it is difficult to explain why the warnings from the rating agencies, which started from mid-2010 when S&P placed Cyprus on negative watch, were ignored. By November of that year, the same agency was the first to downgrade Cyprus. Moody's and Fitch followed in January 2011, by placing Cyprus on negative watch. During 2011 there were 11 successive downgrades. Surely someone should have noticed? Although by 2010 it was too late to contain the excess growth in balance sheets, it was still possible to take actions to mitigate some of the risks.

There is only one possible explanation behind lax regulation and supervision, and it had more to do with the political protection that the banks

---

[2]I must admit that at the time I felt that the IMF's debt sustainability analysis was overly conservative. Specifically, they used a debt to GDP ratio of 100% as the sustainability threshold compared with 120% in the case of Greece. I had a heated argument over this particular issue with the IMF's troika chief of staff, Delia Velculescu. If the IMF had used a higher threshold, the bail-in would have been more limited and, arguably, the toxic fallout from that would have been smaller. Unfortunately, the IMF's view prevailed.

enjoyed than the inability of banking supervisors to understand those risks.[3] The big banks were very much at the core of the 'Cyprus business model', from which many other members of this powerful interest group, including politicians, benefited. The regulator—the CBC—had always been accountable to Parliament. Parliament could and should have scrutinised the CBC over its lax regulation and supervision of the banking system and its oversight of the growing banking risks and the threats to financial stability. To the best of my knowledge, the House of Representatives Finance Committee, rarely, if ever, questioned my predecessor about the risks posed by the banking system. This continued well into 2011, when one downgrade followed another and all rating agencies were warning about banking risks. Conveniently, the House Finance Committee deflected attention from the banks by asking Orphanides to talk about the deterioration in the public finances.

Indicative of Parliament's perverse approach towards banking regulation was the reaction of a key member of a parliamentary committee when I started tightening the regulatory framework soon after I took office. One of the first directives that I amended was the one that allowed banks to circumvent international standards of provisioning, because it included a very lax definition of non-performing loans. Up to that point, and contrary to standard international practice, loans in arrears over 90 days could still be classed as performing if the bank considered them as adequately collateralized. Instead of welcoming the closing of this loophole that led to under-provisioning, as well as misleading accounts and artificially inflated profitability, this politician publicly attacked my actions and described them as an attempt to destroy the banking system. At best, this could be interpreted as a 'laissez-faire' stance towards regulation. At worst, it was reminiscent of how the big banks captured the political system in the United States (see Johnson and Kwak 2010). In the US, the politicians who supported the big banks were promoting the view that 'whatever was good for the big banks was good for America'. In Cyprus, it went further than that. The Bank of Cyprus—I was told many times by different people—was Cyprus. The Governor's duty—I was told by a former Governor—was to protect it 'from too much regulation that Europe wanted to impose'. Such was the audacity of the country's ruling elite. The media, which were dependent on the

---

[3]In fact some of the staff at the CBC did notice well before the credit rating agencies started downgrading the sovereign but were either ignored or assigned other duties.

banks for advertising revenues and soft loans, certainly helped to propagate and legitimise such views among the public.

The foreign inflows that led to the doubling of bank balance sheets during 2005–2010 benefited thousands of introducers, who, however, remained very much in the shadows prior to the crisis. New light was shed on them by a recent interview given by the compliance officer of Bank of Cyprus[4] who revealed that by December 2015 the bank had ditched 90% of the 1601 introducers it had in January 2014. However one looks at this, 1601 introducers was a pretty large number for a country whose labour force is less than half a million people. Another revelation from the same interview was that the bank decreased its 'high-risk client portfolio stemming primarily from the Eastern European countries by 30%' and terminated relations with 1871 of its customers 'solely on compliance grounds'. All this was clearly the result of a much tougher, risk-based, anti-money laundering framework that was introduced in December 2013, as part of the conditionality imposed on Cyprus by the international lenders. No such measures would have been introduced otherwise.

Another important dimension of the 'Cyprus business model', which was downplayed by those who benefited from it, was that it actually gave Cyprus a very bad name internationally as it generated the perception, held by many foreign governments, that Cyprus was 'a playground and money laundering heaven for rich Russians'. While these perceptions may have been somewhat exaggerated, it is a fact that politically connected law firms were among the most successful introducers, perhaps because they had a comparative advantage in developing links with the ruling elites of countries such as Russia and Ukraine. It is also true that many of the largest new shareholders of Bank of Cyprus were politically exposed Russian oligarchs. The stance of the Russian government itself, after the Eurogroup decision of 25 March 2013, is also very telling. Putin welcomed the deal, although it meant that many wealthy Russians—including possibly some of his close associates—lost substantial amounts of money. Medvedev went even further than Putin, when he remarked that 'the stealing of what had already been stolen continues in Cyprus'.[5]

I am not pretending to have easy answers to the question of how policymakers can deter the capture of the regulatory and political process by

---

[4]'BOC's Skandalis: Ethics and profitability go hand-in-hand', *Business Mail*, 20 November 2016. See: http://cyprusbusinessmail.com/?p=36085.

[5]Medvedev was paraphrasing Lenin who had justified the expropriation of capitalists' property by the Bolsheviks by pointing out that they were taking away what had already been stolen.

big banks, especially in cases such as Cyprus where it wasn't just the banks that benefited from the growth in bank balance sheets. Nonetheless, capture was perhaps the single most important cause of the crisis. Media capture was also part of the same equation, as the media painted a very positive image of the banks, the bankers and the regulator at the time when the banking risks were reaching unsustainable heights. If the media were less financially dependent on the banks, they would have been more likely to run objective stories about the growing banking risks and the laxity of regulation, which could have forced Parliament to act differently. Policymakers, therefore, need to be wary of large advertising budgets while supervisors need to scrutinise carefully large loans to media enterprises and other politically exposed persons or organisations.

In Europe, the advent of the Single Supervisory Mechanism (SSM), which now oversees all systemic banks in the euro area, is a very important step forward. The SSM is in a strong position to help address the phenomenon that was observed in Cyprus, whereby large banks prevented better regulation through political and media capture. Only time will tell, however, if the SSM will be effective.

Lesson 3: Educate the General Public About Bail-in and Deposit Insurance

Cyprus was the first country in Europe that applied the principle of 'bail-in', which is now enshrined in the Bank Recovery and Resolution Directive of 2014 that has been adopted by all EU member states. The key aim of the directive is to avoid 'bailouts' that involve the use of taxpayers' money in cases of bank failure. In 2013 not a single cent of taxpayer's money went into saving the two biggest Cypriot lenders. In order to achieve this, the bail-in tool was utilised by which existing shareholders and bondholders were (all but) wiped out and uninsured depositors saw a large proportion of their deposits converted into equity.

Although the bail-in spared the taxpayer—and future generations—from picking up the costs of the failure of Bank of Cyprus and Laiki, which prevented Greek-style austerity, this was not well understood. This may have been because some taxpayers were also depositors, although only 4% of depositors at Bank of Cyprus and Laiki were affected by the bail-in. Many others, especially private sector employees, saw some of their pension savings wiped out because pension funds could not be excluded from the bail-in.

However, even many of the taxpayers who were not affected by the bail-in did not fully realise that they were spared from much harsher austerity, which would have been the case if the banks had been bailed out. At the height of the crisis, I had conversations with many ordinary citizens who complained about the deposit 'haircut'. When I asked them if they had lost money from the bail-in, most replied 'no' but, understandably, they thought it was unfair on those who did. If bail-ins are to acquire the legitimacy the BRRD implicitly (and incorrectly) assumes they have, the public throughout the EU will need to be educated accordingly. Bank depositors also need to better understand the limits and scope of deposit insurance and the implications a bank failure can have on deposits above the insurance limit.

Lesson 4: Clear the Muddled Waters for Smaller Banks and Mutuals

While the Cypriot taxpayer was protected from the failure of the two largest lenders, €1.5 billion of taxpayer money had to be injected into the credit cooperative sector. The economic rationale behind the bailout of the credit coops centred on the following factors: (i) taken together, the credit cooperatives were systemic in that they accounted for over 30% of deposits on the island; (ii) most of the deposits at the coops were below the deposit insurance limit and a bail-in wouldn't have succeeded in generating the required capital and (iii) credit coops had no bondholders or ordinary shareholders.[6] Since a bail-in was not possible, the choice was between bailing them out and allowing them to fail. The latter would have created a bigger bill for the state than the bailout because of the deposit insurance claims. Moreover, failure of the sector would have had disruptive consequences for the rest of the economy and would have been a massive blow to confidence in the entire financial system.

The treatment of the credit cooperatives in Cyprus provides lessons for other small banks and mutuals in Europe, suggesting that the bail-in tool is only of relevance for larger banks. What the BRRD will do for deposit competition between small and large systemic banks remains to be seen. In the case of non-systemic banks or mutuals, the BRRD points towards

---

[6]The mutual legal status of some (but not all) of the credit cooperatives could, in principle, have allowed imposing losses on their members (depositors and borrowers), although this would have caused another major shock without necessarily generating the amounts needed.

winding them up or pushing them down the route of insolvency, which means that deposits above the insured limit stand to lose substantially more than the 8% loss that is envisaged by the BRRD for banks that are resolved (as public money can then be used to recapitalise them). Thus, it appears that the BRRD creates a comparative advantage for larger banks, which, if true, could change the structure and competitiveness of banking in Europe.

Lesson 5: Don't Force Central Banks to do the Dirty Work Without Appropriate Safeguards

Resolving banks is a dirty business. In Cyprus that responsibility fell on the central bank almost by default. There was no other institution that had the technical competence to carry out that work and there was no institution that had the same degree of independence. Only the CBC could carry out resolution actions competently and in a fair, objective and transparent manner. When the resolution legislation was amended to give the government control over the Resolution Authority, the work was still done by central bank staff but the decisions started being driven by political considerations—no doubt the politicians would, of course, argue that whatever they decided was in the country's best interests. However, as political horizons tend to be short-term and linked to electoral cycles, decisions are unlikely to be dictated by considerations of long-term benefits or sustainability. Allowing politicians to make decisions of life and death for banks and bankers sounds like a recipe for politicising banking, much more so than government-ownership of banks that many consider a bad idea.

Although central banks are well placed to carry out bank resolution work, because of their independence, technical competence and high quality human resources, they are neither the only nor necessarily the best institution for this purpose. If the central bank is the supervisory authority, as is often the case, potential conflicts as well as other issues can arise if resolution is also housed under the same roof. The most obvious one relates to delays in taking resolution actions, as these may be seen as supervisory failures. In addition, the experience of Cyprus suggests that central bank independence may come under attack if the central bank is seen to have acquired too many powers. It is also possible, albeit less widely recognised, that central banks without sufficient independence safeguards, can take advantage of the synergy between supervisory and resolution powers to satisfy hidden political agendas (e.g. they can close down healthy banks that are not favoured by politicians or exercise forbearance in case of weak banks that have powerful political patrons). These conflicts can, of course, be addressed through proper segmentation between supervision and resolution, robust governance arrangements within the central bank and strong safeguards for central bank independence. However, this is easier said than done in countries that do not have a sufficiently long history of democratic institutions and respect for the rule of law. Even within the EU, respect for the rule of law is variable, as the experience of Cyprus has shown. In such countries, creating an independent resolution authority with competent staff might be a better way forward.

Lesson 6 (for Europe): Step up the Protection of Central Bank Independence

The erosion of central bank independence in Cyprus was one of the major unintended consequences of the management of the crisis. The CBC was deemed by the international lenders as the most appropriate institution to carry out resolution work, yet, when it came to the crunch the CBC wasn't protected from the toxic political fallout that emanated from those actions. Attacks on its independence started the moment the resolution actions were taken and continued well after my own departure from the helm of the CBC. One wonders the extent to which my successor is able to act independently, in light of the legislative amendments made in the summer of 2013 to the governance of the CBC, which were never corrected, notwithstanding the objections of the ECB.

While the ECB and the Commission systematically expressed their disapproval of these attacks, no concrete action was ever taken to protect the CBC's independence. The Cypriot government and Parliament simply ignored the warnings and legal opinions with few, if any, tangible consequences. Since central bank independence is the foundation of the economic and monetary union, the attacks on independence, which began in Cyprus but spread to other euro area member states, can have serious long-term consequences.[7]

---

[7]See, for example, the commentary in *The Economist*: 'The departure of Cyprus's central bank Governor: a blow to central bank independence'. 10 March 2014. http://www.economist.com/blogs/freeexchange/2014/03/departure-cypruss-central-bank-governor.

Policymakers in Europe need to be vigilant about populist attacks on central banks. In Cyprus, politicians found it easy to legitimise the shifting of powers from the Governor—whose independence is protected by the Treaty—to the central bank's board, which is much less independent and susceptible to political influence. This was partly because of the CBC's perceived supervisory failings and lax regulation during the period 2004–2011. This was all conveniently blamed on the 'excessive powers' of the—independent—Governor who could not be dismissed. Nothing was, however, said about Parliament's responsibility to scrutinise the CBC's actions or inaction to regulate and supervise banks. Had Parliament been more proactive, the crisis could certainly have been avoided.

One view among some key policymakers in Europe that needs to be countered is that the scope of central bank independence should be limited to monetary policy. It has been suggested that when it comes to regulation, supervision or resolution, political influence may be tolerated because the case for independent central banks only relates to monetary policy. This view is dangerous. The reason why independent—but also accountable—central banks are more successful in controlling inflation than elected politicians is that central bankers are appointed technocrats who cannot easily be dismissed and, as such, are not subjected to the pressures of the electoral cycle. Exactly the same argument applies, perhaps even more strongly, when it comes to banking supervision and regulation. If politicians are allowed to influence decisions over regulation, supervision and resolution the likely consequence will be macroeconomic instability through easy credit policies and regulatory forbearance before elections. This could easily result in more frequent crises and bigger costs of 'mopping up' afterwards. Cyprus is, in fact, a case in point. It was because the CBC was under external pressure to keep supervision light, through inappropriate accountability, that the crisis became as big as it did.

In most economies, there is no compelling reason why banking regulation and supervision and bank resolution, as well as monetary policy, should be performed by central banks. If anything, conflicts and other issues can be avoided if there is a separate bank resolution authority with a sufficient degree of independence. If, on the other hand, all these functions are to remain within central banks, what is needed is proper segmentation, robust internal governance and strong independence safeguards. Limiting the scope of central bank independence to monetary policy is a recipe for trouble. If those who are called to do 'whatever it takes' to protect the monetary union do not have the independence safeguards for their actions, it is only a matter of time before the euro starts to unravel. The single biggest lesson from Cyprus is, perhaps, that populism, if left unchecked, can shake the foundations of the monetary union beyond the point of repair.

Bibliography

Lascelles, David. 2013. *Independent Commission on the Future of the Cyprus Banking Sector*, Final Report, 31 October 2013. http://www.centralbank.gov.cy/media/pdf/LSE_ICFCBS_Final_Report_10_13.pdf.

Johnson, Simon, and James Kwak. 2010. *13 bankers: The wall street takeover and the next financial meltdown*. New York: Pantheon Books.

Bibliography

Katsourides, Yiannos. 2014. *History of the Communist Party in Cyprus: Colonialism, class and the Cypriot left.* I.B Tauris: London.

Marsh, David. 2016. *Europe's deadlock: How the Euro Crisis could be solved and why it still won't happen,* Updated Edition, Yale University Press: New Haven and London.

Stephanou, C. 2011. Big banks in small countries: The case of Cyprus. *Cyprus Economic Policy Review,* 5 (1): 3–21.

© The Editor(s) (if applicable) and The Author(s) 2017
P. Demetriades, *A Diary of the Euro Crisis in Cyprus,*
DOI 10.1007/978-3-319-62223-1

Index

© The Editor(s) (if applicable) and The Author(s) 2017
P. Demetriades, *A Diary of the Euro Crisis in Cyprus*,
DOI 10.1007/978-3-319-62223-1

Printed by Printforce, the Netherlands